Case Studies in Adapted Physical Education

EMPOWERING CRITICAL THINKING

Samuel R. Hodge
THE OHIO STATE UNIVERSITY

Nathan M. Murata
UNIVERSITY OF HAWAII AT MANOA

Martin E. Block
UNIVERSITY OF VIRGINIA AT CHARLOTTESVILLE

Lauren J. Lieberman
STATE UNIVERSITY OF NEW YORK AT BROCKPORT

Holcomb Hathaway, Publishers
Scottsdale, Arizona 85250

Library of Congress Cataloging-in-Publication Data

Case studies in adapted physical education : empowering critical thinking / Samuel R.
Hodge ... [et al.].
    p. cm.
  Includes bibliographical references and index.
  ISBN 1-890871-42-7
  1. Physical education for children with disabilities—Study and teaching—Case studies.
I. Hodge, Samuel R.

GV445 .C37 2003
371.9′04486—dc21

2002068821

Copyright © 2003 by Holcomb Hathaway, Publishers, Inc.

Holcomb Hathaway, Publishers, Inc.
6207 North Cattletrack Road
Scottsdale, Arizona 85250
(480) 991-7881
www.hh-pub.com

ISBN 1-890871-42-7

10 9 8 7 6 5 4 3 2

Printed in the United States of America.

CONTENTS

List of Abbreviations

ADD attention deficit disorder

ADHD attention deficit hyperactivity disorder

APE adapted physical education

GPE general physical education

IEP individualized education program

ITP individualized transition plan

FOREWORD

Case Studies in Adapted Physical Education: Empowering Critical Thinking is a splendid contribution to the professional literature of both general and adapted physical education. As I read and reread this book, I keep thinking: "What a many splendored thing! A many splendored way to teach and to learn! A many splendored approach to critical thinking, collaboration, cooperation, and consensus. A many splendored tool for actively engaging individuals with diverse backgrounds in openly sharing their different beliefs and attitudes and their past experiences as they strive to understand and resolve real-life issues and concerns." This book is appropriate for undergraduate and graduate students, for use in in-service training with practicing teachers, and for collaborative interactions with parents, administrators, therapists, and others who are involved in the individualized education program (IEP) process or in the day-to-day adaptations to instruction and all aspects of life that maximize opportunities for all of us to achieve self-actualization.

I highly recommend the case study method of teaching and learning. Exposure to the real-life situations presented in cases introduces students to the many decisions that teachers and caretakers must make each day and the ways that these decisions affect others, both now and in the future. The need for critical thinking skills is made clear, as is the need for empathy and competence in interpersonal relations. Practice with peers, in the emotional safety of a small group discussion, in analyzing case studies and coming to consensus on important points, is tremendously valuable in preparing professionals for the complexity of the real world. Skill in critical thinking, empathy, and interpersonal relations does not happen incidentally as some professors seem to think. These skills must be explicitly taught and repeatedly practiced in progressively more challenging settings and with increasingly more diverse group members.

I was first introduced to the case study method of teaching and learning in my graduate work at Teachers College, Columbia University, in New York City. The pedagogy courses (then called "methods") that I took there were absolutely wonderful, and almost all of professors facilitated learning through the case study method. It was often used as part of a class but sometimes assigned as a homework project that required not only discussion but also the keeping of a personal journal on the experience. Typically the professor designated group members rather than giving us free choice. This strategy assured that each of us was placed with individuals unlike ourselves in culture, ethnicity, socioeconomic class, age experience, gender, ability, and other variables. Of course, New York affords exceptional opportunities for meaningful interactions with all kinds of people! Not all universities can offer such rich experiences in diversity, but students can be taught to role-play and given responsibility for ascertaining that multiple perspectives are considered during the critical thinking process. Guests can be brought into the classroom to provide insight into certain kinds of diversity when the natural environment does not offer enough resources.

While in graduate school, I sometimes wondered if practice in critical thinking via group discussion was a waste of time. I would have much preferred that the professors lecture and highlight "exactly what we needed to know." By the time I graduated, however, I so liked the case method that I chose it for my dissertation. That is because professors repeatedly engaged us in self-evaluation: "What did you learn from the discussion? Which of your beliefs, attitudes, intentions, or actions changed? Why? Why not?" We were expected to keep journals to document increasing competence in critical thinking, empathy, interpersonal relations, and other indicators of growth for ourselves and for group members. I believe that much of my love for teaching and my understanding and appreciation of individual differences came from those early experiences in critical thinking and the wonderful professors who took the time to individually encourage and mentor us but never gave us "the right answers" or highlighted "the most important facts." They taught us to value each other as equal status peers in learning, even though we saw ourselves as different and unique; to share the work of tracing primary sources and finding multiple possible solutions; and to support each other in striving for our personal bests.

I continue to believe that case study discussion, carefully planned and executed, is the best way to teach such processes as critical thinking and effective interpersonal relations. I see these processes as the foundation for good adapted physical activity service delivery. I am delighted that the case method, which decreased in popularity for a few years, is coming back! It is good to know that the pendulum really does swing back and forth, and that good approaches are rediscovered and made even more viable.

I congratulate Samuel Hodge, Nathan Murata, Martin Block, and Lauren Lieberman as pioneers in bringing the case study method to adapted physical education. The cases they have developed are stronger than the ones I studied from and offer tremendous promise. Moreover, the writing team comprises much diversity: that is, they bring a diversity of ideas and perspectives and life experiences. In terms of ethnicity and cultural diversity, the writing team includes three men and one woman, an African American, a Native Hawaiian/Asian American, and two White Americans, one of whom embraces the Jewish faith. Each has had experiences, one way or another, in being a member of a social minority or a marginalized group. Each has advocated strongly for individuals with disabilities and emphasizes the development of beliefs and attitudes that will lead to acceptance and inclusion of *all* persons in sport and physical activity settings. Each is recognized as an exceptional teacher and an outstanding researcher whose work has been published in multiple sources, including the *Adapted Physical Activity Quarterly* and *Palaestra*. The combined scholarship and talent that contributed to this book is truly awesome.

The case studies that Samuel, Nathan, Marty, and Laurie have produced afford outstanding opportunities for learning multiple concepts in numerous ways. I particularly like the care that the authors used in giving ethnically diverse identities to the people in the cases. Furthermore, the distinction between Mrs., Ms., and Miss is made, celebrating the different life styles represented by women who teach. Background information is presented in every case, so that decision-making can be based on contextual variables as well as unique personal needs of everyone in each case. The questions after each case are intellectually stimulating and helpful in many ways.

Because these cases include *general physical educators* as well as various specialists and parents, readers can always find someone to identify with. This enhances interest, helps learners assimilate the frequent changes in federal law, and develops competence in service delivery, advocacy, and research. This book is particularly timely in that the most recent amendments to the Individuals with Disabilities Education Act (IDEA, 1977) mandate that general educators be part of the IEP. The law now requires that the *general physical educator* work with the IEP team either directly or indirectly in addressing (a) how students with disabilities will participate in and progress through the *general physical education curriculum* and (b) how the learning of students with disabilities will be assessed. To manage the ever-growing number of students with disabilities in general physical education and after-school sports, all teachers need to acquire considerable knowledge about supplementary aids, supports, program modifications, and adaptations in environmental and instructional variables that will contribute to safe, successful, joyous physical education for all.

I anticipate that *Case Studies in Adapted Physical Education: Empowering Critical Thinking* will be widely used. I hope that in-service training, all forms of staff development, and conference programs will begin to feature discussions of case studies. I know that professionals who like to write will begin to develop their own cases. Teachers will ask students to think through their most meaningful practicum or service learning experiences and to develop cases illustrating what made these experiences meaningful. I see this book as greatly enriching professional preparation. It has the power to change the way we teach. I look forward to using it with my own students at Texas Woman's University.

CLAUDINE SHERRILL

Author of *Adapted Physical Activity, Recreation and Sport: Crossdisciplinary and Lifespan.*

ABOUT THE AUTHORS

Dr. Samuel R. Hodge is an Associate Professor in the Sport and Exercise Education (i.e., Physical Education–Teacher Education) specialization at The Ohio State University. He has both a masters and a doctoral degree in adapted physical education and pedagogical studies. After seven years as a faculty member in teacher education, he has developed a thorough understanding of teacher pedagogy and has multiple publications to his credit.

Dr. Nathan M. Murata is an Associate Professor in the Department of Kinesiology and Leisure Science at the University of Hawaii at Manoa. Dr. Murata has expertise in both adapted physical education and teacher preparation, and is a nationally certified adapted physical education professional. His research foci have included pedagogy for students with disabilities, training support personnel to work in inclusive contexts, and attitudinal variables regarding the inclusion of students with disabilities in general physical education.

Dr. Martin E. Block is an Associate Professor and Director of the Masters Program in Adapted Physical Education at the University of Virginia. Dr. Block is nationally and internationally recognized as a leading advocate for inclusion with regard to teaching students with disabilities in general physical education contexts. Dr. Block is the noted author of the text *A Teacher's Guide to Including Children with Disabilities in General Physical Education* (2000).

Dr. Lauren J. Lieberman is an Assistant Professor in the Department of Physical Education and Sport at SUNY Brockport. Dr. Lieberman is a sign language specialist. Moreover, her research and service-based interests (e.g., *Campus Abilities*, a developmental sports camp for children who are blind) involve strategies and programming for working with children who are blind, deaf, deaf-blind in physical education, sport, and recreation contexts. Dr. Lieberman is also nationally recognized for her research scholarship regarding peer-tutoring strategies to facilitate inclusion in general physical education classes, and she is the author of multiple publications.

ACKNOWLEDGMENTS

Our special thanks go to Claudine Sherrill of the Texas Woman's University and to the following reviewers, who offered constructive suggestions regarding the manuscript: Rocco Aiello, St. Mary's County Public Schools, Maryland; Ron Davis, Ball State University; Sherry Folsom-Meek, Minnesota State University, Mankato; Ron French, Texas Woman's University; Barry Lavay, California State University, Long Beach; Kimble B. Morton, Diagnostic Center Southern California; Kathy Omoto, Clark County School District, Nevada; Terry L. Rizzo, California State University, San Bernardino; Paul Surburg, Indiana University; and Daniel Webb, Mississippi State University. The book is better as a result of their assistance.

INTRODUCTION

USING THE CASE STUDY METHOD
TO EMPOWER CRITICAL THINKING

We are pleased to introduce case study methodology in adapted physical education (APE) for exploring the challenges and rewards of learning to teach individuals with and without disabilities in a variety of physical activity contexts. Case study methodology is intended to promote an interactive, problem-solving teaching and learning style, addressing realistic problems that occur in APE, general physical education (GPE), and other physical activity settings (e.g., youth sports, recreation, health clubs). The purpose of this book is to provide a series of cases representing various contexts from self-contained APE classes, inclusive GPE (i.e., elementary, middle, and high school; urban, rural, and suburban), and youth sports, to community recreation and health clubs. The cases presented are examples of real-life situations that occur in today's diverse school and community settings and are representative experiences of the authors and practicing teachers who provided realism and meaning to the cases. We conducted interviews and focus group discussions and also observed and/or had informal talks with field-based practicing teachers to develop each case. The information we gathered helped us to develop realistic scenarios that teachers must address in their schools. We used pseudonyms for individuals and locations described in the cases to maintain confidentially.

Real-life teaching scenarios provide critical-thinking opportunities for anyone aspiring to become an APE or GPE professional. Cases within this book are meant to supplement those things that you will learn or have learned through your professional preparation (e.g., method courses, practicum and internship experiences) and actual teaching experiences, which, in turn, will allow you the opportunity to think critically about real-life situations, to question and explore, and to empower yourself in the process. The stories presented herein represent actual cases faced by a diverse group of physical education professionals from across the country. Listen to their voices! You will likely find yourself able to relate to and understand many of these cases; you may find yourself saying, "Yes, this might happen to me." As you interpret these cases, keep in mind that there is no one right answer. These cases are meant to offer you real-life day-to-day experiences of adapted and general physical educators. Allow us to take you on a journey through the case study process.

Case Studies

Case studies methods are used as effective teaching tools to promote discussion, problem solving, and decision making for the realistic concerns of teachers in school settings. Wilson (2000) best states a rationale for using a case studies approach in teacher preparation:

> One strategy for helping physical educators work with administrators, parents, and students of all ability levels is to use the case study approach, and include an adapted physical education (APE) case, in teacher-preparation classes. Teacher educators need to acknowledge the diversity of today's school population, and the complexity of effectively teaching in such an environment (Bolt, 1998). A case study approach encourages preservice teachers to actively generate solutions to real-life challenges, instead of passively receiving theoretical content through lectures (Silverman, Welty, & Lyon, 1992). (p. 37)

Further, Wilson (2000) states that the use of the case study approach "can help physical educators practice ways of safely and successfully including students with disabilities in regular physical education classes" (p. 41).

In recent years, there has been an increased recognition of greater collaboration between APE and GPE professionals (Block & Conatser, 1999; Sherrill, 1998). This book *extends* and *complements* the work of Stroot (2000) and her colleagues in GPE with regard to case studies and is meant to inform both the specialist and generalist in physical education concerning the teaching of students with varied abilities and disabilities. To that end, a collaborative effort was undertaken between (adapted) physical education teacher educators and field-based practicing APE and GPE teachers representing culturally and geographically diverse areas across the United States. Moreover, the authors represent culturally diverse perspectives as teacher educators who have worked together to provide realistic case scenarios that depict life in the schools from the perspective of field-based practicing APE and GPE teachers. It is our hope that these cases will stimulate discussion as well as promote critical thinking and problem-solving skills among APE and GPE preservice and inservice teachers to address the issues reflected in each scenario.

A set of "facilitation questions" follows each case, which includes questions to help guide discussion and critical thinking about important aspects of each scenario. Benefits and limitations of each solution will ideally be discussed in class, again to provide insight into the realization that there is often no "one right answer" to situations that occur in various physical activity environments. These cases are intended to be utilized in a manner that promotes critical thinking and problem-solving skills among and between:

1. Preservice APE and GPE teachers in their experience of real-life situations that occur in various inclusive school settings in a safe and supportive environment.

2. Practicing inservice APE and GPE teachers who are engaged in staff development inservice training, as well as special and general education classroom teachers who are oftentimes responsible for teaching physical education to their students. Such professionals may wish to explore potential solutions to scenarios experienced in working with students with disabilities in similar school contexts.

3. Other professionals who work and/or interact with individuals within physical activity contexts, such as therapeutic recreation specialists,

youth sport coaches, and community recreation and adult health club managers. A number of relevant non-school-related cases are included, making this text useful to these individuals as well.

Each case study depicts a scenario experienced by either an adapted physical educator, general physical educator, or both. Each story unfolds with a vivid description of the main characters; type of school, sport setting, or community facility; the school, sport, or community culture; and other demographic information that will assist you in relating to your current or future experiences. Following each case study are facilitation questions (probes) that ask specifically what the critical issues are, what specific strategy was employed, how the physical education professional and other characters dealt with the issues, and whether you would have done the same thing or something different. The idea behind the use of case studies is not to have your course instructor "tell you" or "find out for you" what the answers might be; rather, it is for you, the education professional, to explain what occurred in each case study. You should think critically, reflect, and feel empowered by exploring answers for each scenario. After reading each case study, stop, reflect, and critically analyze through discussion, interviews, Internet materials, and reading materials what might be suitable resources to extend your thinking for that particular case study. Please remember that not all the practices within each case are exemplary teaching practices; in fact, some should even be avoided. Again, the purpose of the cases is to encourage you to think critically about the various situations, to reinforce that not all practices you will encounter in the schools are best practices, and to allow you to formulate your own ideas about how an issue can be handled. This case study approach is not limited to only physical educators. On the contrary, we have included cases for other professionals who teach, interact, or work with individuals with disabilities in a community environment, recreational setting, private facility, and even at home.

Stroot (2000) and her colleagues developed a set of guidelines for exploring the issues addressed in her case studies book. For our purposes, we have modified those guidelines (p. 3) to help you navigate your way through each case presented in this book. Consider the following:

1. Read each case study thoroughly. Try to respond to the facilitation questions for each specific case. We have provided "Summary of Participants" boxes to help you refer to the key characters in the case.

2. Read through the case a second time with the questions in mind.

3. Identify all issues embedded in the case. Determine whether the case study issues were resolved or unresolved. If a resolution was provided, analyze its likely effectiveness.

4. Identify the types of information you will need to explore these scenarios and critical issues. Gather more information in areas in which you have limited knowledge. For most cases, endnotes are provided with key information or additional resources. In addition, you are encouraged to seek more information through the World Wide Web, library resources, published materials, and practicing teachers.

5. Pick out the key points of the case and identify the salient issues (e.g., behavior management concerns, ethical dilemmas, inclusion practice). Highlight the issues so that you can refer to them later. Make notes in the margins or create a mental note.

6. Discuss the case study with classmates before, during, or after class meetings. Determine whether or not others found similar issues or had similar or different reactions to the cases.

7. Try to provide thoughtful responses to the facilitation questions at the end of the cases. Evaluate the strategies used by the characters in the case. Ask yourself if the strategies represent the best teaching methods based on your prior knowledge from previous classes and available resources (e.g., textbooks, Internet materials, journal articles, personal communication with practicing teachers). Determine what you would do if you encountered a similar set of circumstances.

8. Be prepared to share with others your perspectives on what you might do if faced with a similar situation. Be willing to listen to others' perspectives and ideas.

Centering Themes

The overarching intent of this book is to present cases to be used as a teaching tool for preparing professionals to teach a diversity of individuals with and without disabilities in various physical activity contexts. The concept of *inclusion practice* encompasses the entire book. Moreover, the book is divided into major sections based on three centering themes: (a) *inclusion advocacy and strategies to promote success* (cases 1–20), (b) *behavior management and conflict resolution* (cases 21–24), and (c) *strategies for teaching students with varied abilities and disabilities* (cases 25–40).

Inclusion advocacy and strategies to promote success. This theme addresses specific case studies in which inclusion strategies, ethics, changing attitudes and stereotypical behaviors, inclusion practice, and individualized instruction are highlighted. The fact remains that with the least restrictive environment (LRE) mandate as stipulated in Public Law 105-17 (Individuals with Disabilities Education Act Amendments of 1997), GPE settings should be considered first, before students with disabilities are "automatically placed" in alternative environments (i.e., segregated self-contained classes). More important, with school districts espousing an inclusion philosophy, it is important to address this area and to determine what issues might arise from placing students with disabilities in GPE settings.

Behavior management and conflict resolution. This theme addresses case studies that examine behavior management strategies for proactive and preventive programming and pedagogy, for increasing appropriate student behaviors, for decreasing inappropriate student behaviors, and for conflict resolution methods in physical activity settings. Because it is a well-accepted practice that teachers/practitioners must manage student behavior first, before effective teaching can occur, we include these cases to describe behavior management concerns and some ideas that might be useful in the teaching setting.

Strategies for teaching students with varied abilities and disabilities.

We support a noncategorical philosophy relative to teaching a diversity of students with disabilities. We advocate focusing on a student's ability first, before addressing that student's disability. However, when reading these cases, you will find that disability-specific "labels" were used to describe students. This was done to assist the reader in ascertaining specifically what type of disability is being addressed. We submit that the noncategorical approach implies that specific teaching strategies, personal interactions, attitudes and belief systems, individualizing instruction, behavior management strategies, and thoughtful pedagogy should all be interwoven into effective inclusion practice for students with a variety of abilities and disabilities.

In addition, threaded throughout this book is our recognition of the importance of gender equity and culturally relevant pedagogy. Culturally relevant pedagogy "means that teachers have a moral responsibility to be culturally responsive or to design curricular programs that are responsive to the educational needs of learners from diverse cultural backgrounds" (Sparks, 1994, p. 35). This suggests that culturally relevant pedagogy recognizes the impact of culture, language, ethnicity, gender, and other variables that define students as different (Sparks, 1994). While reading the various cases in this book, we encourage you to explore the question, "What is inside the box?" The *box* in this sense represents an individual's degree of comfort and awareness as it relates to various issues regarding the inclusion of students with disabilities as well as cultural and ethnic diversity.

For some physical educators, inside the box exists traditional gender logic[1] and/or race logic.[2] For instance, societal and cultural expectations based on traditional gender logic for physical activity and sport engagement often lead to differences in participation patterns for girls and boys (Beveridge & Scruggs, 2000). In most cultures, boys usually engage in physical activity and sport to a higher level than girls their same age (Beveridge & Scruggs, 2000). Under traditional race logic, for example, some youth (e.g., African Americans) are perceived as more aggressive, more likely to misbehave, or less intelligent than their peers. We challenge you to go *outside* the box in your efforts to enhance gender equity and promote culturally relevant pedagogy for all students with and without disabilities. A starting point is to analyze your instructional materials to ensure that perspectives and examples from different cultural and ethnic groups are represented with historical accuracy (Sparks, 1994). To assist you further in your efforts toward responsive pedagogy for gender equity and cultural relevance, we encourage you to consult Sutherland and Hodge (2001) and others (Beveridge & Scruggs, 2000; Hutchinson, 1995; Sparks, 1994; Williamson, 1993), who offer guidelines for teaching diverse learners with and without disabilities.

At the end of many of this book's case studies, you will find information (e.g., websites, telephone numbers, reference lists) to help you locate additional information and resources specific to that particular case. In addition, a comprehensive index is provided to enhance your ability to locate cases specific to your needs. The index includes information on cases representing various school contexts (i.e., elementary, middle, and high school).

Conclusion

This case study methodology serves to broaden your ability to work with a diversity of individuals who represent an array of abilities and disabilities. We are encouraged with the opportunities before us as APE and GPE professionals to learn how to effectively integrate content knowledge, pedagogical content knowledge, and "best practices" into our everyday teaching practice. This case study approach offers you a venue in which to think critically about real-life issues and situations encountered in our nation's classrooms, gymnasiums, health clubs, recreational facilities, and sports settings. We aspire to an eclectic approach in addressing these cases, and the conclusion drawn should be viewed as one solution with potentially many other options. We hope that you will use this text to explore issues of diversity and disability, attitude and ethics, behavior management and conflict resolutions, and inclusion strategies that will assist you in becoming more receptive and appreciative of individuals with varied abilities and disabilities. Our intent is to empower you in your thinking as it relates to providing these individuals with safe, satisfying, and successful physical activity experiences. Moreover, we hope that you will share your experiences and thoughts with others and join us as we collectively explore, appreciate, value, and learn more about the myriad abilities and disabilities that individuals demonstrate in physical activity contexts.

Endnotes

1. Traditional *gender logic* led to the conclusion that girls and women were "naturally" *inferior* to boys and men in activity requiring physical skills and cognitive strategies. For example, some people tend to say that a person "throws like a girl" when he or she does not throw a ball correctly, or the coach of a boys' or men's team uses the word *girls* or *ladies* to describe the team (Coakley, 2001).

2. *Race logic* relates to dominant ideas about links between the color of a person's skin and physical activity and sport-related skillfulness and behaviors. For example, teachers and sport coaches often associated dark skin with physical and athletic prowess, and especially with positions on teams for which physical demands are greater than intellectual demands (Coakley, 2001).

Resources and References

Beveridge, S., & Scruggs, P. (2000). TLC for better PE: Girls and elementary physical education. *Journal of Physical Education, Recreation and Dance,* 71(8), 22–27.

Block, M. E., & Conatser, P. (1999). Consulting in adapted physical education. *Adapted Physical Activity Quarterly, 16,* 9–26.

Bolt, B. R. (1998). Encouraging cognitive growth through case discussions. *Journal of Teaching in Physical Education, 18*(1), 90–102.

Coakley, J. J. (2001). *Sport in society: Issues and controversies* (7th ed.). Dubuque, IA: Irwin McGraw-Hill.

Hutchinson, G. E. (1995). Gender-fair teaching in physical education. *Journal of Physical Education, Recreation and Dance, 66*(1), 42–47.

Sherrill, C. (1998). *Adapted physical activity, recreation and sport: Cross-disciplinary and lifespan* (5th ed.). Dubuque, IA: WCB McGraw-Hill.

Silverman, R., Welty, W. M., & Lyon, S. (1992). *Case studies for teacher problem solving.* New York: McGraw-Hill.

Sparks, W. G., III. (1994). Culturally responsive pedagogy: A framework for addressing multicultural issues. *Journal of Physical Education, Recreation and Dance, 65*(9), 33–36, 61.

Stroot, S. A. (Ed.). (2000). *Case studies in physical education: Real world preparation for teaching.* Scottsdale, AZ: Holcomb Hathaway.

Sutherland, S., & Hodge, S. (2001). Inclusion of a diverse population. *Teaching Elementary Physical Education, 12*(2), 15–17.

Williamson, K. M. (1993). Is your inequity showing? Ideas and strategies for creating a more equitable learning environment. *Journal of Physical Education, Recreation and Dance, 64*(8), 15–23.

Wilson, S. (2000). Disability case studies: Learning to include all students. *Journal of Physical Education, Recreation and Dance, 71*(4), 37–41.

Changing Attitudes and Stereotypical Beliefs

Most of the boys at Southern Middle School, like many boys their age, are sports crazy. Sports, sports, sports—that's all they seem to talk about. You can hear the boys at lunch talking about their favorite sports teams, whether it's their local high school or their favorite college or professional team. You can see them at recess dividing into teams and playing football or soccer or basketball. Moreover, many boys at Southern play on community-sponsored sport teams, and the exceptional athletes play on one or more of Southern's interscholastic teams. Sometimes it seems that all the boys at Southern are involved in sports in some way.

Well, almost all the boys. The boys in Mr. Jackson's class, a self-contained class for middle school students with severe disabilities, don't seem to have caught the sports bug like the other boys at Southern. All of the boys in Mr. Jackson's class have severe cognitive impairments (i.e., severe mental retardation). Some are able to walk and even run whereas others have physical disabilities that require them to use wheelchairs. None of the students can read or write, but some of the students can talk and even say short sentences. Because of the severe nature of their disabilities, the school district has chosen to self-contain these students for the majority of the day with Mr. Jackson and two teacher assistants. However, Mr. Jackson does take the boys out of school once a week to work on functional skills such as grocery shopping, accessing fast-food restaurants, and using local recreation facilities such as bowling alleys and miniature golf courses. These opportunities give his students a chance to interact with workers in the community who do not have disabilities.

As prescribed in their individualized education programs, there also are times during the day when the boys are included in activities with their peers without disabilities. For example, the boys are included in general education recess, lunch, music, and physical education. Mr. Jackson is careful not to bring all the boys in his class to these activities at the same time. Rather, he brings only one to two students at a time, and the students are always accompanied by Mr. Jackson or one of his teacher assistants. Mr. Jackson has told the parents of these students as well as the general education teachers that these inclusionary experiences are good opportunities for his students to learn how to develop appropriate behaviors and social skills. In addition, Mr. Jackson has noted that these inclusionary opportunities should help peers without disabilities appreciate students with disabilities more and learn to be more empathetic of these students. At least that is what should happen according to the special education classes Mr. Jackson took in college and the books he has read about inclusion.

Unfortunately, Mr. Jackson is not seeing the types of positive responses from peers without disabilities that he thought he would see. In fact, he is seeing the opposite effects. At recess, boys without disabilities quickly divide themselves into teams and play games. While Mr. Jackson has tried to include his students in these games, students without disabilities simply refuse to let these other boys play. Mr. Jackson has not pushed the recess issue too much since it is free time for students without disabilities. Forcing them to include his students just doesn't seem right. But he has noticed that the boys without disabilities have started to tease his students, and although this teasing has been mostly name-calling and taunting, Mr. Jackson can see that it is beginning to bother his students. Mr. Jackson decides to move his students to a different part of the playground to avoid those few boys who tease his students, but running away from the situation just doesn't seem to be the best solution.

Interestingly, the teasing directed at Mr. Jackson's students is also directed at some other children who are not inclined toward athletics. It seems that children who are different because they wear glasses, are a little overweight, or have trouble playing games are also ostracized. For example, Mr. Jackson notices that two boys whom he recognizes as students with learning disabilities (who go to a resource room next door to his class) are usually left out of games and teased. One of these boys really likes sports and tries to play with the students without disabilities. But even when he is allowed to play, his peers never pass him the ball, they push him out of the way, and they call him names.

Inclusion in general physical education (GPE) has not fared like Mr. Jackson had hoped, either. The GPE teacher, Mrs. Springer, is receptive enough to having Mr. Jackson's students attend her classes (as long as they are accompanied by Mr. Jackson or one of his teacher assistants). Yet, students without disabilities almost never interact with his students. When Mrs. Springer asks students to find partners, Mr. Jackson's students either have to partner with each other or with Mr. Jackson or one of his teacher assistants. The social opportunities that Mr. Jackson had hoped for are virtually nonexistent, and students without disabilities cannot possibly be learning to be more accepting or empathetic in this setting. Even worse, some of the boys walk by students from Mr. Jackson's class and whisper things in their ears such as "hey, retard" and "loser." When Mrs. Springer tries to place students with disabilities on teams, their peers start to moan and complain "I don't want them on my team" or "Oh great, we're going to lose." And when Mrs. Springer makes changes to the games in order to accommodate the students with disabilities, many of the students without disabilities complain "It's not fair," and "That's going to the ruin the game."

For example, when the class was at the end of a basketball unit, Mrs. Springer wanted her students to apply the skills that they had learned to a game situation. Her plan was to divide the class into six teams of five players each and then play a round-robin tournament. She knew that if she let her students pick teams, the students in Mr. Jackson's class would be picked last. So she divided the class herself, trying to evenly distribute skilled and less skilled players. But when she placed one of Mr. Jackson's students, Billy, on a team, the team's members began to complain that they were going to lose because of him. Mrs. Springer told the players that Billy could shoot at his lower basket, but they still complained. Mr. Jackson told them that he would help Billy, but they just rolled their eyes at Mr. Jackson.

Mr. Jackson realizes that inclusion in physical education is not working out like he had anticipated, but what can he do? He had hoped that simply placing his students with disabilities into GPE would result in the other students befriending his students, but clearly this isn't happening. Mr. Jackson knows that he has to do something to change these negative attitudes. Mr. Jackson first consults some colleagues in the school district who have had more success with the social aspects of inclusion. He then goes to the library at the local college to find some books and articles that talk about ways to improve attitudes of students without disabilities toward their peers with disabilities. Finally, he searches on the Internet to find information on disability awareness, famous people with disabilities, and attitudes toward disabilities.

The result of Mr. Jackson's efforts is a wealth of information and ideas to try to change the attitudes of students without disabilities. He now has a list of famous people who have disabilities, including actors Tom Cruise (he has a severe learning disability and attended a special school for a while) and Danny Glover (he was in a class for children with mental retardation through high school and did not learn to read until he left school), and basketball stars Sean Elliot and Alonzo Mourning (kidney disease).

Mr. Jackson also has some role-playing ideas that might help his students understand what it is like to have a disability. For example, because some of Mr. Jackson's students use wheelchairs, he could bring in a wheelchair and have students without disabilities take turns trying to shoot baskets, move across the field, or throw a football. Because all of Mr. Jackson's students have trouble understanding even simple directions, he could try to explain the rules of a new game without speaking. This would show students what it might be like to have mental retardation. Finally, because one of Mr. Jackson's students has a visual impairment, he could blindfold students and have them try to shoot baskets or run the bases in baseball to see what it might be like to be blind.

Mr. Jackson also could lead a discussion on the concept of "handicapping" and why allowing athletes to have "handicaps" makes games more equitable for players of different abilities. For example, in golf, players who are not very good can still be competitive against much more skilled players because of handicapping. A player with a 10 handicap would get 10 strokes from his playing partner. Most golf courses have different tee boxes for different levels of players. The blue, or championship, tees are for the most skilled players, and these tees are farthest from the hole. Other tees usually include white tees for average golfers, gold tees for senior golfers, and red tees for female and junior golfers.

Mr. Jackson could lead a discussion on the specific students who are included, what they like and dislike, and how they feel when they are teased and excluded. This would then lead to a discussion on what peers without disabilities can do to welcome and befriend these students with disabilities. For example, one of the students who is often teased, Tommy, looks and moves very differently than his peers. Although Tommy can walk, he walks slowly and often veers off to the side because of vision problems. Tommy also has a birth deformity that makes his head look different from that of typically developing students. But Tommy really loves basketball, especially the repetitiveness of dribbling and walking with a basketball. He also has learned how to pass a basketball to his peers and shoot a basketball into a 6-foot-high basket with only verbal cues. Tommy really gets excited when he or his peers scores a basket, and he loves giving and getting "high fives." With some simple modifications, he could play in a basketball game and have fun without negatively affecting the game.

Mr. Jackson could bring in guest speakers who have disabilities but who are accomplished athletes as well. For example, he knows that there is a high school student with mental retardation who won a gold medal in tennis at the World Special Olympic Games. He has also heard of a person in a neighboring town who is paralyzed from the waist down and uses a wheelchair yet completed the Marine Corp Marathon in Washington, D.C. And there was a recent story in the local newspaper about a 12-year-old girl from another middle school who became a state champion in gymnastics even though she was born profoundly Deaf.

Mr. Jackson clearly has a lot of ideas, but which one of these activities would help peers without disabilities become more accepting toward Mr. Jackson's students in GPE? As noted earlier, the students without disabilities at Southern Middle School are an athletic bunch who love sports. Mr. Jackson needs to find activities that would be interesting to these sports-crazed students yet still change their attitudes toward his students. Mr. Jackson is ready to get started.

QUESTIONS

Preparing for Learning & Teaching

1. What is the primary issue in this case?

2. What are some of the factors that contributed to this issue?

3. Why do you think many of the students without disabilities tease Mr. Jackson's students, and why do you think many of them do not want Mr. Jackson's students to play in their games and be on their teams?

4. Do you think students who are caught teasing or taunting the students in Mr. Jackson's class (or for that matter, any other student in the school) should receive punishment for their behavior? If yes, what kind of punishment and why?

5. Could Mr. Jackson and Mrs. Springer have done something before Mr. Jackson's students were included in order to prevent the teasing and taunting that occurred on the playground and in the gym? If so, what?

6. Mr. Jackson found a lot of activities to present information that might change the attitudes of students without disabilities toward peers with disabilities. Which of the activities discussed in this case would be most effective given the scenario? Why do you think these types of activities would be the best?

7. Can you think of other activities that you, as either the special education teacher or GPE teacher, could present to the students that would make them more understanding and accepting of peers with disabilities? Explain.

8. Do you think the activities you chose to present would work for elementary-aged children? If not, why, and which activities would you present and why?

9. How would you present modifications to games such as basketball so that peers without disabilities would accept them?

The Limits
of Behavior
Management
Techniques

CASE 2

Ms. Cooper has just completed her masters degree in adapted physical education (APE), and she is excited about starting her first job as the APE specialist for Lincoln County Public Schools. She is particularly looking forward to working with a lot of different students with disabilities (she was told that her caseload would be between 30 and 40 students), teachers, parents, and administrators in Lincoln County's eight elementary and three middle schools and one high school.

Ms. Cooper arrives at the school district's "new teachers' orientation" hoping that she will find some other new teachers whom she can befriend. As luck would have it, Ms. Cooper sits next to Mr. Collins, a new special education teacher hired to work with students with severe disabilities at one of the middle schools. Like Ms. Cooper, Mr. Collins has just completed his masters in special education, and he too is excited but a little nervous about his first teaching job. He tells Ms. Cooper that he gained a lot of experience working with children with severe physical disabilities through his internship at a rehabilitation center as well as children with severe mental retardation through his internship at a local school. However, he confesses that he has had the least amount of experience working with students with autism, and he knows that he will have two children with autism in his class. Ms. Cooper, on the other hand, has had a fair amount of experience working with students with autism through her internship in a special class for such students. In addition, she worked at a camp for children with autism over the summer. Ms. Cooper tells Mr. Collins that, since she would be working with the students in his class anyway, she would be happy to help him in any way that she can with these two children.

Ms. Cooper makes a point of visiting Mr. Collins's classroom first thing the next morning and begins to learn about his students. The files on the two children with autism are very thick, since both children had been in the school system since preschool. Ms. Cooper and Mr. Collins leaf through the two files together, finding things such as each student's assessment reports, individualized education programs (IEPs), medical and psychological reports, and progress reports from the previous teacher. For one of the students with autism, Donald, nothing stands out in the reports.

By contrast, behavioral issues jump out at the two teachers as they start looking through Linda's file, the other student with autism. Linda also is 13 years old, but she is nonverbal. Reports note that efforts have been made to use sign language and pictures to help her to communicate, but neither was particularly effective. The school district's autism specialist noted in her report that Linda's lack of expressive communication could be causing some of her behavioral outbursts. This autism specialist also noted that, while Linda understands simple two-to-three-step directions, she often seems to get confused when her routine is changed. For example, the report notes one incident when music had to be canceled because the music teacher took a group of 8th graders to a concert. Linda was accustomed to going to music at 11:15 on Mondays and Wednesdays, and she threw a huge tantrum when her routine was changed. Similarly, the report notes that when school is canceled for teacher workdays or inclement weather, Linda becomes upset and is very difficult to control when she returns to school. As Ms. Cooper and Mr. Collins look through the various reports in Linda's file, they begin to see that her behaviors include self-abuse (e.g., hitting her head with her fist, banging her head against the wall, biting her hand) as well as aggression toward others (e.g., scratching, biting, hitting, grabbing at clothes).

Ms. Cooper and Mr. Collins look at each other for several seconds before Mr. Collins says, "Looks like Linda is going to be a real challenge this year!" Ms. Cooper agrees, noting that she had worked with a child like Linda at camp: "The most difficult thing is to remain calm and not get angry when the child attacks you." She suggests that Mr. Collins contact the autism specialist as soon as possible to get a better handle on Linda and to hear her recommendations for behavior intervention. Since she worked with Linda during the previous year, she surely would know Linda's unique behaviors, what types of things tend to set her off, what type of class structure seems to be most effective, and what behavior plan was in place.

By chance, the autism specialist walks into the room at just that moment along with a tall, burly-looking man. The autism specialist, Mrs. Clark, introduces herself and the gentleman, Mr. Johansen. She notes that Mr. Johansen, who recently retired from the military, has been hired as Linda's new teacher assistant. Mr. Collins and Ms. Cooper introduce themselves, and for the next several minutes Mrs. Clark gives a quick overview of Linda. Her particular concern is for the safety of the staff who work with Linda. She recalls several incidents last year in which Linda tried to scratch and bite the teacher assistant, special education teacher, speech therapist, and APE specialist. She tells the three of them that Linda had to be restrained at least a dozen times last year during particularly bad episodes.

When Mrs. Clark finishes her review, she tells Mr. Johansen, Mr. Collins, and Ms. Cooper that she would be happy to talk with them in more detail about Linda at any time during the school year.

All three teachers look at each other and think, "This is going to be an interesting year with Linda." Ms. Cooper says that she has gone through some special training to help de-escalate students and, when necessary, restrain students to prevent them from hurting others as well as themselves. Mr. Johansen says that he also has received similar training, and that he would be happy to show Mr. Collins some of these restraining techniques.

The first day of school arrives, and Ms. Cooper goes to Mr. Collins's school to set up the gym. She has prepared a lesson that focuses more on individual skills than group activities, although she does plan for a group warm-up. Ms. Cooper anticipates that setting up a clear, consistent routine is critical for Linda and many of the other children in Mr. Collins's class, so she creates a schedule board with various pictures of activities that can be easily moved up and down along the schedule board. She plans on starting class every day with the same warm-up routine, at least for the first few months of school, so students like Linda will have some consistency. Ms. Cooper knows that the first few days will be the hardest because the students have been away from school all summer long, and they will have a new classroom teacher and teacher assistants as well as a new APE specialist. Mr. Collins brings the class down to the gym with Mr. Johansen walking alongside Linda and two female teacher assistants walking alongside the rest of the class. As they walk into the gym, Ms. Cooper points to circles on the floor where she wants each child to sit. All of the children comply, but Linda looks around the room several times before she sits down. Ms. Cooper introduces herself to the class and asks the students to introduce themselves to her. Some students need extra prompting, and Linda and one other child need an assistant to tell Ms. Cooper their names.

After everyone introduces themselves, Ms. Cooper quickly reviews the schedule for the day using her schedule board. She then asks the students and teacher assistants to stand up and run two laps around the gym for the first part of warm-ups. To her surprise, everyone stands up on just a verbal cue, even Linda. However, while the other students begin to run, Linda turns toward Mr. Johansen and tries to scratch him and then head-butts him. He quickly grabs Linda, turns her around so that she is facing away from him, and then twists and pulls Linda's arm so that her arm is bent behind her back with her hand pulled toward the back of her head. This causes Linda to shriek, but it also keeps her from hurting him. Although Mr. Johansen's actions are quick and effective, he clearly is hurting Linda. Ms. Cooper walks over to him to ask what he is doing, and he tells her that he is restraining Linda using the special restraining technique that he learned from a previous job at a school for children with behavior disorders. Ms. Cooper looks at Mr. Collins, who smiles and says, "Isn't this great. Mr. Johansen really seems to have a handle on how to deal with Linda's aggressive behavior." Thinking back to the special training that she received in restraining children who were out of control, Ms. Cooper specifically remembers her instructor telling her and the other future teachers that under no circumstance is it appropriate to inflict pain on a student and that pain compliance techniques were reserved for law enforcement personnel. Clearly, that is exactly what Mr. Johansen is doing to Linda.

Class continues, and Linda vacillates back and forth between participating in activities and trying to attack Mr. Johansen. He continues to thwart these attempts by placing Linda in the same painful armhold used during warm-ups. At one point Ms. Cooper sees tears rolling down Linda's face, and she knows that Mr. Johansen, whether intentionally or not, is hurting Linda. When class is over Ms. Cooper walks with the class back to Mr. Collins's classroom. She waits until he has a free moment and asks to have a word with him in the hallway. The two go out into the hallway, and she tells him, "I am concerned for Linda's safety. I really feel that the 'restraining technique' Mr. Johansen is using is causing her a great deal of pain." Mr. Collins agrees that Linda might be experiencing a little bit of pain but says, "Mr. Johansen and I feel that Linda needs to feel a little pain in order to understand how her outbursts affect people around her." Ms. Cooper gathers her thoughts for a moment and then, as nicely as possible, says, "I disagree. You should never inflict pain on a student, as I learned in my restraint training program. I realize that you and Mr. Johansen may not know that there are effective, non-painful ways to control an assaultive student. Can you see that some people witnessing that would consider it a clear case of child abuse?" She also wonders if Linda's parents had been informed of and agreed to pain compliance as part of Linda's behavior intervention program, so she asks Mr. Collins. He tells her that Linda's parents had not been informed, but that, according to him, they generally agreed to any behavior program that he felt would help Linda. Upset by this answer, Ms. Cooper tells him: "I think you should inform Linda's parents about this specific program. I don't think they would want to see Linda in pain." Mr. Collins suddenly becomes defensive: "Thanks for your input, but we really have a handle on it. I have to get back to my class now."

Ms. Cooper heads back to the gym to clean up. She feels she should quickly report this incident to someone in order to protect Linda. Ms. Cooper herself believes it is a clear case of child abuse since Mr. Collins says that Linda "needs to feel a little pain in order to understand how her outbursts affect people around her." However, Ms. Cooper realizes that Mr. Collins and Mr. Johansen are not going to be happy if she reports it to the principal, to child protective services, or to Linda's parents. She also wonders if the autism specialist and/or building principal agreed to use of a pain compliance technique. Ms. Cooper is in a quandary. She knows that she has to do the right thing, but wonders about the best course of action.

Endnotes

1. For information about alternate behavior management techniques, see the endnote about the Mandt System on p. 30. You could also consult such programs as Nonviolent Crisis Intervention, www.crisis prevention.com/, and Professional Assault Response Training (PART), www.pretext.co.za/naccw/training.mtml#PART/.

QUESTIONS

Preparing for Learning & Teaching

SUMMARY OF PARTICIPANTS

Ms. Cooper, APE specialist

Mr. Collins, special education teacher

Donald, 13-year-old student with autism

Linda, 13-year-old student with autism

Mrs. Clark, school district autism specialist

Mr. Johansen, Linda's teacher assistant

1. What is the primary ethical issue in this case?

2. What are some of the factors that contributed to this issue?

3. From a legal standpoint, is it all right to inflict pain on a child as part of his or her behavior intervention program? Why or why not?

4. From an ethical standpoint, is it all right to inflict pain on a child as part of his or her behavior intervention plan? Why or why not?

5. Is it worthwhile for Ms. Cooper to try to change Mr. Collins's mind about the behavior intervention plan? If so, what might she say or do to change his mind?

6. Whom should Ms. Cooper go to first to try to deal with this problem? What are the consequences of going to this person? Why?

7. Is there something that Ms. Cooper could have done immediately to protect Linda?

8. As an advocate for Linda, should Ms. Cooper be concerned about what might happen to Mr. Collins or Mr. Johansen? Why or why not?

9. Can Ms. Cooper be held legally liable if:

   a. Linda's parents find out that pain is purposely and repeatedly used?

   b. Someone else reports child abuse and it is discovered that Ms. Cooper failed to report suspected child abuse?

   c. If Linda is injured by the painful restraint technique while in Ms. Cooper's presence?

   d. If Linda is injured by the painful restraint technique while not in Ms. Cooper's presence?

10. Could Ms. Cooper be fired or disciplined by the district for reporting the incident to Linda's parents or child protective services?

11. Could Ms. Cooper be fired or disciplined by the district for not reporting the incident to her administrator, Linda's parents, or child protective services?

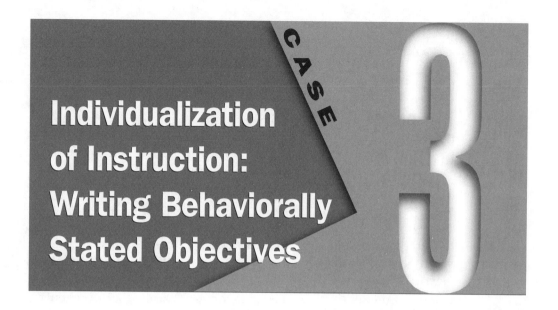

Individualization of Instruction: Writing Behaviorally Stated Objectives

C A S E 3

Mr. Joseph is a veteran teacher with more than 17 years of experience teaching general physical education in a large urban school district. Recently he attended the New York State Alliance for Health, Physical Education, Recreation and Dance Conference. While there, Mr. Joseph attended a session entitled "Writing Behaviorally-Stated Objectives for Students with Disabilities from Culturally Diverse Backgrounds."[1] The two presenters for that session both had years of public school experience teaching students with disabilities from culturally and ethnically diverse backgrounds. Similarly, Mr. Joseph's physical education classes comprised students with and without disabilities from culturally and ethnically diverse backgrounds. Mr. Joseph enjoys his teaching position and is becoming increasingly aware of the need to learn more about providing culturally sensitive and relevant pedagogy in physical education. According to Mr. Joseph, his being "a White American male teaching mostly ethnic minority kids in an urban school district" has led to his increasing awareness of the need to be culturally sensitive. In other words, his heightened awareness is what motivated him to attend this particular session.

At the conference, the presenters state that the purpose of the session is to provide those in attendance with information and practical ideas on how to write behaviorally stated objectives for students with (and without) disabilities from culturally diverse backgrounds. Mr. Joseph immediately realizes that he has selected the right session for his needs. Further, they state that Public Law 105-17, Individuals with Disabilities Education Act Amendments of 1997 (IDEA, 1997) guarantees children and youth with disabilities in the United States, ages 3–21, a free, appropriate education in the least restrictive environment and encourages states to provide early intervention services for infants and toddlers, ages 0–2, by offering financial incentives. The presenters continue with several key points:

- IDEA (1997) requires that special education, including physical education, be made available to all students with disabilities

- The inclusion movement, which advocates for students with disabilities to be educated in general education with same-age peers, has been considered "one of the most powerful educational movements in the last decade of the 20th century" (Winnick, 2000, p. 22).

- At the school level, these two factors have resulted in the inclusion of more and more students with disabilities within GPE classes (Sutherland & Hodge, 2001).

- In fact, some students of color ("minorities") are 4.5 times more likely to *receive* special education services than their White American peers (IDEA, 1997).

- From a moral and professional standpoint, physical educators should consider gender equity and culturally relevant pedagogy for *all* students with and without disabilities.

The presenters discuss the importance of writing culturally relevant[2] behaviorally stated objectives to successfully include diverse learners with disabilities in GPE contexts. Furthermore, they suggest that a key issue to consider when teaching a student with a disability is being aware of the IEP relative to physical education goals. For specific instructional strategies, the presenters encourage the audience to read more about this topic from Block (1996, 2000), and Sutherland and Hodge (2001). At that point, they explain that individualization of instruction according to Jansma and French (1994) involves testing, assessing, planning, and instruction that focuses on the individual needs, interests, and abilities of students with disabilities, usually with emphasis on those students with moderate to more severe conditions. Moreover, they explain that this requires individualized task analysis, which involves a sequencing of skills outside the repertoire of a specific learner, based on the individual's developmental-functional level, needs, and learning characteristics (Jansma & French, 1994).

Mr. Joseph is impressed by this presentation and hopes to learn more. He raises his hand and asks, "What about writing PE objectives?" "Good question," responds the lead presenter, who then introduces the process of lesson planning to include students with moderate to severe disabilities using the ABCD model[3] for individualization of instruction. This model, the lead presenter further explains, calls for four primary components: ABCD. Briefly defined, these four components refer to (a) the *audience*, which generally represents the student with a disability, (b) the *behavior*, to be emitted by the target student, (c) the *conditions* under which the behavior(s) will occur, and (d) the *degree*, representing the criteria or criterion of expected success for the target student (Jansma & French, 1994).

Next the lead presenter talks about the need to test and assess students to determine their present level of psychomotor performance as it relates to physical activities. According to the presenters, after reviewing a student's IEP, consulting relevant IEP team members regarding annual goals and objectives for a particular student, and establishing the present level of performance (i.e., testing to gather baseline data), the teacher is ready to develop unit and lesson plans following the ABCD model as well as to write the physical education component of an IEP for that student. Mr. Joseph and others attending the session are then provided with an example of a simple lesson plan[4] using the ABCD model.

Lesson Plan

PRESENT LEVEL OF PERFORMANCE

Ashanti uses a same-sided throw pattern (verbal request).

LESSON OBJECTIVE

Given a verbal cue, Ashanti will throw a tennis ball using overhand opposition to the instructor 20 feet away, 3 of 4 attempts.

PROGRESSION

1. Using footprints in opposition, when given a verbal request Ashanti will step and throw a tennis ball overhand toward a 3 foot × 3 foot target 10 feet away with the instructor providing a physical prompt at the stepping leg, 8 of 10 attempts.

2. Using footprints in opposition, when given a verbal request Ashanti will step and throw a tennis ball overhand toward a 3 foot × 3 foot target 10 feet away with the instructor providing only a verbal prompt, 8 of 10 attempts.

3. (Remove or "fade" footprints.) When given a verbal request Ashanti will step and throw a tennis ball overhand toward a 3 foot × 3 foot target 10 feet away with the instructor's verbal prompt as needed, 8 of 10 attempts.

4. When given a verbal request (stress "hard" throw), Ashanti will step and throw a tennis ball overhand toward a 3 foot × 3 foot target 15 feet away with the instructor's verbal prompts only as needed, 8 of 10 attempts.

The presenters ask the audience to identify the specific ABCD components of the sample lesson. Marlene states that Ashanti represents the "A" for audience. Others raise their hands, and Kathy says "overhand throw" is the "B" for behavior. The energy and participation within the room is high. Mr. Joseph suggests that several aspects of the progressions represent the "C" for conditions. These are "using footprints in opposition," "verbal request," "a tennis ball," "the 3 foot × 3 foot target 10 feet away," and "the instructor with either physical or verbal prompting." "Excellent responses!" exclaims one presenter. "Now, what about 'D' for degree?" "Is it 8 of 10 attempts?" asks Ron. "Exactly right," replies the presenter. "Now you all can see that writing culturally relevant behaviorally stated objectives is as easy as ABCD!"

The presenters then divide those attending the session into small groups and give each group a large sheet of paper and markers. Each group's task is to draft a lesson plan that contains present level of performance, behaviorally stated objectives (progressions), and a short-term objective for the group's assigned student. Their respective lesson plans must enable the assigned student to engage in high levels of motor activity participation within an inclusionary physical activity context. Each group is assigned one of the following students:

- Ebony is an African American 4th-grade student who has spastic, diplegic cerebral palsy (paralysis affecting similar parts on both sides of the body) and uses a manual wheelchair for mobility. Ebony has difficulty with speech, so she uses a communication board. She also is considered moderately mentally retarded.

- Young-Ryuel is a Korean-born 2nd-grade student who is severely visually impaired. Young-Ryuel has never received GPE at school; rather, he has received orientation and mobility training during physical education.

- Ikara is a Native Hawaiian 12th-grade high school student who has a condition known as spina bifida and uses a wheelchair in most situations. She is learning how to use long leg braces and crutches.

- Cynthia is a White American 7th-grade middle school student who is visually impaired (legally blind) and uses Braille (classroom notes are recorded for her). Cynthia is unable to see the teacher's demonstrations.

The group members work on their tasks of writing culturally sensitive and relevant behaviorally stated lesson plan objectives. Several minutes later, the session continues with a spokesperson from each group coming to the front of the room to share the lesson plan that the group has developed, and she or he points out the ABCD components within the plan's progressions. After all the groups have a turn to discuss their lesson plans, the presenters praise everyone for their high-quality work. They conclude the session by showing everyone how the ABCD model could be used in developing IEP objectives.

Endnotes

1. Hodge, S. R., & Murata, N. M. (November 2000). *Writing behaviorally-stated objectives for students with disabilities from culturally diverse backgrounds.* New York State Alliance for Health, Physical Education, Recreation and Dance Conference. Unpublished conference presentation.

2. Culturally relevant pedagogy "means that teachers have a moral responsibility to be culturally responsive or to design curricular programs that are responsive to the educational needs of learners from diverse cultural backgrounds" (Sparks, 1994, p. 35). This suggests that culturally relevant pedagogy recognizes the impact of culture, language, ethnicity, gender, and other variables that define students as different (Sparks, 1994).

3. Jansma and French (1994) provide a complete discussion of the ABCD model for lesson planning and individualization of instruction.

4. The sample lesson plan was adapted from Jansma and French (1994, p. 79).

Resources and References

Block, M. E. (1996). Modify instruction: Include all students. *Strategies* 9(4), 9–12.

Block, M. E. (2000). *A teacher's guide to including students with disabilities in general physical education* (2nd ed.). Baltimore: Brookes.

Individuals with Disabilities Education Act Amendments of 1997, Pub. L. No. 105-17, Sec. 601, 111 Stat. 40-41 (June 4, 1997).

Jansma, P., & French, R. (1994). *Special physical education: Physical activity, sports, and recreation.* Englewood Cliffs, NJ: Prentice Hall.

Sparks, W. G., III. (1994). Culturally responsive pedagogy: A framework for addressing multicultural issues. *Journal of Physical Education, Recreation and Dance, 65*(9), 33–36, 61.

Sutherland, S. L., & Hodge, S. R. (2001). Inclusion of a diverse population. *Teaching Elementary Physical Education, 12*(2), 15–17.

Winnick, J. P. (2000). *Adapted physical education and sport* (3rd ed.). Champaign, IL: Human Kinetics.

NOTES

QUESTIONS

Preparing for Learning & Teaching

CASE 3

SUMMARY OF PARTICIPANTS

Mr. Joseph, physical education teacher

Ashanti, student example in lesson plan

Marlene, audience participant

Kathy, audience participant

Ron, audience participant

Ebony, assigned student for lesson plan

Young-Ryuel, assigned student for lesson plan

Ikara, assigned student for lesson plan

Cynthia, assigned student for lesson plan

1. What issues exist in this case?

2. What is individualization of instruction? What is individualized task analysis?

3. Can you identify and discuss the four components of the ABCD model for writing behaviorally stated objectives?

4. What practical applications and benefits can be derived from using the ABCD model for unit and lesson planning? IEP development? How is this model different or similar to the style of unit and lesson planning you currently use?

5. What are some concerns or disadvantages associated with using this model in physical education?

6. Can you write a lesson plan for Ebony, Young-Ryuel, Ikara, and Cynthia using the ABCD model? What about for students with disabilities in settings that you are familiar with at your school, at a practicum site, at a recreational facility, or in the community?

7. What legal requirements exist with respect to teaching students with disabilities in physical education settings? What is your understanding of Public Law 105-17 relative to this issue?

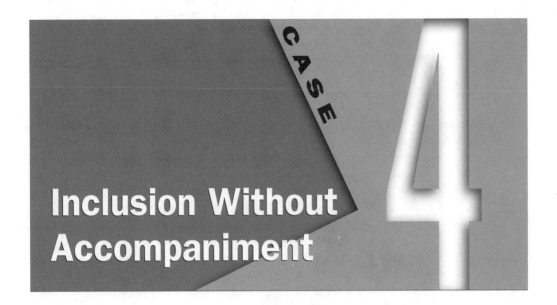

Inclusion Without Accompaniment

School administrators and teachers are becoming more and more receptive of inclusion practice for students with disabilities. Most administrators and teachers at Parkview School Complex are no different. In fact, at Parkview most of these educational professionals embrace an inclusion philosophy in that all students can learn, get along, and respect each other. This philosophy is also reflected in the district's mission statement; it addresses appreciable differences for all persons and supports the myriad ways that students learn. Crane Park Middle School is one of only two middle schools in Parkview School Complex. These schools, along with their feeder elementary schools, comprise a total of 11 schools (1 high school, 2 middle schools, and 8 elementary schools). Teachers who work in the Parkview School Complex have an average of 15 years of teaching experience, with 85 percent of its teachers with master's degrees. The community is affluent with a good mixture of diverse cultures. Although the distribution is not equal across the board, Parkview is considered more diverse than other comparable complexes nearby. One would think that a complex like Parkview would wholeheartedly embrace an inclusion philosophy. To some extent this is true; however, several mechanisms need to be in place before a true inclusion philosophy can be fully adopted.

Mr. Alvarez is the regular physical education teacher at Crane Park Middle School. He is new to the school but has taught physical education for more than 8 years. Mr. Alvarez is an energetic and enthusiastic teacher. Students enjoy his Latino songs, and he often uses them in his classes. Mr. Alvarez is also inclined to teach any student who is placed in his PE class. Although he did not receive much training in APE, he knows that specialized instruction in the form of modifications and adaptations is needed. In fact, he generally would adapt most of his physical education lessons. Mr. Alvarez has one stipulation regarding inclusion of a student with disabilities in his class: "I would like to receive some type of report (medical or motor present level of performance) on the student. And should the student or I need any assistance or support, either or both would be provided." Mr. Alvarez has attended several IEP meetings, so he knows that physical education is always a topic of discussion. He participated in these IEP meetings in order to inform the group as to what his physical education program is like, to indicate his expectations for students, and to describe the eventual outcomes that all students should obtain. He feels comfortable that he was able to address specific physical education needs for students.

Mr. Alvarez is teaching his 7th graders an aerobics lesson by having them do Tae Bo via an instructional videotape. In addition, Mr. Alvarez assigns the class into groups to come up with their own creative aerobic fitness routine. The routine will be videotaped and used for assessment purposes, parent–teacher conferences, and open house functions. About halfway through the class, Mr. Alvarez notices that Ms. Easton, the vice principal, is standing by the gym door with a mother, father, and girl. The girl seems in wonderment, as she holds her hands by her mouth and makes unusual noises. Ms. Easton waves for Mr. Alvarez to joint them. As the class continues to follow the Tae Bo video, Mr. Alvarez walks over to Ms. Easton, smiles, and shakes her hand. Ms. Easton introduces Mr. Alvarez to Mr. and Mrs. Miller and their daughter Lisa. Mr. Alvarez shakes both parents' hands and then extends his hand to Lisa. Lisa immediately starts screaming and tries to run away. Mr. Miller quickly grabs Lisa. Ms. Easton, quite shaken by the high-pitched scream, says, "Alfredo, Lisa Miller is a new student who just moved into our school district. We are currently getting her situated and introducing her to her new teachers." Suddenly, the smile from Mr. Alvarez's face disappears. "Oh . . . ," he replies. But before he can get another word out, Mrs. Miller informs him that Lisa has Asperger disorder. A look of uncertainty appears on Mr. Alvarez's face. "Asperger disorder . . . I've never heard of it," he replies. Mrs. Miller explains that Asperger disorder is something like autism, but Lisa functions at a much higher level. Only one thought races through Mr. Alvarez's mind—"autism." His questions about this girl must wait, however, because the videotape is over and his 7th graders are becoming restless and noisy. The class period is about to end, so Mr. Alvarez quickly excuses himself and debriefs the students on their lesson and previews the next day's lesson. He informs them that they will soon have to demonstrate their routines, so they need to be prepared.

Ms. Easton suggests that they walk toward the lockers so that they can continue their discussion. She says, "Lisa will be starting school tomorrow and we have assigned her to your period 5 class." As the Millers try to keep Lisa from running away, Mr. Alvarez tries to appear pleasant. Clearly, he is not thrilled by this venture. Mrs. Miller tries to downplay Lisa's condition. "Lisa is a bright girl, enjoys watching television, plays with the family dog, and likes to be with friends. She came from another public school where she was well received and did extremely well." Mr. Miller adds, "Lisa does have her moments, but with some structure she will be fine." At that point, the bell rings, and Mr. Alvarez excuses himself and returns to his classroom.

The same day after school, Mr. Alvarez goes to see Ms. Easton. He is clearly not happy: "Ms. Easton, I know we espouse an inclusion philosophy, but shouldn't we at least have a meeting? An IEP meeting would be nice, because I don't know the extent to which Lisa is able to participate in PE class. What other classes does she have?" Ms. Easton replies, "Lisa has art with Mr. King and special education with Ms. Bell. Lisa is a very capable young lady and I'm sure she'll do just fine." Mr. Alvarez asks, "Can I at least see her present level of performance or some form of assessment information?" Ms. Easton replies, "Lisa's IEP is on its way from South Hill Complex, so it may take a few days." "A few days! How am I supposed to teach her when I know absolutely nothing about her?" bellows Mr. Alvarez. Ms. Easton tries to calm down Mr. Alvarez: "You will be just fine. Lisa's condition does not impede her from participating in physical education. Plus, according to the Millers, Lisa had regular physical education back in South Hill." Stunned, Mr. Alvarez returns to his office. Although he is a firm believer in the inclusion philosophy, he starts to second-guess the implications of inclusion, especially since he is not prepared to receive Lisa in class. She may very well have received regular physical education at one time, but he certainly would have appreciated a little more information about her.

That night, Mr. Alvarez reads about Lisa's condition. He also contacts Ms. Sato, the APE teacher in the district. However, Ms. Sato is out of town at a conference and won't be back for a week. As Mr. Alvarez continues to read about Asperger disorder, he becomes more and more distressed: "How could the school immediately accept a student without knowing her background? How could a student arrive in the middle of the semester without any follow-up information? How could the school literally 'dump' Lisa into my PE class without any information, support, or input from me?" It just wasn't right. Despite his initial negative judgments about Lisa, Mr. Alvarez knows that at this point he can do little about it. Although the situation might not be fair to him and the other period 5 students, Mr. Alvarez acknowledges that he and his period 5 class now need to be prepared for Lisa or any student with a disability. His growing concern now focuses on all the students in his period 5 class, not just on providing appropriate physical education to Lisa. Mr. Alvarez feels that the "cavalry" has abandoned him.

NOTES

QUESTIONS

Preparing for Learning & Teaching

1. What is the primary issue in this case?

2. What are some of the factors that contributed positively and negatively to this case?

3. Why did Mr. Alvarez perceive Lisa's disability as a problem? What was his main concern?

4. Do you agree or disagree with how Mr. Alvarez reacted? Was it appropriate? How do you think you would have reacted in such a situation?

5. Do you think Mr. Alvarez truly believed in an inclusion philosophy or was his "belief" conditional?

6. Was Mr. Alvarez's demand for medical and educational (i.e., IEP present level of motor performance) reports unreasonable? Why or why not?

7. When Mr. Alvarez acknowledges that his period 5 class needs to be "prepared," what does he mean?

Support Personnel: Roles and Training

J eremy is only 5 years old, small for his age, with the most angelic face, big blue eyes, and a smile that makes everyone around him melt. So why is this adorable little boy causing such turmoil at Bluestone Elementary School? From the principal to the custodian, everyone at Bluestone is concerned about Jeremy. And Jeremy isn't even a student at Bluestone! It is only May and Jeremy isn't scheduled to enter kindergarten until the fall. Nevertheless, everyone at Bluestone knows about Jeremy, and they want to know how to deal with this little boy.

Why all the fuss about one little boy? Jeremy isn't quite what he appears, and he certainly isn't a typical 5-year-old. When Jeremy was 2 years old, he was diagnosed with autism by his pediatrician. He was then referred to the Stony Cliff School District, where he was tested by special education staff and determined to be a child with a developmental delay. Stony Cliff immediately initiated an individualized family service plan (IFSP) meeting. It was determined that Jeremy would receive itinerant, in-home special education and occupational therapy by a special education teacher and occupational therapist provided by Stony Cliff. This in-home service seemed to work fairly well, although the teacher and therapist saw glimpses of Jeremy's unpredictable and violent behaviors. When Jeremy turned 3, he was placed in a preschool class for children with developmental disabilities that was housed in another elementary school in the school district. Preschoolers from all over the school district were brought to this one site for special education classes. This special preschool program and its staff have a good reputation in the school district, but the staff has never dealt with anyone quite like Jeremy.

It is at this special preschool that Jeremy's behaviors begin to worsen and become almost uncontrollable. He is only 3, but his preschool special education teacher, Mrs. Jump, as well as the two teacher assistants, the speech and occupational therapists, and even the principal are very intimidated and even afraid of Jeremy. The reason for everyone's fear is his violent behaviors, which include biting, scratching, kicking, and screaming. His teacher and teacher assistants have scratch and bite marks on their hands and arms, and more than once the principal has been summoned to the preschool classroom to help restrain Jeremy. An autism specialist, Ms. Fisher, was called in several times to work with Jeremy and help the staff deal with him. Ms. Fisher had some good ideas including creating a daily schedule, learning simple ways to communicate with Jeremy and to help him communicate, managing behavior, and learning how to make transitions clearer to Jeremy. These changes seem to help Jeremy a little toward the end of his first year in preschool as well as his second year of preschool. But he still has at least 3 violent outbursts a day (as many as 10 on a really bad day), and the staff feels that he is going to have a difficult transition to kindergarten in the fall.

Jeremy's IEP meeting is scheduled for June 1, and everyone at Bluestone is interested in the outcome of this meeting. After Jeremy's parents and the other key members of the IEP team are introduced, the meeting commences with a review of Jeremy's present level of performance. This includes information on Jeremy's cognitive, social, behavioral, speech, fine motor, and gross motor skills. The results of the assessment are presented without a great deal of comment—everyone knows that Jeremy is delayed in virtually every developmental area. There is some discussion regarding Jeremy's violent behaviors and their frequency as well as regarding how a large, general education class might affect these behaviors and the staff's ability to deal with these behaviors.

The discussion then focuses on Jeremy's IEP goals and objectives. After several minutes of discussion, all team members agree upon one goal per area (i.e., cognitive, speech, motor) and three to four objectives per goal. There really is surprising consensus on the goals and objectives between Jeremy's parents and the other team members, and the IEP meeting is progressing better than most had expected. Besides the developmental goals and objectives in the cognitive, speech, and motor areas, there are several objectives that deal with Jeremy's behaviors, including dealing with frustration and confusion, handling transitions from one activity to another as well as one setting to another, communicating appropriately when he is tired or doesn't want to participate in activity, and communicating the need for time away from the group or some sensory stimulation. Everyone agrees that helping Jeremy develop more appropriate behaviors is the most important aspect of his IEP.

Next on the agenda is a discussion of special education services, related services, and accommodations that Jeremy will need to help him reach his goals and objectives. Given Jeremy's significant delays and his behaviors, it is determined that he will receive special education services from a special education teacher 50 percent of the time. The other portion of his school day will be filled as follows: speech twice per week for 30 minutes per session, occupational therapy twice per week for 30 minutes per session, and APE twice per week for 30 minutes per session. Jeremy's special educator, adapted physical educator, teacher assistant, and related service personnel will also receive consultative support from Ms. Fisher twice per month for 30 minutes through a bimonthly team meeting. One of the major accommodations that Jeremy will receive is a full-time teacher assistant.

Finally, the discussion moves to placement options. Mr. Riley, the special education teacher at Bluestone, spends several minutes outlining the various placement options available to Jeremy from full-time regular class placement with full-time support from Mr. Riley and his new teacher assistant, Mr. Ball, to full-time special education placement. The team members discuss the pros and cons of each placement and then amicably agree that Jeremy will spend most of his day in a special education class with pull-in opportunities for story time (Jeremy likes to hear teachers read stories), recess, lunch, physical education, and art. These pull-in opportunities will be supported by Mr. Riley or Mr. Ball, and these integrated opportunities will be based on his tolerance level for these integrated activities and any negative effect that he might be having on the general education children.

As the meeting concludes, Jeremy's parents thank the team and in particular Mrs. Jump and her teaching assistants for all that they had done for Jeremy over the past two years. One of his parents' concerns is whether or not the staff at Bluestone has the necessary training to carry out this fairly complex educational program. Mr. Riley, the speech therapist, the occupational therapist, the adapted physical educator, general physical educator Mr. Adams, and art teacher Mrs. Grant admit that they have had very little experience with children with autism, particularly those with severe behavior problems. Jeremy's parents also are concerned that Mr. Ball will most likely need extensive training. They question who will provide this training, what type of training will be provided, when it will be provided (sometime that summer or in the beginning of the school year), and how much ongoing training will be provided. Jeremy's parents are particularly concerned about his transition to Bluestone and the importance of having everyone trained in one plan when school starts.

Mr. Riley looks to Ms. Fisher. She says that she would be happy to do some of the staff training, but first she wants members of the IEP team, including Jeremy's parents and former preschool teacher, to outline the types of training that they feel are needed for Jeremy. Everyone is silent. Then Mrs. Grant says that she is concerned for her safety and the safety of her other children. She feels that she needs some training in how to de-escalate and restrain Jeremy if he is having a tantrum, and that she needs to learn some basic self-defense so that she can protect herself without harming Jeremy. Mr. Adams as well as the other therapists all nod their heads in agreement. Mr. Adams also asks about training in how to create and use picture schedules with Jeremy. It seems that from their conversations during the IEP meeting picture schedules are reasonably effective with Jeremy, and Mr. Adams wants to learn more about this technique and how it might be used in physical education. Mrs. Grant and the other therapists again nod in agreement.

Then Mr. Riley asks about communication. Jeremy is nonverbal, but he uses basic signs and pointing to convey what he wants. He seems to understand some one-word sentences, but Mrs. Jump had also used basic signs, gestures, and pictures. Mr. Riley feels that all the staff working with Jeremy should have training in how to communicate with him. Finally, Jeremy's parents want all the staff to watch a video on autism that they can provide so that everyone will have a better understanding of autism in general and why children with autism behave the way that they do.

Ms. Fisher takes notes on all of the suggestions for training. She says that she could teach the staff about picture schedules and how to help Jeremy with transitions. She then asks Mrs. Jump if she could teach staff members at Bluestone some of the basic signs that Jeremy knows and generally how to communicate with him. Mrs. Jump gladly agrees. Mr. Riley says that a certified MANDT[1] trainer works in a private school located within the school district, and that this person might be willing to conduct MANDT training (MANDT training focuses on de-escalation, restraint, and self-defense for children and adults with behavior problems). One major, final question that needs to be answered is, When would all this training take place? It is already June, and there are only two more weeks of school. The parents (and rightfully so) want to have everything in place when Jeremy walks into Bluestone in the fall. That means training will have to take place during the summer. The staff anxiously looks at each other in such a way as to say, "I don't want to give up my summer to learn how to deal with this little boy!" Ms. Fisher closes the meeting by suggesting that everyone go home, check their calendars and consult with their families, and then choose possible dates for summer training.

Endnote

1. The Mandt System® is a systematic training program developed by David Mandt and designed to help prevent people from losing control and, if necessary, de-escalate people when they have lost control. The program believes that until the person is de-escalated, no training (e.g., behavior program, etc.), learning, or work will take place. The entire philosophy of The Mandt System® is based on the principle that all people have the right to be treated with dignity and respect. The Mandt System® blends well with traditional behavior management approaches. The system teaches the use of a graded system of alternatives that use the least amount of external management necessary in all situations. Professionals learn to recognize the "crisis cycle" and how to manage students through verbal and non-verbal strategies. They also learn ways to provide appropriate physical assistance and, when necessary, restraints in a variety of settings while keeping the student, the teacher, and others in the area safe.

   For more information, contact David Mandt & Associates, P.O. Box 831790, Richardson, TX 75083-1790, Phone: (972) 495-0755, Fax: (972) 530-2292. http://mandtsystem.com/h_version.htm

QUESTIONS
Preparing for Learning & Teaching

1. What is the primary issue in this case?

SUMMARY OF PARTICIPANTS
CASE 5

Jeremy, 5-year-old with autism

Mrs. Jump, preschool special education teacher

Ms. Fisher, autism specialist

Mr. Riley, special education teacher

Mr. Ball, teacher assistant

Mr. Adams, general physical educator

Mrs. Grant, art teacher

2. Should the staff be required to attend a summer training session to prepare them for Jeremy? Should the school district pay the staff for this summer training?

3. Is it appropriate for parents to ask all the staff to watch a video as part of their training?

4. What is MANDT training? Is this the type of program that the staff should learn? Who should pay for the MANDT training? Are there other programs similar to MANDT that might be effective in this situation?

5. If the school district did not have an autism specialist, who could be contacted to provide training?

6. Regarding ongoing training, do you think that twice monthly meetings are enough, or should some other mechanism be in place?

7. Who should train and supervise the teacher assistant? When Mr. Ball accompanies Jeremy to GPE, who is responsible for Jeremy's program, behaviors, skill work, modifications, and so forth?

Creating and Conducting a Self-Contained Adapted Physical Education Program

6

M r. Jacobs, or Coach Jacobs as he likes to be called, is not exactly known as a go-getter in his school. He comes to work on time, does his job teaching physical education at Adams Middle School, and leaves at the required time each afternoon. However, he'll tell anyone who asks that teaching physical education to 6th, 7th, and 8th graders isn't what he envisioned himself doing for 20 years. Rather, he studied physical education so he could coach football. And, in fact, Mr. Jacobs is a very good football coach. In his 20 years of coaching at Northwood High School, his teams have won 10 district championships, 3 regional championships, and one state title. Thirty of his players received scholarships to play college football, and more than 90 percent of his players graduated from high school. He is well known and well respected in the community for his football program. Teaching middle school physical education is something Coach Jacobs has to do so that he can coach.

Not that Coach Jacobs is a bad physical education specialist. The program he runs has a nice mix of fitness, sports, and lifetime leisure activities. Additionally, he tries hard to teach skills and concepts rather than just "rolling out the ball." Although he does create opportunities for regulation basketball and soccer games in his classes, he usually has the students practice the skills first. He is good at seeing what the students are doing correctly and incorrectly He is also good at taking the organizational skills he establishes at his football practices and applying them to the skill work he does with his students. For example, he is accustomed to having his football players work at stations on skills needed for their particular position, so he is very comfortable creating learning stations in the gym so that students can work on different aspects of a sport. Coach Jacobs's students respect him, mostly because of his almost celebrity-like status as a football coach. But they also respect him because he runs a pretty good physical education program.

As noted earlier, Coach Jacobs is not a go-getter at his school. He does his job, but he never tries to implement new ideas or programs. For example, his school is the only middle school in the district that doesn't participate in the Jump Rope for Heart Program. Also, many other middle school physical educators create and conduct running clubs, intramural sports programs, and other PE-related activities during the school day and after school, but Mr. Jacobs never seems to have the time or interest for these special programs. Mr. Peterson, principal of Adams Middle School, has suggested that he start a fitness club for the increasing number of overweight students and even found time in Coach Jacobs's schedule for this program during the school day. But Coach Jacobs somehow managed to get out of it—he likes his schedule, and he doesn't want to change it.

Coach Jacobs's comfortable schedule is about to change. He has noticed that over the past five years or so more students with disabilities have been included in his PE classes. In general, Coach Jacobs doesn't mind having these students in his PE classes, as long as they can follow his directions and keep up with the other students. He does occasionally make modifications when he feels it is appropriate and not too difficult. Like the time he had a student with Down syndrome in one of his classes. He let the student stand closer to the basket when shooting, he would often repeat directions to this student when he seemed confused, and he tried to encourage the other students to pass the ball to him and include him in games. There was also the time he had a student who was Deaf in one of his classes. This student managed fairly well by having a peer who knew enough sign language to repeat directions.

Lately, students with more severe disabilities have been coming to Coach Jacobs's PE classes. These students are usually accompanied by a teacher assistant, so they never really cause Coach Jacobs any problems, but they never really seem to fit in, either. For example, two students with autism, Billy and Charles, do warm-ups with the rest of the class with the help of the teacher assistant, but they are not able to keep up with the pace of the warm-up routine. Cooper, a student with severe cerebral palsy, is taken out of his chair during warm-ups and stretched on a mat. And Jaquin, a student with severe mental retardation, requires an incredible amount of prodding and pulling just to get him to sit up and try any of the warm-up activities.

Skill activities are even more difficult for these students with severe disabilities. The teacher assistants help them join their classmates and then help them do the skill work, but the skill level of these students is nowhere close to that of their peers. Modifications are so great that peers who are partnered with these students end up helping them rather than actually practicing the skills themselves. Coach Jacobs often wonders if the skill activities are even appropriate for these students. After all, Cooper will never be able to play soccer or any of the sports that are part of the middle school physical education curriculum, and Billy, Charles, and Jaquin don't seem interested in most of the activities. Even when they are interested, Coach Jacobs believes that it would take a lot more than a four-week unit for these students to make any significant gains in their skills. For example, Billy likes to dribble a basketball, and he seems interested in shooting as well. But Coach Jacobs believes it is going to take Billy a long, long time to master these and other basic basketball skills, and he isn't even sure Billy will ever learn the basic rules of the game.

Games are especially difficult for these students with severe disabilities. For example, during a game Billy and Charles often just stand and stare at their fingers as if they don't even realize what is going on around them. Jaquin often just sits down in the middle of the game and refuses to move or play. And Coach Jacobs is concerned that in the heat of the game some of the students without disabilities will run into Cooper's wheelchair. This is middle school, and the students are bigger, faster, and stronger than those in elementary school. It is impossible for the students with severe disabilities to keep up. When the other students are involved in games, the easiest thing for Coach Jacobs to do is have Billy, Charles, Jaquin, and Cooper participate in activities with their teacher assistant on the sidelines or just watch and cheer for the other students. He realizes that these students are not getting the attention they should, but he feels he is doing the best he can for everyone involved. Coach Jacobs thinks these students would be better served if they were enrolled in a specially designed physical education program in a small group rather than in his general physical education class with 60 other students.

Well, it turns out that Coach Jacobs is not the only one who feels these students with severe disabilities should receive at least part of their physical education in a separate, specially designed program. The parents of these children have wondered what their children were getting out of GPE. At several IEP meetings, Mrs. McGraw, the special education teacher, and Coach Jacobs are unable to answer some of the parents' questions about GPE. After one particularly contentious IEP meeting, Mrs. McGraw walks down the hall with Coach Jacobs and asks him, "What do you think the students with severe disabilities really need in physical education?" He replies, "I honestly don't think they are benefiting at all from GPE, and I think they should have a separate program." Mrs. McGraw agrees and heads back to her classroom. Coach Jacobs figures this is the end of the discussion.

The next day, Coach Jacobs is summoned to Mr. Peterson's office. When he arrives Mrs. McGraw is already there. He sits down and Mr. Peterson tells them, "I have heard from several parents and from Mrs. McGraw that GPE is not appropriate for some of the students with more severe disabilities." Coach Jacobs responds, "I agree and I've felt this way for several months now." Mr. Peterson then catches Coach Jacobs by surprise: "I have released you from your bus duty at the end of the day, and during that time you will conduct a specially designed physical education program for Billy, Charles, Jaquin, and Cooper." Dumbfounded, Coach Jacobs stammers out an argument including statements that he did not know what do to with these kids, that he was not trained, and that the school district should hire a certified APE specialist. Mr. Peterson doesn't disagree and tells him that he understands his concerns. However, Coach Jacobs is qualified to conduct this program according to the state, and he will ensure that each student will have their own teacher assistant and funds will be provided for extra equipment. He also tells Coach Jacobs that he will support his needs to attend conferences or observe other physical educators in the district who run similar programs. Mr. Peterson says that since it is early December, it would probably be best to just wait and start the program when school resumes after the holiday break. As Coach Jacobs rises from his chair, Mr. Peterson says, "I have the utmost confidence that you'll figure out what to do. I know it might be difficult at first, but I also know that you'll run a great APE program."

Coach Jacobs walks back to his office, sits down at his desk, and begins to think about how to run an APE program for Billy, Charles, Jaquin, and Cooper. He only has four weeks to create this APE program and get it up and running, and he doesn't have a clue what to do.

QUESTIONS

Preparing for Learning & Teaching

SUMMARY OF PARTICIPANTS

Mr. Jacobs, or Coach Jacobs, physical education teacher

Mr. Peterson, principal

Billy, student with autism

Charles, student with autism

Jaquin, student with severe mental retardation

Cooper, student with severe cerebral palsy

Mrs. McGraw, special education teacher

1. What is the primary issue in this case?

2. What are some of the factors that contributed to this issue?

3. According to federal law and to your state law, who is "qualified" to provide APE services to students with disabilities? Do you think this is right?

4. What are some preliminary things Coach Jacobs should do to prepare for this program? Why do you think these things are important?

5. Whom should Coach Jacobs contact to get some ideas? Where are these people (in the school, in the school district, in the state, somewhere in the country)? Why are these important people to contact?

6. What other resources (e.g., websites, books, articles) should Coach Jacobs use? Why are these important resources?

7. Do you think that Coach Jacobs should do the same activity with each student, or should each student have his or her own individual plan? Why?

8. If you think that each student should have his own individualized program, how should Coach Jacobs go about deciding what to teach each student? Why?

9. After Coach Jacobs has a general idea of what to teach, how can he break down this general plan into more teachable components? For example, if it is determined that one of the boys would play basketball, how could Coach Jacobs decide specifically what skills this student already has, what he needs to work on, and how to work on it?

10. If you think that each student should have his own individualized program, how can such a program be implemented. In other words, how can Coach Jacobs organize this special class that includes all four students so that each student is working on his own individual program?

11. Because parents were not happy with the previous physical education program and because they know that Coach Jacobs's program is new, they might want regular reports to see how well the program is doing. How can Coach Jacobs report to the parents on a regular basis as to what he is doing, and how well their children are doing?

Consultation Between Generalist and Specialist in Physical Education

Bill loves the independence he has as the only physical education teacher at Smithtown Elementary School. No one tells him what to teach, how to teach, or even how to discipline his children. Dr. Stephenson, the principal at Smithtown, even allows Bill to make his own schedule. Bill has created a basketball and soccer league for 4th and 5th graders during lunch and recess two days per week; a pull-out program for children with mild disabilities the last period of the day two days per week; and a jump rope team on Friday afternoons, which he also runs. Yes, Bill loves his independence.

Bill isn't necessarily opposed to working with others, but he had a bad experience a few years ago that has left him very cautious about seeking outside help. It was Bill's 5th year of teaching elementary physical education, and he had developed a nice routine and structure for his program. Then his principal told him that Michelle, a child who used a wheelchair, would be in his 4th-grade class in the upcoming year. In addition, one of the county's APE specialists would be coming to work with this child and help Bill 2 days per week. Bill was excited about having another colleague in the gym with him to discuss ideas and just to talk. Unfortunately, Jessica Moore, the APE assigned to work with Michelle, was not what he had expected. She was very confident and brash and quick to voice her opinion to Bill not only about Michelle but also about how to teach GPE. There was very little give-and-take or team problem solving—Jessica simply told Bill what to do. He never really got the chance to tell her about his feelings or concerns, and he did not appreciate being told how to teach. Fortunately for Bill, Michelle moved to another school in midyear, along with Jessica.

Brooke is a 3rd grader at Smithtown who is perhaps the best-known student in the school. She has big blue eyes and beautiful blonde hair that is always neatly pulled back into a long braid. She loves to run, climb on the playground equipment, and swing on the swings. However, behind this beautiful exterior is a very troubled girl. Brooke has autism, and she often seems terribly tormented by her disability. There are days when she cries inconsolably for no apparent reason. Other days she lashes out at her teachers and her peers, trying to scratch, bite, or punch them. And some days she seems fine and happy but will suddenly run out the back door and into the woods behind the school.

Bill has some unique problems with Brooke in physical education. Even though Mrs. Phillips, her teacher assistant, always accompanies Brooke to PE class, Brooke has a particularly difficult time in the gym setting. For one thing, like most gyms, the one at Smithtown is a large, vacuous space that has terrible acoustics. On most days Brooke gladly enters the gym and has no problems with the noise level. However, on other days she enters hesitantly. Then, as the noise level begins to rise, she becomes noticeably irritable. This irritability often rises to the point where Brooke will cover her ears, scream, and then run to the exit. Bill isn't sure what to do with Brooke during these episodes. For the past few months her screaming has occurred more often and seems to be even louder and more distracting to the other students. When Brooke becomes too distracting Bill simply asks Mrs. Phillips to take her for a walk around the building. Also, Brooke sometimes seems to be doing well when suddenly, for no apparent reason, she will lash out at Mrs. Phillips or a peer. Understandably, Bill is concerned about the safety of Mrs. Phillips and the other students. He has a few rules for physical education, including treating teachers and peers with respect. Clearly, striking out at a teacher assistant or another student violates this rule. Bill isn't sure how this rule should apply to someone like Brooke, who probably cannot comprehend its meaning.

Even on the best of days when Brooke is lucid and relatively compliant, her motor skills (at least the type of motor skills used in physical education such as ball skills, moving in space, and working with peers) are significantly delayed. Brooke tries to throw or catch with peers or play dodging and fleeing games, but she just can't keep up. Bill tries a few modifications such as giving her a different ball and allowing her to stand closer to another student when playing catch. He also allows Mrs. Phillips to guide her in dodging and fleeing games. Still, he isn't satisfied with how well Brooke is being included, and he wonders if she is benefiting from physical education at all. In addition, Brooke's inclusion seems to slow the games down, and Bill wonders how this might make the other students feel about physical education.

Bill knows that he needs the expertise of an APE specialist who has had training and experience with children with autism, but his last experience with one wasn't very positive. With great reluctance, Bill calls the director of special education and arranges to have an APE specialist consult with him about Brooke. He requests a different person this time and is relieved to hear that Nancy Cohen will be the consultant. Bill has never met Ms. Cohen, but he has heard from other PE colleagues that she is very pleasant, knowledgeable, and helpful. The plan is for Ms. Cohen to observe Brooke one day in GPE class and then briefly talk with Bill. They will then set up a lengthier meeting to discuss the problems he is facing.

Ms. Cohen arrives about 10 minutes before Brooke's class. With a quick nod to Bill, she takes a seat on the corner of the bleachers so as to be as inconspicuous as possible. Before Brooke's class begins, Bill introduces himself to Ms. Cohen and quickly explains that he has created some throwing stations for Brooke's class. After warm-ups, the class will break into four groups and go through the stations. At the end of class, he will play a game of "clean out your backyard" to reinforce throwing. He also tells Ms. Cohen what Brooke looks like and notes that Mrs. Phillips, her teacher assistant, will accompany her.

Brooke's class arrives a few minutes later, with Brooke and Mrs. Phillips bringing up the rear. As it turns out, Brooke is having a pretty good day. She enters the gym without any problems, finds her squad with a cue from Mrs. Phillips, and sits with her squad. She then does her best to follow Bill during warm-ups (which consist of stretches and strength activities while students stay in their squads). Although she isn't able to do the activities exactly like him, Brooke clearly tries to imitate Bill and the other students. She occasionally makes noise and jumps up and down, but she seems to do this because she is happy. After warm-ups, Bill explains the four stations. Brooke turns her body away from him and taps the floor with her hands and rocks gently from side to side. She is quiet most of the time although she does scream once. Again, this seems to be a "happy scream."

Bill then assigns each student to one of the four stations. They are to follow the directions posted on the wall at each station. Brooke gets up and walks to her assigned station with an extra cue from Mrs. Phillips. Brooke's station requires students to find a partner and bounce and catch a playground ball back and forth. Mrs. Phillips decides to be Brooke's partner, and she and Brooke bounce and catch the ball fairly well. Brooke needs a lot of extra cues to bounce the ball, but she eventually gets the hang of it. Ms. Cohen notes that there is no real interaction among Brooke and her classmates.

After a few minutes at the first station, Bill blows his whistle. The students stop what they are doing and sit down (Brooke sits after Mrs. Phillips gives her an extra cue). Bill then tells the children to walk and rotate to their next station. The next station for Brooke requires the children to throw yarn balls at a suspended parachute. Brooke walks to this station without any problems. Mrs. Phillips hands a yarn ball to Brooke, positions her toward the parachute, and then cues her to throw. Brooke throws the ball at the parachute, but without much force. Ms. Cohen notices that the other students at Brooke's station really enjoy throwing the ball very hard. She also notices that they are getting loud and quite competitive at grabbing the yarn balls on the floor.

Mrs. Phillips picks up another yarn ball and hands it to Brooke, but Brooke won't take it from her. Instead, she tries to scratch Mrs. Phillips. Mrs. Phillips backs away but Brooke again tries to scratch her. "No scratching!" says Mrs. Phillips in a firm voice, and she grabs Brooke by the wrists. Brooke then attempts to head-butt Mrs. Phillips. Mrs. Phillips lets go of Brooke's wrists, backs away, and firmly says, "No hitting!" But that doesn't stop Brooke. Mrs. Phillips again takes Brooke by the wrists and walks her toward the gym door. Brooke squirms and fights but she seems to calm down a little as she leaves the gym. Bill glances over at Ms. Cohen and shrugs his shoulders. Brooke doesn't return to PE class that day.

At the end of class, Ms. Cohen helps Bill clean up the gym. He asks her, "Well, what do you think of Brooke?" She replies, "I see why you contacted me. It looks like Brooke can be a real handful." She continues, "I have seen a lot of children with autism, and Brooke looks like one of the toughest. You should be given an award for keeping her in GPE as long you have!" Bill suddenly feels a little better about himself and decides that he is going to like working with Ms. Cohen. Ms. Cohen then asks him, "Do you have any idea why Brooke suddenly attacked Mrs. Phillips after starting the class so well?" He thinks for a moment and then says, "Maybe it was all the commotion of the balls flying around." Ms. Cohen agrees and says, "Children with autism often have trouble in crowded spaces because of tactile defensiveness. Maybe Brooke was worried that she would be bumped by a peer." Bill smiles and thinks to himself, "Hey, maybe I have a better handle on this than I thought." The two of them set up a meeting for the next week on Tuesday at 2:30 to talk about Brooke.

On Tuesday Ms. Cohen arrives at Bill's office a few minutes before 2:30, enabling her to see the end of the special PE class he put together for children with mild disabilities. As Bill walks into his office, Ms. Cohen tells him what a nice job he did with that special class. He smiles and thanks her and then says, "What have you got for me that will solve my problem with Brooke?" "I wish it were that easy," she says with a smile. She then explains the consultation model she uses. She notes that it is a collaborative model in which the two of them would be equal partners in solving the problems with Brooke. Ms. Cohen's contribution would include listening to Bill and trying to understand his concerns. In addition, she would share her knowledge about children with autism in physical education and help him find information on the Internet and elsewhere. She also has some good contacts with both autism and APE groups, with whom they could discuss ideas. Finally, she could train Bill on some specific techniques that he might find useful when dealing with Brooke.

Ms. Cohen tells Bill that he has a lot to contribute as well: "Only you can describe your specific concerns regarding Brooke. You have a better handle on your class structure, environment, curriculum, the temperament of Brooke's classmates, and even how Brooke reacts in many situations." Bill seems very impressed that he is going to be a partner in the process rather than simply having to listen to someone tell him what to do. This puts him at ease. However, he questions his role again: "I thought *you* were supposed to tell *me* how to deal with Brooke." Ms. Cohen grins and says, "That's the typical response I get from general physical educators when I consult. However, working together as a team proves to be the most effective way to consult. You and Mrs. Phillips would have to buy in to any program that was developed, so I feel you both should be part of the development team." Bill nods and says, "Okay, let's get started."

QUESTIONS
Preparing for Learning & Teaching

1. What is the primary issue in this case?

2. Why was Bill hesitant about seeking consultation?

3. What are some of the things Ms. Moore, the first APE consultant, did that Bill did not like? Why do you think this turned him off? What would have been a better way for Ms. Moore to handle this situation?

4. What are some of the little things that Ms. Cohen did during the entry phase that put Bill at ease about the consultant relationship?

5. Why do you think Ms. Cohen chose to use a collaborative consultation approach rather than simply analyze the situation and tell Bill what he needed to do? Why do you think she felt it was important to include the special education teacher and Mrs. Phillips in the process rather than just Bill?

6. Within this collaborative model, what is the role of the APE specialist? What is the role of the GPE specialist?

7. Although it appears that the consultation between Bill and Ms. Cohen will go well, what are some potential barriers or problems that can occur in the consultation process? How can these be overcome?

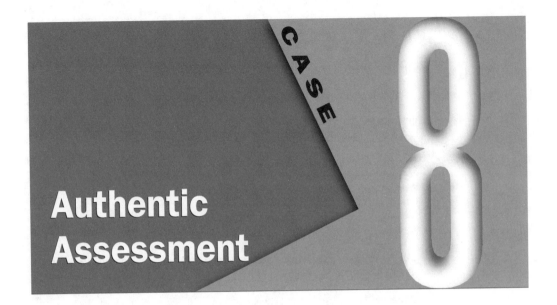

Authentic Assessment

Ms. Cody is an elementary school physical education teacher in her first year of teaching. She takes pride in her new job and loves her students. She has had extensive experience teaching at summer soccer and cheerleading camps. She loves her school and the physical education curriculum and is working well with her teaching partner, Mr. Datillo. Mr. Datillo has been at this school for 23 years and has a strong grasp on the curriculum. The school has a very well-rounded curriculum, which includes project adventure, hiking, snowshoeing, juggling, cooperative games, and orienteering, along with more traditional elementary units. Mr. Datillo is an excellent teacher and won the state teacher of the year award his 10th year of teaching. He is still very involved professionally, often is a presenter at state conferences, and accepts student teachers at least one semester a year. Mr. Datillo is especially proud of the rubric assessment he is currently implementing (see Example 1). The state elementary physical education task force developed general rubrics for each of most of the units that are taught. This is a form of *authentic assessment*:[1] it is an on-going assessment in a real-life situation. Criteria are presented ahead of time and children know exactly what is expected.

Utilizing the rubrics is very motivational for the children and helps Mr. Datillo keep accurate records of performance in their portfolios. The school had very few students with disabilities in the past, because the school had no ramp and there are three floors to the building. The school had only one class with some children with mental retardation and autism. This year the district installed ramps and an elevator at the school. As a result, three students who use wheelchairs and two who use walkers now attend the

EXAMPLE 1
Underhand Throw Rubrics

TASK	UNDERHAND THROW

Task description   Student will underhand throw to peer.

Scale components   Task analysis of form of step with opposite foot, release in front, weight shift forward, and follow-through.

LEVEL/COLOR	RUBRIC DESCRIPTORS
1/Red	Student will attempt to underhand throw a beanbag to peer standing 10 feet away.
2/Orange	Student will underhand throw a beanbag using a step with the opposite foot most of the time.
3/Yellow	Student will underhand throw a beanbag using a step with the opposite foot, and a release in front of the body most of the time.
4/Green	Student will underhand throw a beanbag using a step with the opposite foot, release in front of the body most of the time, and shift his or her weight forward during the throw most of the time.
5/Blue	Student will underhand throw a beanbag using a step with the opposite foot, release in front of the body, shift his or her weight forward during the throw, and follow through most of the time.
6/Indigo	Student will underhand throw a beanbag using a step with the opposite foot, release in front of the body, shift his or her weight forward during the throw, and follow through to partner 10 feet away.
7/Violet	Student will underhand throw a beanbag using a step with the opposite foot, release in front of the body, shift his or her weight forward during the throw, and follow through hitting an 8 foot by 8 foot target 15 feet away three out of five attempts.

Specific adaptations:

school. Ms. Cody feels comfortable modifying the curriculum for children with disabilities, yet she has no idea how to document their performance with the current assessment instrument. In addition, she is concerned about being in compliance with the law if she has no documented assessment for them.

The first three units of the year, Ms. Cody's class just went through the usual units using already established rubric assessments. Ms. Cody modified what she could for the students in her class who use wheelchairs and crutches. She felt okay about these modifications, but she felt much better about her modification for the children with autism and mental retardation. For example, during a kicking and soccer unit she had the students in wheelchairs perform throw-ins and block whatever came to them during drills or a game. The children with mental retardation had peer tutors who demonstrated and gave them feedback during the unit. For the juggling unit there were few modifications for the students who use wheelchairs, and the children who use crutches juggled while sitting. The students with mental retardation started out with scarves and balloons and used smaller progressions. Ms. Cody felt she was getting the hang of it, but she knew they were still being left out in some ways.

Mr. Datillo recently attended a statewide assessment workshop offered through the state association. In this conference the instructor covered assessment and how to modify rubrics for children with disabilities. Mr. Datillo shares the information with Ms. Cody when he returns. She is so relieved that she finally understands how to include the students who had been left out of the assessment loop for so long. Ms. Cody chooses her new project as a curriculum modification portfolio along with rubrics, websites, and lesson plans. She solicits Mr. Datillo's advice for the curriculum modifications, and they put their heads together to modify their existing rubrics. As Ms. Cody creates the rubrics for the current unit, she tests them out with her class and asks the students for feedback. The students love being part of the development process and have some great ideas. For example, when Ms. Cody wants to modify the jump rope unit, she asks the children with and without disabilities what they could do and how they would break up the levels. The students come up with the idea that they could put a rope on the floor and jump over it, crawl over it, or swing it at a low level and step over it, and it would still be considered part of the jump rope rubric. A few children don't have the patience to think of the steps in jumping rope and they become off task. This is a distraction for part of the group, so Ms. Cody adds questions and even has them get in a wheelchair or use crutches and asks them how they could be part of the rubric. The class (including the students who were acting out) suggests that students with crutches could fold two ropes in half and swing the rope with both hands to music. One child with hemiplegia cerebral palsy could swing the rope with one arm and have a peer hold the other end and swing the rope for him. Two of the children in wheelchairs could swing the rope over the chair and push their chairs over the rope. These ideas are incorporated into the existing rubrics in the way of rubrics extensions (see Examples 2 and 3).

The previously easiest rubric is now in the middle of the rubrics and there is a level on the rubrics for every child in the class. For the catching unit the rubrics were predominantly describing the product scores for catching. Basically, students had to count the number of completed catches and from how far away. This was only successful for about two-thirds of the children in Ms. Cody's classes. Ms. Cody had read about a rubrics analysis in an article, so she adds a specific task analysis rubrics to that unit so the students could achieve a level for their performance or form as well as how many catches they had from any distance. With this system the students could get a score and improve no matter what their catching ability.

Mr. Datillo adopts most of the adaptations and rubrics from Ms. Cody's project, and he is thrilled about how well all the students were included. Mr. Datillo and Ms. Cody continue to modify each unit and all the rubrics for their program, and they are soon asked to share their success at a Parent Teacher Association (PTA) meeting and at their local physical education conference as "Best Practices."

EXAMPLE 2

Jump Rope

TASK	JUMP ROPE
Task description	Student will perform the act of rolling, walking, hopping, or jumping over a rope at any height.
Scale components	From one time over one way to jumping forward and backward once or twice around.

LEVEL/COLOR	RUBRIC DESCRIPTORS
1/Red	Student will crawl, roll, walk, and jump over a rope placed on the floor up to 1 foot.
2/Orange	Student will step or jump forward over a rope placed 1 foot off the ground either stationary or swinging. Student will swing rope folded in half forward and backward with one arm.
3/Yellow	Student will bring rope over head with arms and step or roll over rope once. Student will swing rope folded in half forward and backward using both right and left hands.
4/Green	Student will bring rope over head with arms and step or roll over rope 2–20 times.
5/Blue	Student will jump rope (or wheel over rope) swinging rope over head backward 1–20 times.
6/Indigo	Student will jump rope to music forward, backward, and crisscross for 1–5 minutes.
7/Violet	Student will jump rope to music either alone or with a partner to music for 6–20 minutes.

Specific adaptations:

EXAMPLE 3
Underhand Throw with Extensions Rubrics

TASK	UNDERHAND THROW
Task description	Student will underhand throw to peer.
Scale components	Task analysis of form of step with opposite foot, release in front, weight shift forward, and follow-through.

LEVEL/COLOR	RUBRIC DESCRIPTORS
1/Tan	From seated position student will attempt to bat balloon palm up at waist level.
2/Gold	From seated position student will bat balloon and/or make circle with streamer at waist to shoulder level.
3/Red	From standing or sitting student will attempt to underhand throw a beanbag to peer standing 5–10 feet away.
4/Orange	From standing or sitting student will underhand throw a beanbag using a step with the opposite foot most of the time.
5/Yellow	From standing or sitting student will underhand throw a beanbag using a step with the opposite foot and a release in front of the body most of the time.
6/Green	From standing or sitting student will underhand throw a beanbag using a step with the opposite foot, release in front of the body most of the time, and shift his or her weight forward during the throw most of the time.
7/Blue	From standing or sitting student will underhand throw a beanbag using a step with the opposite foot, release in front of the body, shift his or her weight forward during the throw, and follow through most of the time.
8/Indigo	From standing or sitting student will underhand throw a beanbag using a step with the opposite foot, release in front of the body, shift his or her weight forward during the throw, and follow through to partner 10 feet away.
9/Violet	From standing or sitting student will underhand throw a beanbag using a step with the opposite foot, release in front of the body, shift his or her weight forward during the throw, and follow through hitting an 8 foot by 8 foot target 15 feet away three out of five attempts.

Specific adaptations:

Endnote

1. Authentic assessment is an assessment strategy that promotes students' participation in "applying skills and knowledge to solve real world problems, giving the task a degree of authenticity. The tests attempt to measure the acquisition of knowledge from a holistic standpoint" (Lund, 1997, p. 25). Students are asked to "demonstrate a thoughtful understanding of the problem, thus indicating mastery of a concept (Wiggins, 1989) as they apply and use their knowledge" (Lund, 1997, p. 25). Further, "tasks are set in meaningful contexts with connectivity to real world experiences and school-based ideas" (Lund, 1997, p. 25).

Resources and References

Block, M. E., Lieberman, L. J., & Conner-Kuntz, F. (1998). Authentic assessment in adapted physical education. *Journal of Physical Education, Recreation, & Dance, 69*(3), 48–56.

Goodrich, H. (1997). Understanding rubrics. *Educational Leadership, 54*(4), 14–17.

Lieberman, L. J., & Houston-Wilson, C. (2002). *Strategies for inclusion: A handbook for physical educators.* Champaign, IL: Human Kinetics.

Lund, J. (1997). Authentic assessment: Its development and applications. *Journal of Physical Education, Recreation & Dance, 68*(7), 25–28, 40.

Siedentop, D. (1994). Authentic assessment through sport education. In D. Siedentop (Ed.), *Sport education: Quality PE through positive sport experiences* (pp. 115–118). Champaign, IL: Human Kinetics.

Wiggins, G. (1989). A true test: Toward more authentic and equitable assessment. *Phi Delta Kappan, 69*, 703–713.

Wiggins, G. (1997). Practice what we preach in designing authentic assessment. *Educational Leadership, 54*(4), 18–25.

QUESTIONS

Preparing for Learning & Teaching

SUMMARY OF PARTICIPANTS

CASE 8

Ms. Cody, physical education teacher

Mr. Datillo, Ms. Cody's teaching partner

1. What was the initial problem in Ms. Cody and Mr. Datillo's curriculum?

2. What did Ms. Cody do to change this?

3. Why did the assessment system have to be changed?

4. What is authentic assessment, and what is a rubric?

5. What kinds of rubrics have application to APE and/or inclusive GPE?

6. What law would have been violated had Ms. Cody or Mr. Datillo not changed the assessment system?

7. How does the new rubrics system tie in with IEP development?

8. How would you modify rubrics for your current or future situations?

9. What other assessment tools would you use?

10. What teaching techniques would you use? How would you document progress on the new rubrics?

11. What other resources would you use?

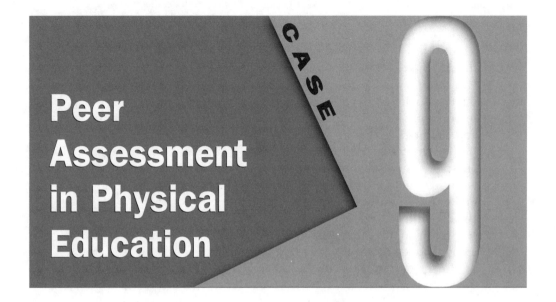

Peer Assessment in Physical Education

CASE

9

Tyrese Howard is a general physical education teacher at an urban middle school in Cleveland, Ohio. He firmly believes that assessment is one way to enhance the teaching–learning process for his students in physical education. He understands that assessment combines the processes of collecting test data and interpreting what his students know and can do. Tyrese uses assessment strategies to determine whether or not his students are progressing toward planned lesson and unit objectives. In fact, his favorite assessment strategies are authentic[1] and peer[2] assessments because he can use these practical strategies on a regular basis to assess an entire class in a short period of time.

In using peer assessments, Tyrese allows each student or group of students to assess peers' performance. He knows that by doing this his students will develop their skills to evaluate motor performances and gain a sense of trust and responsibility in giving and receiving feedback. Before using peer assessment tasks, Tyrese establishes the performance criteria for a particular lesson, and during class his students are then instructed to assess their peers' performances regarding the identified criteria. These students can then provide feedback to their peers either orally or through the use of a task card, rating scale, or checklist.

Tyrese's understanding of how best to use peer assessment was confirmed recently in a physical education journal article that he read. The article's authors suggested that in order for students to assess one another effectively the physical education teacher should first teach them how to appropriately do so. The authors pointed out the importance of communication in using peer assessment. Tyrese is pleased to know that he is on the right track in terms of seeking ways to effectively communicate performance expectations and outcome objectives to his students. He is also aware that his students will vary in terms of their skillfulness to perform the assessment tasks accurately and to communicate with one another effectively. Tyrese believes, as stated in the article, that using peer assessment also helps develop an understanding of teamwork, fosters shared responsibility for learning, promotes respect, enhances communication, and builds trust.

Tyrese's first-period class comprises a culturally and ethnically diverse group of students, including one student with a disability, Anthony. Anthony has a learning disability concomitant with attention deficit disorder (ADD) and hyperactivity and has been included in this class since the beginning of the school year. Anthony is typically developing in terms of psychomotor, behavioral, and intellectual functioning. However, he is easily distracted and tends to "get off task" frequently.

In the current individual and dual sports (e.g., tennis, badminton, racquetball) unit, students are engaged in tennis participation as taught within a sport education curriculum model. As was the case in previous units, Tyrese continues to emphasize ways to promote group cooperation, team membership, and sport participation. At the start of the "preseason" component of the current unit, Tyrese introduced the students to the fundamental skills of tennis, such as proper handgrips, footwork, execution of forehand and backhand ground strokes, and proper serving techniques. For the rest of the time spent in this tennis unit, Tyrese allowed the students to engage in singles and doubles match play and to take on tennis-related roles, such as the chair umpire, linesperson, ball boys and girls, or the "U. S. Davis Cup" captain.

In using peer assessment within this tennis unit, Tyrese introduced the students to proper handgrips (i.e., Continental, Western, and Eastern) for executing forehand and backhand ground strokes. Further, he instructed the students on specific critical elements to look for as he demonstrated proper grip and footwork for executing both forehand and backhand ground strokes. Tyrese was cognizant about emphasizing those critical elements of executing ground strokes that would later be assessed by the students during their peer assessment tasks.

After performing a series of forehand and backhand ground stroke demonstrations, Tyrese grouped the students into small groups of three to four to watch each other perform these same tennis strokes. Again, the students were reminded about the specific critical elements that they should look for while watching their peer partners practice the ground strokes. Each student was instructed to carefully watch and practice the ground strokes with the critical elements of performance in mind, and to try their best to assess accurately their peers' performance. Per Tyrese's request, his students rotated roles, as performer (i.e., person being evaluated), as observer and evaluator (recorder), and as activity partner. In other words, one student took on the role of performer (i.e., executed the tennis strokes), a second student served as the observer and evaluator of her or his peer's performance, while a third peer ("activity partner") hit the tennis balls back and forth across the net to her or his peer. These roles were demonstrated and practiced within each group of students prior to the actual peer assessments. Before each class, Tyrese ensured that ample equipment was available for each student's use (i.e., plenty of tennis balls and racquets) and that the tennis courts were available and ready (i.e., no standing water on the courts) for play.

Tyrese likes to take advantage of the school's block schedule of 70-minute class periods. On the first day of the tennis unit, he uses the first 5 minutes of the class to briefly review previous content, introduce the day's lesson objectives (i.e., executing tennis forehand and backhand ground strokes), and review the use of peer assessments with his students. For the next 10 minutes, Tyrese provides instructions, engages in a series of demonstrations (handgrips, and proper footwork for executing forehand and backhand ground strokes), and emphasizes what critical elements the students should watch for as their peers attempt to execute the strokes. Further, Tyrese checks for understanding using reiteration (i.e., students are asked to describe the critical elements of the demonstration to one another) and shadowing (i.e., students are asked to demonstrate the skills) strategies (Rauschenbach, 1994), techniques he had learned while in college. For the next 15 minutes, Tyrese allows the students to engage in practice opportunities. This is followed by the students engaging in actual peer assessments for about 20 minutes. Then Tyrese allows the students to participate in either singles or doubles match play for the remaining class time. This leaves about 2 minutes to end the class.

Specific to the peer assessments, "partner helping partner" assessment rubrics are used to score performances. These assessment rubrics consist of skills to be observed (critical elements) and assessed during each of the students' performances of the identified tennis skills (i.e., handgrips, footwork, forehand and backhand ground strokes). Each student has his or her own scoring rubric that is used by the person in the role of evaluator.

Later that day, Tyrese reviews the peer assessment sheets and discovers that his students did a good job of providing feedback to their peer partners and did so with accuracy and appropriateness. He does, however, feel that some of the feedback is too general. Tyrese decides that the next time he uses peer assessment, he will again explain and point out to his students the importance of providing specific feedback statements. Nevertheless, he is pleased that several students provided specific written feedback to their peer partners that was useful in helping them improve the execution of their ground strokes (e.g., "Step forward and follow through your stroke"). When students did provide specific feedback, it tended to be brief, clear, and direct, such as "Bend your knees" and "Keep your head up and eyes on the ball." Tyrese is also pleased to see that Anthony had successfully engaged in the peer assessment tasks. Anthony even seemed to have enjoyed the opportunities for group interactions and role responsibilities, which had helped to keep him focused and on task throughout the class period.

Moreover, it was encouraging that, based on the feedback his students gave him during class closure, Tyrese's use of peer assessment tasks had enhanced a sense of community and trust among his students in two important ways. First, the students had begun to trust their classmates' ability to assess their performances, and second, the students including Anthony had begun to show signs of developing trusting relationships as they interacted in cooperative ways with one another. In fact, Anthony had recently said, "I trust what my partner said, because I trust her." Tyrese is now convinced that if given proper instructions, appropriate demonstrations, specific performance criteria, and opportunities to practice, students—including those with learning disabilities—can accurately assess their peers' performances, are capable of providing specific feedback, are accountable, and can develop a sense of trust among their peers.

Endnotes

1. Authentic assessment is an assessment strategy that promotes students' participation in "applying skills and knowledge to solve real world problems, giving the task a degree of authenticity. The tests attempt to measure the acquisition of knowledge from a holistic standpoint" (Lund, 1997, p. 25). Students are asked to "demonstrate a thoughtful understanding of the problem, thus indicating mastery of a concept (Wiggins, 1989) as they apply and use their knowledge" (Lund, 1997, p. 25). Further, "tasks are set in meaningful contexts with connectivity to real world experiences and school-based ideas" (Lund, 1997, p. 25).

2. In physical education contexts, peer assessment is an assessment strategy whereby students evaluate the performance(s) of their classmates (Butler & Hodge, 2001; Melograno, 1997).

Resources and References

Butler, S. A., & Hodge, S. R. (2001). Enhancing student trust through peer assessment in physical education. *Physical Educator, 58*(1), 30–41.

Dana, T., & Tippins, D. (1993). Considering alternative assessments for middle level learners. *Middle School Journal, 25*(2), 3–5.

Hill, G., & Miller, T. (1997). A comparison of peer and teacher assessment of students' physical fitness performance. *Physical Educator, 54*, 40–46.

Lund, J. (1997). Authentic assessment: Its development and applications. *Journal of Physical Education, Recreation & Dance, 68*(7), 25–28, 40.

Melograno, V. J. (1997). Integrating assessment into physical education teaching. *Journal of Physical Education, Recreation & Dance, 68*, 34–37.

Radford, K. W., Schincariol, L., & Hughes, A. S. (1995). Enhance performance through assessment. *Strategies, 8*, 5–9.

Rauschenbach, J. (1994). Checking for student understanding—Four techniques. *Journal of Physical Education, Recreation & Dance, 65*(4), 60–63.

Siedentop, D. (Ed.). (1994). *Sport education: Quality PE through positive sport experience.* Champaign, IL: Human Kinetics.

Wiggins, G. (1989). A true test: Toward more authentic and equitable assessment. *Phi Delta Kappan, 69*, 703–713.

Zhu, W. (1997). Alternative assessment: What, why, how. *Journal of Physical Education, Recreation & Dance, 68*(7), 17–18.

Acknowledgment

The authors wish to thank Scott A. Butler for his input on this case. Scott is a GPE teacher at Windsor Academy Elementary School within the Columbus Public School District in the greater Columbus, Ohio, area.

NOTES

QUESTIONS

Preparing for Learning & Teaching

SUMMARY OF PARTICIPANTS

Tyrese Howard, physical education teacher

Anthony, student with learning disability concomitant with ADD and hyperactivity

1. What issues exist in this case?

2. What are authentic assessment and peer assessment?

3. What steps should a teacher follow to use peer assessment strategies effectively?

4. What guidelines should a teacher follow in determining the student groupings and "peer partners"?

5. What is a scoring rubric?

6. Did Tyrese use peer assessments effectively in his class?

7. What accommodations were required, if any, for Anthony?

8. What practical applications and benefits can be derived from the use of peer assessments?

9. What are some concerns or disadvantages associated with using peer assessments in physical education?

10. Can a teacher "trust" students' abilities to evaluate one another? If so, what must the teacher do to ensure accurate and reliable data?

11. Do you think students can learn to trust one another by way of peer assessments? What conditions would allow this to happen and what conditions would prevent this from happening?

12. What legal requirements exist regarding assessing students with disabilities in physical education settings? What is your understanding of Public Law 105-17 relative to this issue?

Synergism in Adapted Physical Education

Reminiscing about the recent staff development workshop that he had attended, Mr. Cosmo, a seasoned football coach and veteran physical educator of 20 years, thinks that the information was good, but attending one workshop with no follow-up was useless and unproductive. He isn't sure if he is correctly fulfilling the physical education goals and objectives of his students' IEPs. This workshop had dealt with including all students in GPE classes. The speaker had spoken eloquently about individualization, adaptations and modifications, curricular changes and the use of supports. While all this information appeared worthwhile and interesting, Mr. Cosmo ponders if it is as easy as the speaker had implied. He wonders, "Why doesn't he come into my class and show me?" Others who had attended this workshop were probably pondering the same question about their unique situation. During the workshop, a fellow physical educator had blurted out, "I've got a kid with a ventilator in my class, and I'm scared to death about working with him." Mr. Cosmo is wondering how he can best deliver physical education to one of his students, Bret, while addressing all of Bret's IEP goals and objectives.

Bret, a 9th grader, is like any other student—funny, tireless, wanting to please all his teachers—and he tries really hard in PE class. In fact, Bret tries extremely hard in all his classes. The unique thing about Bret is that he has severe mental retardation and related medical issues. His concomitant disabilities impede him from participating in general education classes on a full-time basis, but, when appropriate Bret is included with peers without disabilities. He particularly enjoys hanging out with Mark, Keone, and Wynn (peers without disabilities). Mr. Cosmo believes that Bret should be included in his PE class and, in fact, that all students should have some type of physical education. Bret's disability is a concern, however, because the skills and concepts being taught in Mr. Cosmo's PE class appear to be too difficult despite the adaptations and modifications that he has made. Mr. Cosmo keeps wondering, "How should I handle Bret's physical education program?" As he ponders this dilemma, Mr. Cosmo admits that he doesn't know everything about Bret's condition. Although the workshop he attended mentioned that the recent reauthorization of the Individuals with Disabilities Education Act of 1997 stipulated participation in GPE in the IEP meetings, Mr. Cosmo believes that it is nearly impossible to attend all IEP meetings. However, because he believes that every student should be given equal opportunity to participate in GPE first and foremost, he decides to make every attempt to attend as many IEP meetings as he can and seek assistance whenever possible.

Arriving at school, he notices that Ms. James, the paraprofessional, is having a difficult time getting Bret off the school bus. Bret is being stubborn and noncompliant, hitting, screaming, and yelling at the top of his lungs. Ms. James asks the bus driver and the bus aide for assistance. After what seems like an eternity, Bret calms down and walks quietly with Ms. James to class. Mr. Cosmo, shocked by this display, wonders how Bret will behave in PE class. Mr. Cosmo heads through the gym to his office. It's his prep period now, and he must plan his PE class for Bret and others who are in need of adaptations and modifications. Mr. Cosmo's mind races with questions: "What if Bret becomes angry? What if he is having a bad day, like this morning? What if he doesn't want to listen to me? What if he becomes violent and starts hitting the other students?" As the day wears on, such "what if" questions became more prevalent, elevating Mr. Cosmo's stress level.

Mr. Cosmo acknowledges that he needs to do more with Bret's physical education program. Initially, he revisits his physical education curriculum. The curriculum is conducive for Bret and all students because of its lifetime physical activity concept. Similarly, it addresses standards and performance benchmarks highlighted by the board of education. Curricular changes are not immediately needed. Mr. Cosmo then decides to contact a few colleagues (fellow physical educators) who are in similar situations around the district. The message he receives is clear: perhaps Bret should receive APE instead of being included in GPE. His colleagues go as far as to suggest reconvening the IEP meeting to have Bret removed from GPE for a myriad of reasons. They feel that an APE setting with a smaller teacher/student ratio might be more appropriate.

Although Mr. Cosmo appreciates his colleagues' input, he still believes that his GPE class is better suited than an APE class. His frustration leads him to inform the school principal about his situation. The principal suggests that he contact the district APE specialist for feedback and suggestions. Thinking "outside of the box," Mr. Cosmo elects to contact a host of individuals to assist him with Bret's physical education program. From previous experiences working with others, Mr. Cosmo believes in synergism—that the combined efforts of others are greater than the sum of efforts of an individual.

Mr. Cosmo contacts the school district adapted physical educator, Mr. Little; the physical therapist, Ms. Wong; the behavior management resource teacher, Mr. Kealoha; and Bret's special education teacher, Ms. Loo. He vehemently wants to have a meeting with everyone as soon as possible. Fortunately, Mr. Little, Mr. Kealoha, and Ms. Loo are available and willing to help. Mr. Cosmo had difficulty reaching Ms. Wong, so he left a voice message. The earliest a meeting can take place is the next day after school. This means that Mr. Cosmo will have to address Bret's physical education program alone—at least for now. The next day could not come soon enough.

At the meeting, Mr. Cosmo stresses that he wants Bret in his class as well as to succeed and enjoy physical activity during and after school. Fortunately, everyone that Mr. Cosmo contacted either was on Bret's IEP team or had experience working with Bret. Mr. Kealoha, the behavior management resource teacher, suggests that Mr. Cosmo try a schedule of reinforcement for Bret and his classmates. This schedule of reinforcement would offer Mr. Cosmo a varying degree of items that would be rewarding to Bret and even to the class. For example, Mr. Cosmo could start out by reinforcing the students' behavior through a tangible reward system (certificates of award, choice of physical activity, student of the week). Social reinforcers such as high fives, positive verbal reinforcement, and nods of approval could then replace tangible reinforcers. Another suggestion was to use proximity control whereby Mr. Cosmo would teach near Bret. Ms. Wong, the physical therapist, says that Bret is capable of using standard equipment (i.e., regulation volleyballs and basketballs) but may need to use larger softballs for tracking during the softball unit. She also suggests that Bret should participate in an aquatics program, because the aqua therapy that Bret is currently receiving appears to be effective and beneficial; she then alludes to specific gains in movement activities using water as the medium. Ms. Wong offers to assist Mr. Cosmo at least once a week during his PE class. Her involvement would be along the lines of providing feedback and suggestions for improving the activity, and not interfering with class.

Ms. Loo, the special education teacher, acknowledges that Bret's disability sometimes impedes his success in his other subject areas, but that he is a good student. She recommends that Bret be assigned a peer buddy from class, particularly Keone because they get along quite nicely; that a hand signal be used as an attention getter for Bret; and that the tasks be repeated and the skills modeled as a visual if necessary. If further support is necessary for success, Ms. Loo could occasionally send her paraprofessional, Ms. James, to class to assist. She notes, however, that she seldom has Ms. James work one-on-one with Bret, so she doesn't wish to portray a sense that Bret requires this type of assistance. In fact, she wishes to minimize the intrusiveness toward Bret. According to Bret's parents, Ms. Loo, and Ms. James, all parties wish to instill and promote an independence that may lead to a better quality of life for Bret. Other suggestions are offered such as varying equipment and using lots of demonstration, cues, prompts, and established routines. Mr. Cosmo recognizes that these suggestions alone might not be enough, because he's already tried them.

Mr. Little, the adapted physical educator, expresses that he could work with Bret on specific skills prior to his participation in GPE class. He would make sure that Bret has the necessary skills to assist him during class. Such preteaching of skills could enhance Bret's success in GPE. This service would be more ancillary to what Bret already is receiving. Mr. Little wishes to make clear that this method is by no means suggesting that Bret should be receiving APE alone. The information generated from these individuals is enlightening and helpful. Mr. Cosmo decides that he will use all this information to plan Bret's physical education based on the activity that is currently being taught.

The next day in PE class, Mr. Cosmo feels optimistic and upbeat about Bret's physical education program. However, during this class, Bret becomes extremely difficult to manage. He is angry, stubborn, and refuses to listen to instructions. Mr. Cosmo, not wanting to disrupt the others in class and lose his teaching momentum, has Keone take Bret aside and sit with him until he settles down (special educator Ms. Loo's suggestion). Bret sits quietly with Keone, and Mr. Cosmo continues teaching. After a few minutes, Bret appears ready to rejoin the class. Mr. Cosmo asks Keone to work with him for this modified game. Bret is doing extremely well so Mr. Cosmo approaches him and says with a smile, "Terrific, Bret. You are doing a fantastic job releasing the ball!" (behavior management resource teacher Mr. Kealoha's suggestion on using positive verbal reinforcement). The class ends with a modified version of the entire game. Bret is attentive, waits his turn when his team isn't playing, and cheers for the others.

For the next few PE classes, Mr. Cosmo sets up a schedule of reinforcement that he uses for all his students. This strategy, which was recommended by Mr. Kealoha, turns out to be effective and positive. Mr. Cosmo eventually assumes proximity control over Bret during class. Ms. James, the paraprofessional, comes by to see how Mr. Cosmo and Bret are doing. Mr. Cosmo asks her if she would like to assist him with this particular lesson because of the safety issues involved. She readily obliges. While keeping an eye on Bret, Ms. James moves from one group to another helping all the students in the class with their skills. Bret is doing well and doesn't really need Ms. James's assistance. But, as part of the agreement among all parties involved, Ms. James is there to make sure that Bret experiences success in his PE class.

Just as things appear to be going so well, Bret has an emotional outburst. He screams, yells, and swings at anyone who comes near to him. Of course, this extremely volatile situation is of great concern to everyone. Ms. Loo informs Mr. Cosmo that Bret's related medical condition is worsening and that his doctor is considering placing him on medication to address this condition. "How will this affect his performance in school, especially in physical education?" ponders Mr. Cosmo.

Bret's doctor assures the teachers that they should not be overly concerned: the medication is used to help Bret's medical condition without major side effects. However, the doctor does mention that further modifications in his physical education program might be needed. The doctor informs the school nurse of Bret's situation and how she can assist in monitoring his performance in school, particularly in physical education. She can also assist with dispensing the medication during school. Mr. Cosmo sighs with relief. He will continue to implement the suggested modifications and adaptations that the others had recommended. He realizes that others are there to assist him and his physical education program for the betterment of all students. As a result, Mr. Cosmo takes extreme care in documenting Bret's activity and progress for IEP evaluation.

QUESTIONS

Preparing for Learning & Teaching

SUMMARY OF PARTICIPANTS

Mr. Cosmo, football coach and physical educator

Bret, 9th-grade student with severe mental retardation and related medical issues

Mark, friend of Bret

Keone, friend of Bret

Wynn, friend of Bret

Ms. James, paraprofessional

Mr. Little, school district adapted physical educator

Ms. Wong, physical therapist

Mr. Kealoha, behavior management resource teacher

Ms. Loo, Bret's special education teacher

1. What is the primary issue in this case?

2. What issues led Mr. Cosmo to seek assistance? How did he approach the fact that he requested assistance?

3. From a practitioner's viewpoint, would you agree or disagree with the way Mr. Cosmo's workshop in APE was conducted? Why or why not?

4. Attending all IEP meetings in order to be in compliance with the Individuals with Disabilities Education Act's mandating general education participation is not always feasible and practical. What strategies could you use to ensure prominent discussions about physical education at these meetings?

5. How would you describe synergy in your setting involving physical education for students with disabilities?

6. What potential barriers might impede synergism?

7. Is synergy a concept that can be employed and embraced by other educators and related services personnel at your school or site? Why or why not?

8. What important role did each member of the team play in preparing Bret's IEP program? What strengths did each member bring to the IEP?

Peer Tutoring for Physical Education

Mrs. Fernandez is an elementary school teacher at Hill Elementary School. She has taught physical education there for 4 years and loves the school and the students. She teaches with Mr. McLaughlin, who has been at the elementary school and coached at the high school for more than 22 years. Her background is in physical education and coaching with a concentration in APE. She is currently studying to take the Adapted Physical Education National Standards (APENS) Certification Examination[1] in June and is looking forward to being certified in APE.

It is the end of May and Mrs. Fernandez has been working on Sylvia's IEP for weeks. Sylvia is in 4th grade and has spina bifida. She uses a wheelchair but can walk slowly for short distances with her crutches and her ankle-foot-orthotics. Sylvia has been in a self-contained APE class with other children with disabilities since she came to Hill Elementary School in the 1st grade. Currently, she is in a class with three other children who have disabilities. Two of these children, Juan and Samantha, are in the 2nd grade and Zachary is in the 3rd grade. Juan has autism and is hard to keep on task. Mrs. Fernandez spends most of her time in the self-contained class trying to get Juan to pay attention. Samantha has diplegic cerebral palsy and walks independently with a scissor gait, and Zachary has Down syndrome.

Sylvia attends the IEP meeting along with her parents, the classroom teacher, the nurse, the physical therapist, and the special education director. The meeting goes very well, and it appears that Sylvia is meeting or exceeding all of the goals and objectives identified for her in most subjects.

In physical education, Mrs. Fernandez is impressed with Sylvia's improvement in fitness and locomotor skills. Mrs. Fernandez asks Sylvia, "Do you want to change any of your goals and objectives or is there anything else you would like to work on?" Sylvia has been dreaming of being in the GPE class with her peers for the past few years and voices her opinion: "I'm tired of hearing the other students talk about all the fun they have in Mr. McLaughlin's class. I'm also tired of being left out at recess. I'm ready to be part of the GPE class. Being in the class with all the younger kids makes me feel like a baby." This starts a long discussion about the physical education schedule, goals and objectives of the GPE class, and the goals and objectives for Sylvia. The time allotted for the meeting runs out, and the group decides to convene again in two weeks to finish addressing some other issues. Mrs. Fernandez thanks Sylvia for her honesty and tells her that she will do what she can to ensure that Sylvia gets what she wants.

For the next week, Mrs. Fernandez worries about how she will include Sylvia in Mr. McLaughlin's class successfully. Right now, the students accept and like Sylvia, but how will Mr. McLaughlin's students react to her? He has never had a child with a disability in his classes before. Mr. McLaughlin will have no idea what to do. If he spends time one-on-one with Sylvia, will the other students lose instruction and feedback? Mrs. Fernandez poses this question on the APE list serve and reads through her APENS study guide for answers. On the APE list serve, four professionals respond with the idea of setting up a peer tutor program and provide references on peer tutoring. In addition, Mrs. Fernandez reads about setting up peer-tutoring programs in the APENS manual.

Mrs. Fernandez thinks of at least four students in Sylvia's class who could serve as excellent peer tutors, and she creates peer tutor training material from an inclusion textbook.[2] With her action plan she is prepared for the next IEP meeting. In that meeting, Mrs. Fernandez presents the peer-tutoring idea and Sylvia is thrilled. One of Sylvia's major concerns is that she might not have a partner when they do activities in twos. But peer tutoring will solve that problem. The IEP team agrees and the new schedule will take effect the next fall.

Mrs. Fernandez doesn't want to wait until the start of the new school year to get the program off the ground. She asks permission from her administration to implement the program, and it doesn't take much to gain their full support. She decides to start by asking who would like to be a peer tutor for the four "preferred" students she has in mind. To her surprise as well as Sylvia's, 14 students (including the 4 preferred students) volunteer to participate in the program. Mrs. Fernandez is thrilled and quickly sends letters home to the parents to get permission. The program will start at the beginning of the following school year. During the summer Mrs. Fernandez completes the training packets and expands the program to include tutors in her self-contained program.

At the beginning of the next school year, one student has moved and one decides he doesn't want to do the program, but three others sign up and she has to put five more on the waiting list. Mrs. Fernandez trains 15 students during their lunchtime or recess for three weeks. Mr. McLaughlin sits in on the training so he will know what to expect in his classes. The training consists of (a) disability awareness, (b) communication techniques, (c) instructional techniques, (d) feedback techniques, (e) evaluation techniques, (f) scenarios, and (g) written tests. Sylvia is also part of the tutor training. The class is using reciprocal peer tutoring, and she needs to know how to tutor her peers too. The two students who have permission to work in Mrs. Fernandez's self-contained class with Juan need extra tutoring because of his extensive behavioral needs. When the tutor training is completed, the tutors start to implement what they have learned. Mrs. Fernandez finds that she and Mr. McLaughlin have to give cues and feedback to the tutors to ensure appropriate instruction and feedback. They also find that having the tutors arrive a few minutes before class to cover instructional cues and the content of the lesson is helpful. After a few weeks, Mr. McLaughlin is having trouble because several students have been arguing over who will be the tutor next. Mrs. Fernandez and Mr. McLaughlin make a monthly schedule of the self-contained APE class and the inclusive GPE class so that the peer tutors know exactly when their turn will be and for how long. This also helps Sylvia know with whom she will be working.

Mrs. Fernandez finds that she has to assist Mr. McLaughlin with modification to his units, but that Sylvia isn't shy in asking for what she needs. Sylvia knows the benefits of asking for what you want. For example, during a parachute unit, Mr. McLaughlin usually had the children practice their locomotor skills around the large circle of the parachute with them holding on with one hand. But he knew this would be a problem for Sylvia while pushing her chair. So Sylvia and her tutor suggested doing the locomotor skills around the circle *without* holding on to the parachute, then picking up the parachute for activities directly involving the parachute. When they tried this it appeared that Sylvia was slower than most of the class, so Mr. McLaughlin created two circles, an inside circle and an outside circle, and the students went to the circle of their choice. At least one-third of the students joined Sylvia in the inside circle.

Mrs. Fernandez's self-contained class is going very well also. Juan is on task most of the time, and she is able to give attention to Samantha and Zachary. Mrs. Fernandez recruits two more of the peer tutors to come to her class so they can play small-sided games. She is even thinking about including Zachary in the GPE class with peer tutors the next fall.

The evaluation of the students with disabilities is more efficient than ever. With the 5th graders observing and recording the students' performance, Mrs. Fernandez knows the number of turns they had, their level of performance, and how many sit-ups and push-ups they did in each class. Her IEPs are very thorough and she is able to spend more time assisting Mr. McLaughlin as well as planning and teaching. The peer tutor program is a success and she is soon asked to help set up one in the neighboring elementary school. Sylvia is included every year and she never has to attend a self-contained class again.

Endnotes

1. For information and application materials regarding the APENS Certification Examination call 1-888-APENS-EXAM, contact apens@twu.edu, or visit the APENS website at www.twu.edu/o/apens.

2. See Lieberman & Houston-Wilson (2002), *Strategies for Inclusion*, below.

Resources and References

PEER TUTOR PROGRAM PLANNING

Barfield, J. P., Hannigan-Downs, S. B., & Lieberman, L. J. (1998). Implementing a peer tutor program: Strategies for practitioners. *Physical Educator, 55*(4), 211–221.

Block, M. E. (1995). Use peer tutors and task sheets. *Strategies, 8,* 9–14.

Block, M. E., Oberweiser, B., & Bain, M. (1995). Using classwide peer tutoring to facilitate inclusion of students with disabilities in regular physical education. *Physical Educator, 52,* 47–56.

Houston-Wilson, C., Lieberman, L. J., Horton, M., & Kasser, S. (1997). Peer tutoring: An effective strategy for inclusion. *Journal of Health, Physical Education, Recreation, & Dance, 68*(6), 39–44.

Lieberman, L. (1999). Peer tutoring strategies. In *Physical education methods for classroom teachers.* Champaign, IL: Human Kinetics.

Lieberman, L. J., & Houston-Wilson, C. (2002). *Strategies for inclusion: A handbook for physical educators.* Champaign, IL: Human Kinetics.

DISABILITY AWARENESS

Wilson, S., & Lieberman, L. J. (2000). DisAbility awareness in physical education. *Strategies, 13*(6), 12, 29–33.

PEER TUTOR RESEARCH

Barron, A., & Foot, H. (1991). Peer tutoring and tutor training. *Educational Research, 33,* 174–179.

Houston-Wilson, C., Dunn, J. M., van der Mars, H., & McCubbin, J. A. (1997). The effect of peer tutors on motor performance in integrated physical education classes. *Adapted Physical Activity Quarterly, 14,* 298–313.

Lieberman, L. J., Dunn, J. M., van der Mars, H., & McCubbin, J. A. (2000). Peer tutors' effects on activity levels of deaf students in inclusive elementary physical education. *Adapted Physical Activity Quarterly, 17,* 20–39.

Lieberman, L. J., Newcomer, J., McCubbin, J. A., & Dalrymple, N. (1997). The effects of cross-aged peer tutors on the academic learning time in physical education of students with disabilities in inclusive elementary physical education classes. *Brazilian International Journal of Adapted Physical Education, 4*(1), 15–32.

Webster, G. E. (1987). Influence of peer tutors upon academic learning time–physical education of mentally handicapped students. *Journal of Teaching in Physical Education, 7,* 393–403.

QUESTIONS

Preparing for Learning & Teaching

1. What was the initial problem with Sylvia's self-contained APE class?

SUMMARY OF PARTICIPANTS

Mrs. Fernandez, physical education teacher

Mr. McLaughlin, Mrs. Fernandez's teaching partner

Sylvia, 4th-grade student with spina bifida

Juan, 2nd-grade student with autism

Samantha, 2nd-grade student with diplegic cerebral palsy

Zachary, 3rd-grade student with Down syndrome

2. What did Mrs. Fernandez do to resolve this problem?

3. Why did the self-contained APE class have to be changed? Could it have been left the way it was? Why or why not?

4. What is peer tutoring and why was it successful in this particular situation?

5. What APENS learning standard does peer tutoring fulfill?

6. How did the new peer tutor program assist with IEP development?

7. How would you include a peer tutor program in your current or future situations?

8. If the teacher were using groups of three, what guidelines would you suggest for grouping? Why? How do these relate to contact theory as a meaningful, positive, cooperative, ongoing activity?

9. What would you add to a peer-tutoring training program if Sylvia were Deaf?

10. What other inclusion strategies would you use?

11. What other teaching techniques would you use along with peer tutoring?

12. How would you assist your tutors in documenting progress?

13. What other resources would you use?

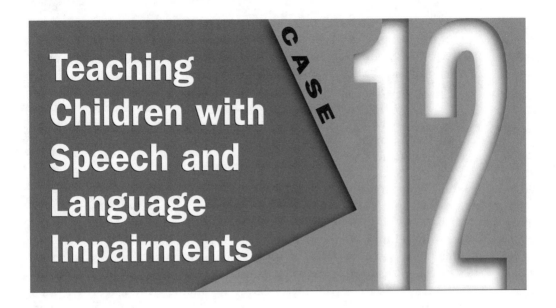

Teaching Children with Speech and Language Impairments

12

Ms. Mendoza is the Honolulu public school district's APE resource teacher at Shaw Elementary School. Shaw Elementary has classes for kindergarten through 5th grade; although there is no preschool unit for typically developing children (children without disabilities) at this school, it does house a preschool unit for children (ages 3–5) with developmental delays. In that unit those preschoolers receive special education services primarily because of their speech and language impairments. Teaching these preschoolers physical education is very rewarding for Ms. Mendoza. However, she is less confident in her ability to provide them with content that emphasizes and reinforces speech–language usage in physical education. Several of these preschoolers' IEPs require that speech–language concepts be reinforced in all content areas throughout the school day. Ms. Mendoza is prepared with strategies to teach the motor domain to these children, but facilitating language use creates a problem. The problem from Ms. Mendoza's perspective is how to incorporate language into her teaching. She is excited, yet ambivalent about what to expect because of the demands required of her by the IEP teams.

School policy advocates including children in all aspects of school life. It is the school district's position that inclusive education is beneficial and helpful, and school personnel also support this concept. Since Shaw Elementary does not house a preschool unit for typically developing children, Ms. Mendoza believes that the Head Start preschool program located directly across the street would be a good place to teach both children with developmental delays (from Shaw Elementary School's preschool unit) and children without disabilities (from Teddy Bear Head

Start preschool unit) together. Before acting on this, Ms. Mendoza seeks input from the preschool unit classroom teacher and school building principal at Shaw Elementary School, as well as from the director at Teddy Bear Head Start Program. Each of them feels that having typically developing same-age peers and preschoolers with developmental delays in the classroom together is an excellent idea. Ms. Mendoza hopes that the preschoolers without disabilities who have age appropriate speech–language development will serve as role models for her students with speech–language impairments.

Ms. Mendoza knows that children will mimic each other, particularly in the area of motor performance. Yet, she still has to promote speech–language development in her teaching. She goes to Teddy Bear Head Start to inform them about attending PE class. The classroom teachers excitedly have the children line up by the door to prepare to cross the street to Shaw Elementary School for PE class. In the meantime, Ms. Mendoza returns to her special education preschool classroom.

It is 8:45 A.M. and the preschoolers are sitting in a circle with their teacher Ms. Aiu and Ms. Cathy, the paraprofessional. All eight preschoolers have developmental delays, with Tory, Chad, and Kami having severe and pronounced speech–language impairments. Tory has a receptive language disorder that makes following multitask directions (e.g., picking up a ball and throwing it) difficult. He drools profusely, so occasionally he wears a bib to physical education. Ms. Aiu and Ms. Cathy will always be sure to change the bib prior to PE class. A medical specialist diagnosed Chad with a functional communication disorder that could not be accurately described. Ms. Aiu suspects that Chad was physically traumatized when he was about 2 years old. He also stutters severely and slurs his speech. Similarly, Kami rambles words that have no meaning and often is incoherent. She was identified as having dysarthria, an articulation disorder caused by a neuromuscular impairment. This apparent lack of motor control doesn't allow her to produce sequenced sounds.

The severity of these speech and language impairments is coupled with other distinguishing impairments that make up developmental delays in preschoolers, such as impairments that impede a child's ability to concentrate on a given task, to follow directions, and/or to communicate verbally. The severity and nature of these impairments are of concern to the respective IEP team members.

Upon seeing the adapted physical educator arriving, Ms. Aiu announces to her class that Ms. Mendoza is here for their PE class. Excitedly, the children form a line and wait patiently for Ms. Mendoza. Ms. Mendoza verbally directs the children to an outside space adjoining the class. She has already set up colored cones and colored spots in order to establish boundaries and personal space and for her classroom management. Colored playground balls are also readily available and visible.

Contemplating how she will promote language in her teaching, Ms. Mendoza acknowledges that she knows very little about how to facilitate speech and language development with children who have speech and language impairments. Ms. Mendoza, however, does understand that if she infuses concepts from the typically developing preschoolers' lessons it will strengthen her physical education lessons by reinforcing language.

Immediately prior to the lesson, Ms. Aiu asks Ms. Mendoza, "What are the children going to do today?" Ms. Mendoza responds, "They will participate in a tag game with concepts and words learned on their recent visit to the aquarium." Ms. Aiu feels that this is an excellent idea; she had been hoping that the PE lessons would be woven into her thematic lesson for the week. Ms. Mendoza asks Ms. Aiu for several key words and concepts that are difficult for the children. Ms. Aiu confers with Ms. Cathy and they decide that names of sea animals would be a good link with their current lesson in class. Ms. Aiu tells Ms. Mendoza about the various names of ocean sea animals that are housed at the aquarium.

The PE lesson begins as soon as both classes arrive and the students are all seated. At 9:10 A.M., Ms. Mendoza guides the preschoolers in stretching exercises and then proceeds with her first objective of the lesson. She creates a game called eels and fishes. Several preschoolers are assigned as eels while the others are fishes. The objective of this lesson is to work on locomotor (e.g., hopping and galloping) skills coupled with arm and hand motion (to mimic fish swimming) through a game of tag. The eels are to tag "swallow" the fishes before they reach one of the colored spots (symbolic of a hole in a coral reef).

When the children pretending to be fishes stand on the colored spots, which serve as a safe haven, those children pretending to be eels continue hopping and galloping within the boundaries. Fishes eventually have to swim (hop, slide, or gallop) to another hole in the coral reef. These preschoolers are already familiar with this game, so they know the objective and have a lot of fun. However, the problem of trying to get these children to verbalize language as they participate in this lesson instead of screaming and yelling still exists. This is the challenge posed to Ms. Mendoza.

Periodically, Ms. Mendoza stops the game and probes for responses from the preschoolers. She asks, "Who can tell me the name of a fish? Who can tell me the colors of the fishes? Who can show me how a fish swims in water? Who can describe what an eel looks like?" Ms. Mendoza especially hopes for responses from Tory, Chad, and Kami, because of their IEP goals. But even with teacher and paraprofessional prompting, expressive language from these three students is not coherent and often disoriented. As frustration mounts, Ms. Mendoza becomes more determined to elicit coherent and understandable responses from these children. At 9:45 A.M., Ms. Mendoza draws the class to closure. She asks the children about what they learned, reinforcing skills and concepts about names of sea animals and how they related to the PE lesson. Ms. Mendoza feels that this was a good lesson but knows that she still hasn't achieved her goal. Unfortunately, her probing still isn't successful in promoting language for any of the children with disabilities.

Before her next class, Ms. Mendoza confers with Ms. Chang, the speech–language pathologist at Shaw Elementary School. Ms. Chang informs her that these preschoolers, especially Tory, Chad, and Kami, need to have language development as part of their overall educational program, and that everyone working with these children should promote as much expressive language as possible. Her rationale for this is that the more these children are able to verbalize, the more prone they will be to learning new skills, tasks, and concepts. In fact, Chad's mother wants to transition him into kindergarten next year, so age appropriate expressive and receptive language is deemed critical. Acknowledging that movement serves as an infrastructure for preschool development, Ms. Chang notes that physical education should be the catalyst for which speech and language development should occur. She provides Ms. Mendoza with some strategies that could facilitate receptive and expressive language development: "Allow time for the children to respond to your questions, at least three to five seconds, instead of directing the answer. Infuse the use of colors into your teaching. Ask the children to hop to the 'blue' cone, or gallop to the 'green' cone. Also have the children repeat the task that you want them to do. Continue to probe and model the correct responses, if necessary." Interestingly, once Ms. Mendoza implements these strategies, the preschoolers are able to listen and follow verbal prompts and phrases from her and their peers. The latter indirect method (following peers) of facilitating language is beginning to be effective.

Yet another problem that Ms. Mendoza faces is behavior management of the entire class. Despite the inclusive policy at Shaw Elementary School, managing the behaviors of the Head Start preschoolers proves to be a challenge to Ms. Mendoza's physical education pedagogy. On occasion, Ms. Mendoza asks the Head Start teachers and aides to assist with their children, so that she can work more closely with the preschoolers with developmental delays on their skills. For instance, during a particular lesson, Ms. Mendoza probes the children on colors. As she waits for their responses, the typically developing children say the color out loud; this doesn't allow their peers with speech–language impairments a reasonable opportunity to respond. Ms. Mendoza ponders, "How am I supposed to ask questions and probe for answers when the Head Start children immediately blurt out the correct or sometimes incorrect answers?" Getting the preschoolers with speech and language impairments to be expressive, as per their IEP, is quite a challenge indeed.

The next session couldn't come soon enough. Ms. Mendoza contemplates her teaching strategy for the day. She understands that reemphasizing what is previously taught promotes spiral learning, which helps preschoolers to learn and maintain concepts. However, she still faces the question: "How can I get the preschoolers with speech and language delays to be more expressive, while not having the other children yelling out words and phrases?" Ms. Mendoza arrives at the preschool class with her equipment and finds that the children are not ready because of a late breakfast. This allows enough time to consult with the Head Start teachers about the lesson for the day. She crosses the street to the Teddy Bear Head Start preschool to meet with Ms. Ryan, a classroom teacher. They discuss the situation and decide to have each child raise his or her hand before giving any answers. This strategy will be beneficial because it will make the children listen and follow directions and teach them skills that they need to transition into kindergarten. Ms. Ryan relays this strategy to her teacher assistants. Ms. Mendoza returns to the Shaw Elementary special education preschool class to set up the environment and equipment for the PE lesson.

The lesson is similar to the last regarding a game, colors, and locomotor skills. The difference this time is that all preschoolers (both special education and Head Start) must raise their hand, be called upon, and then answer the question. Classroom teachers and aides are asked to prompt the children on raising their hand. Although time-consuming, this lesson goes much smoother with less behavior problems exhibited. In fact, Ms. Mendoza feels that this has been a very successful lesson overall because she was able to call on Chad and Tory. Both Chad and Tory were able to use expressive language when called upon without interference from the other preschoolers. However, Kami was still having difficultly expressing herself in a meaningful and coherent way despite the amount of time and prompts given. Eventually, Ms. Mendoza is able to select more children to answer questions. Considering the amount of trial and error she has gone through, Ms. Mendoza feels that she is making strides in promoting language in her PE classes.

As Ms. Mendoza reflects on this particular lesson, she realizes that the strategies learned from Ms. Chang, the speech–language pathologist, and classroom teachers Ms. Aiu and Ms. Ryan made a tremendous difference in how she presented her information, and how the preschoolers responded. Most useful, Ms. Chang's hints appear to have made a tremendous difference. Ms. Mendoza decides that all children could benefit from more language development. Her strategy from now will be to employ questions-and-answers instruction to help the children be able to think critically about what they are doing, how they are doing it, and why they are doing it, and more important, to promote receptive and expressive language for all preschoolers of all abilities.

QUESTIONS

Preparing for Learning & Teaching

1. What is the primary issue in this case?

CASE 12

SUMMARY OF PARTICIPANTS

Ms. Mendoza, APE teacher

Ms. Aiu, preschool teacher

Ms. Cathy, paraprofessional

Tory, preschooler with receptive language disorder

Chad, preschooler with functional communication disorder

2. What are some of the factors that contributed to this case?

Kami, preschooler with dysarthria

Ms. Chang, speech–language pathologist

Ms. Ryan, classroom teacher

3. Do you think the inclusive learning environment that Ms. Mendoza created fit in with the inclusion philosophy espoused by Shaw Elementary School?

4. What issues did Ms. Mendoza encounter that caused anxiety and stress? How did she alleviate such stresses?

5. What strategies did Ms. Mendoza employ that would be helpful from a practitioner's standpoint? Can you think of other suggestions?

6. What other related service personnel could Ms. Mendoza collaborate with to facilitate preschoolers' IEPs?

7. How can educators manage behaviors of preschoolers with and without developmental delays in an effective and efficient way in order to address the objectives of the lesson?

8. What could the classroom teachers do to assist Ms. Mendoza in teaching physical education? Do you think she should have taken all the children to PE class alone?

9. What was the overall outcome of the lessons taught by Ms. Mendoza at the end of this case study? What other suggestions could you offer her regarding speech–language techniques and behavior management?

CASE

Technological Applications in Physical Education

R eading a billboard on his way to work, Mr. Lee asks himself, "How am I going to keep up with technology in my teaching?" Not a day goes by that he doesn't hear students discussing the recent revolution of a faster computer, the newest video games with three-dimensional graphics, and much more. On-line capabilities, access to the World Wide Web, and high-tech video games have inundated recent dialogue among his students. More important, from his vantage point, Mr. Lee wonders, "How will I be able to teach students who utilize assistive devices for learning within a physical education context?" This questions runs through his mind over and over.

Mr. Lee is a seasoned veteran who has taught GPE on the leeward side of Oahu for 15 years. He firmly believes in continuing his professional development and, in fact, holds a master's degree in physical education and is always on the lookout for workshops to attend to augment his teaching, especially those involving technology. Despite his best efforts he still believes that the day will come when a student will arrive in his PE class with a device "somewhere out of Star Wars." Much to Mr. Lee's surprise that day is about to arrive.

On this particular day, while Mr. Lee is engaging students from his 10th-grade PE class in a badminton unit, Ms. James, the school's special education teacher, approaches him and asks if one of her students, Kawika, can participate in his classes. She tells him that she is making this request because Kawika's mother wants him to be included with typically developing peers. Mr. Lee, an advocate of quality physical education for all students, immediately thinks that including a student with a disability in his PE classes is a good idea. Moreover, he knows that badminton is a lifetime recreational sport that all students could benefit from now and throughout their adult life.

81

Mr. Lee tells Ms. James, "I'd be more than happy to support her request." But before he can say another word, Ms. James begins to describe Kawika: "Kawika is a pleasant and cheerful teen with mental retardation concomitant with mild cerebral palsy and is nonambulatory and nonverbal. He has physical limitations, but he does have some mobility in his upper extremities, although his movements are spastic with limited control. On the bright side, he can control the movement of his wheelchair. Kawika can also communicate with a communication board attached to a laptop computer. He can understand and slowly process verbal commands and is able to respond with his laptop by pushing selected switches for voice activation."

Mr. Lee stares in disbelief. He thinks, "How can this student participate in my class with such a device? How would he be able to participate freely with the other students? Wouldn't running into Kawika's wheelchair hurt the others in class? Who's going to pay for the laptop computer should it break in class?" Feeling overwhelmed, Mr. Lee blurts out these questions to Ms. James. Noticing his anxiety, Ms. James tells him she feels that of all her students, Kawika is capable of being included in GPE class. She also tells him that the situation is still at the dialogue stage and that no official placement decision regarding physical education can occur without reconvening the IEP team.

Mr. Lee already knows a little about Kawika. On previous occasions, Mr. Lee has watched Kawika as he maneuvered his wheelchair with relative ease in the cafeteria. His chair did appear to be large and awkward with some strange object located on his tray table. Mr. Lee continues to ponder the question, "How will I be able to have Kawika participate in badminton?" Later that day and during his prep period, Ms. James encourages Mr. Lee to visit with Kawika in her classroom.

Before any placement in physical education can occur, Mr. Lee knows that an IEP meeting must be held to discuss Kawika's case. Ms. James tells him that the IEP meeting will reconvene the next afternoon and asks him to attend. Sensing that this IEP meeting is important and a requirement for general educators to attend, Mr. Lee readily agrees.

At the IEP meeting, Mrs. Bailey, Kawika's mom, says that she wants Kawika to mingle and "hang out" with peers his own age, and to participate in physical activity because all he does is watch television when he comes home. She wants him to have some type of activity outside of the home. Mr. Lee points out that his class is currently in a badminton unit and that he believes that this might work, because it is a lifetime recreational activity and all his students appear to enjoy playing it. Mr. Lee discusses the rest of his physical education curriculum with Mrs. Bailey. He explains that 10th graders would be participating in a fitness unit as their final activity for the semester. This means that Kawika could participate in badminton and finish out the semester in a fitness unit with his peers.

However, the question of the usefulness and applicability of his assistive technology does pose a problem. Mr. Lee is concerned that he isn't knowledgeable about assistive technology but he is willing to learn. The IEP team members indicate that they will do everything possible to support Mr. Lee and Kawika in physical education. Upon completion of the IEP meeting, Ms. James indicates that she will provide Mr. Lee with an in-service on the usage of Kawika's assistive device.

The next morning, Mr. Lee arrives at Ms. James's classroom eager to find out more about these technological devices. Kawika is already there, eating breakfast. Ms. James explains about the laptop computer, voice activation mechanism, and switches. The box at the bottom of Kawika's chair on the backside is the battery pack that supplies all the power to his chair and computer. Every night, Mrs. Bailey must recharge the battery pack on the wheelchair. The laptop computer is a common Hewlett-Packard model with auditory voice projection. To activate specific single-phrased words such as *yes, no, thank you, yours, mine, left, right, hungry, bathroom, classroom,* and *office,* Kawika must touch picture objects and phrases on his communication board. A four-inch wobble control switch, which can move forward, backward, or side to side, is attached to the right armrest for mobility purposes.

Standing firm on his philosophy of quality physical education for all students, and after acquiring more information about assistive technologies, Mr. Lee decides to preview Kawika's IEP, paying particular attention to the motor domain. Interestingly, the IEP notes more visible strengths than weaknesses. For example, through assistive technology Kawika can communicate freely and is able to move from one point to another with relative ease and precision, while appearing cheerful and pleasant. As the next day approaches, the thought of having Kawika in class becomes less worrisome. Mr. Lee's lesson focuses on doubles play in badminton. He has already covered basic fundamental drills such as forehand stroke, backhand stroke, and serving. Since a round-robin tournament is about to begin, doubles would be an excellent way to have Kawika participate. Mr. Lee approaches Keith, one of the more skilled players in the class, and asks if he is willing to be partners with Kawika. Keith, who has a sister with Down syndrome and therefore is no stranger to interacting with persons with disabilities, readily agrees.

First and foremost are the safety issues involved with Kawika, Keith, and the rest of the 10th-grade class. In that light, the day's lesson employs the following strategy: Keith will play and cover the entire back half of the court. Kawika will man the front row of the court. Cones will be placed on both sides of their part of the court to mark the halves, thus allowing Kawika to see where the boundaries are relative to the front and back rows. Keith will not move into the front row until Kawika calls "yours" or "mine" through his voice-activated laptop computer. Additionally, the birdie will be allowed to "touch" the ground and Keith will be allowed to help Kawika make contact with the birdie.

A special bracket with Velcro strips is used to secure the racket (face up) to Kawika's wheelchair. In this way, Kawika will be able to move his chair toward the birdie and make contact with it. Such precision (moving and stopping at a space) will help with an IEP annual goal for Kawika. The concept of how using Velcro strips applies to the definition of assistive technology is really not that difficult to master. Interestingly, the more Mr. Lee is able to accept this fact, the easier it becomes to accept and try novel ideas relative to assistive technologies.

At 10:30, Mr. Lee's badminton class is about to begin. Classmates Keith, John, Renee, and Kristy are there early, helping Mr. Lee set up the courts.

Kawika arrives dressed in his PE clothes. At 10:35, the rest of the class arrives. Mr. Lee has everyone line up in alphabetical order for roll call. Roll is quickly taken and the students search for their partners. Keith approaches Kawika and says to him, "Let's stay at this first court." Kawika, with his voice-activated laptop, replies, "Okay." Within a few minutes, everyone has a partner and is transitioning onto their respective courts. There are only six courts, so two sets of partners are assigned as officials for selected games. Keith and Kawika are slow to get started because Kawika's racket keeps falling down. Once another Velcro strip is used, they are ready to begin.

Claire and Kevin, the opposing team, serve first. As Claire serves, the birdie flies well beyond Kawika and into the back row. Keith easily hits the birdie back to the opposing team. Claire makes an underhand scooping motion to hit the birdie back over the net. This time the birdie approaches the front row. Sensing that Kawika is having some difficulty tracking the birdie, Keith yells to him, "Your left, your left." Instantaneously, Kawika replies, "Yes, yes," and maneuvers his wheelchair into the vicinity of the approaching birdie. Unfortunately, he misses the birdie by a few feet.

Keith grabs the birdie and hits it back over to Kevin. Occasionally, Kawika is able to make contact with the birdie during flight. Most of the time, however, Keith assists him by stopping the birdie in flight and allowing Kawika to make contact, and then, dropping the birdie on his racket, Keith hits it to the opposing team. Although this might appear trivial, what's important is that Kawika is using his voice-activated device more and more. He is able to say "yes" and "thank you" more often. His processing appears to be improving, with movements becoming more fluid. Moreover, the laptop and voice activation device didn't impede Kawika's ability to participate. They continue to play for the entire period, while Mr. Lee keeps a close watch over Kawika and Keith. He notices that Keith's voice is loud and direct, and that Kawika is replying to each and every prompt. The rest of the class is oblivious to what is occurring on the first court. In fact, they don't even pay much attention to the mechanical, almost robotic voice emitted from the laptop. Mr. Lee is quite surprised and is sure that the others will be asking questions about how and why Kawika was in class.

At the end of class, Mr. Lee approaches Keith and Kawika and asks, "Who won?" Smiling, Keith replies, "We did!" Yelling from the other court, Claire and Kevin refute, "No, we did!" Before a full-blown argument can ensue, Mr. Lee gathers everyone for a quick debriefing of the doubles game and previews the lesson for the next day. Then he excuses everyone to go change out of their PE clothes. Putting his hand on Kawika's wheelchair, Mr. Lee asks him, "How did the class go today?" Kawika replies, "Yes, fun. Thank you." Ms. James then walks into the gym and takes Kawika back to class.

Sitting in his office after the class, Mr. Lee is enthused by technology and how it has helped Kawika participate in PE class. He acknowledges that advances in technology have permeated into the physical education setting. Mr. Lee no longer feels overwhelmed by Kawika and his assistive devices. In fact, his perception of the use of assistive technology has become more positive as a result of witnessing what one student with disabilities was able to accomplish with a little high-tech help.

QUESTIONS

Preparing for Learning & Teaching

SUMMARY OF PARTICIPANTS

Mr. Lee, GPE teacher

Ms. James, special education teacher

Kawika, 10th-grade student with mental retardation concomitant with mild cerebral palsy

Mrs. Bailey, Kawika's mother

Keith, John, Renee, Kristy, Claire, Kevin, Kawika's classmates

1. What is the primary issue in this case? Are there related issues? If so, what are they?

2. What are some of the factors that had a positive or negative impact on this case?

3. What was Mr. Lee's initial reaction regarding the inclusion of Kawika in GPE when first approached by Ms. James? Why did his reaction change?

4. What specific technological devices are mentioned in this case? Can you distinguish these devices as either low or high tech?

5. How comfortable would you feel about one or several of your students using such devices in physical education? If your prior knowledge were limited regarding assistive technology, what could you do to improve and enhance your knowledge base?

6. What mediating factors were present with respect to the use of assistive technology in this case? Would you say that Mr. Lee supports implementing assistive technology in his GPE class?

7. In addition to the use of assistive technology, what other gains resulted from Kawika's inclusion in Mr. Lee's GPE class?

8. What would you describe as the overall attitudes and behaviors of Kawika's peers without disabilities (e.g., Keith) toward him in this GPE class?

9. Can you identify other technological devices that might be seen or used in physical education?

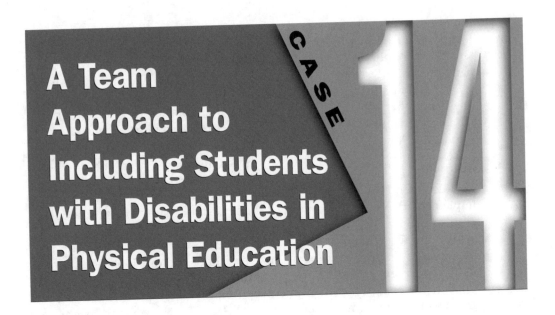

A Team Approach to Including Students with Disabilities in Physical Education

Lincoln Elementary is located in an affluent suburb approximately 10 minutes (by car) from downtown. Local support for the school has grown, as the result of families moving out of the city. Along with this growth comes more and more specialized services and instruction for students, particularly for students with special needs. At Lincoln Elementary there is a relatively larger population of students with special needs enrolled than at other schools in the district.

On this particular morning the weather is warm and humid. Ms. Angie, the district adapted physical educator, is elated because today she starts her aquatics unit. In recent years, the popularity of the aquatics unit with students and teachers has been enormous. In addition to teaching students how to swim, Ms. Angie emphasizes "drown-proofing" techniques aimed at assisting children with survival tactics should they find themselves in a body of water. Recently, however, the local school board raised liability concerns over the aquatics program. Despite these warnings, Lincoln Elementary's principal, Mr. Jones, and Ms. Angie are determined to maintain the aquatics unit for all 3rd graders.

There are three 3rd-grade classrooms at Lincoln Elementary, with each class having 24 to 29 children. There is also a fairly large contingent of children with an array of special needs. Most of the students receiving special education services receive APE as well. Other than sharing facilities, Ms. Angie has little to do with these children. However, Ms. Angie will soon become part of a cadre of teachers and professionals whose purpose is to include Mitch in the aquatics unit.

Mitch, a 3rd grader, has spastic cerebral palsy with moderate mental retardation. He is nonambulatory and has a slight hearing loss. His IQ is 75, and both cognitively and physically, Mitch requires assistance with many daily life activities. During his recent IEP meeting, Ms. Thom (Mitch's mother) voices that she wants Mitch to be included in the aquatics program. She has heard that all 3rd graders are receiving aquatics, and she wants the same opportunities for her son. The IEP team members consist of Ms. Thom, Mr. Jones, Ms. Bennett (special education teacher), Mr. Rob (paraprofessional), Mr. Donovan (physical therapist), Ms. Chan (occupational therapist), Ms. Clark (speech–language pathologist), and Ms. Angie. As the IEP team members discuss the extent to which the aquatics program can be implemented, Ms. Thom is under the impression that the IEP team doesn't wish to provide Mitch with the swimming program that all the typical 3rd graders are receiving. Mr. Jones states, "There is a huge liability issue with the aquatics program in general, and the school board is looking into modifying and even canceling the program." Ms. Thom adamantly expresses, "All 3rd graders at Lincoln Elementary are provided with this aquatics program, so why can't my son be included?" "Ms. Thom, everyone here is very supportive of providing services to Mitch. We all want what's best and we should examine all reasonable options," replies Ms. Bennett. Agitated, Ms. Thom asks, "What's so unreasonable about having my son receive aquatics like everyone else? And please don't patronize me." Ms. Chan intervenes, "There is some information about the benefits of an aquatics program for persons with limited mobility. I can bring it to the meeting if you wish." Mr. Donovan, nodding his head knowingly, concurs with Ms. Chan: "An aquatics program might be beneficial to Mitch. I remember working with patients in a rehabilitative clinic whereby aqua therapy was used. The patients felt really positive about that and even demonstrated more flexibility and mobility." Ms. Angie interjects, "How about collaborating on what might work for Mitch, instead of examining what we cannot do. Mr. Jones, I fully understand your plight about liability issues. However, Ms. Thom is legally right in that all 3rd graders are receiving aquatics, and so should her son." Mr. Jones, sitting red faced and vividly annoyed, says, "I think this IEP meeting should be postponed until tomorrow in order to address the aquatics issue."

The next day, everyone from the IEP team returns to discuss the final components of the meeting. Ms. Bennett quickly asks, "How can we assist Mitch in receiving aquatics?" Ms. Angie replies, "Mitch will need one-on-one instruction during the aquatics unit. Since the unit runs twice a week for 3 weeks, I could come to each lesson with Mitch and work with him along with the other 3rd graders." Ms. Chan says, "I could assist Ms. Angie with strategies prior to the aquatics unit. Some strategies might even be beneficial for all the children, not only Mitch." Echoing Ms. Chan's comments, Mr. Donovan states, "I can offer support and assistance to Ms. Angie over the course of the aquatics unit. It will be interesting to see if water increases Mitch's fluidity and mobility as opposed to land-bound movements. I would be available only once a week, however." As the IEP team discusses the possibilities of offering Mitch the same aquatics program as the other

3rd graders, issues of support, accommodations, and equipment are addressed. The team agrees that everyone including the pool staff can work with Ms. Angie during the aquatics unit. Despite everyone's enthusiasm, though, no one had bothered to consult the local community recreation pool staff, who host the pool where the 3rd-grade aquatics program is carried out. Ms. Angie quickly suggests, "I will talk with Mr. Pang, the pool manager. He has been very supportive of our swim program for years, so I don't think it will be problem." Everyone agrees that this is a good idea.

The local community recreation pool is clean and generally provides a pleasant atmosphere for learning and recreational swimming. As the first day of instruction approaches, Ms. Angie goes to the pool to make sure that all the necessary equipment is available. She discusses in detail how she will handle including Mitch in the aquatics class. She also suggests that Mitch participate with Mr. Farrell's 3rd grade class, because he has the smallest number of children. Mr. Farrell will therefore need to be included in the IEP team meetings and discussions.

On the first day of instruction, Ms. Angie, Mr. Farrell, Ms. Chan, Ms. Bennett, Mr. Rob, and Mr. Donovan are all present. As Ms. Angie provides the ground rules for this unit to Mr. Farrell's 3rd-grade class, Ms. Chan sits with Mitch. As Mr. Farrell's class enters the water, Ms. Chan places a personal flotation device (PFD) on Mitch and has Mr. Donovan and Mr. Rob assist him into the water. The PFD is to be used only sparingly—ideally, only on the first day. Upon touching the water, Mitch's muscles tense immediately and he becomes spastic. The water is rather cool (72°F), thus triggering this reaction. Eventually, as Mr. Pang organizes the class for bobbing and breathing drills, Ms. Angie works with Mitch doing similar drills.

Ms. Angie gives Mitch verbal cues and prompts. Mr. Donovan suggests that she hold her hand by Mitch's belly button to keep him in a prone position. After Mitch immerses his head into the water, he surfaces spitting water and choking and coughing. Ms. Angie warns, "Mitch, don't drink the water. Hold your breath. Here, watch me." Ms. Chan is assisting the other children with different grips when bobbing, and breathing techniques as they hold on to the side of the pool. The children are having a great time, while learning various drown-proofing techniques. Assisted by Ms. Angie, Mitch finally appears to be catching on. He really seems to be enjoying himself. Ms. Chan repeatedly tries to reach Mitch and Ms. Angie to see how they are doing, but with the other 25 children in the water, this is an impossible feat. Ms. Bennett stands nearby to assist Mitch and Ms. Angie whenever necessary. The pool staff, including the lifeguard on deck, curiously observe everyone, especially Mitch and Ms. Angie.

As the class ends, Mitch is all smiles. Ms. Bennett and Mr. Rob quickly help Mitch out of the water and into the locker room. On the pool deck, Ms. Angie, Ms. Chan, and Mr. Donovan quietly discuss the day's session. Ms. Angie expresses how concerned she was when Mitch "hit" the water and became spastic. However, she notes that as soon as he began moving, his range of motion and flexibility increased. As part of Mitch's PE goals and objectives, Ms. Angie suggests that eventually, they should remove the PFD to allow Mitch the opportunity to move freely without any restrictions. Ms.

Angie and members of the IEP team will work closely with Mitch (one-on-one assistance) as supports in order for him to continue to be included in this aquatics program.

QUESTIONS

Preparing for Learning & Teaching

1. What is the primary issue in this case?

2. What are some of the factors that contributed positively and negatively to this case?

3. How was Mitch's disability a problem? Was Mitch's disability the main issue of concern in this case? From whose perspective?

4. What contributed to Mitch's involvement in the aquatics unit? Who was influential?

5. Do you agree or disagree with the manner in which Mr. Jones reacted? Was it appropriate? Do you think that Ms. Thom and the other IEP team members handled his reactions appropriately?

6. What were Mr. Donovan and Ms. Chan's contributions to improving Mitch's participation in this aquatics unit? Do you think they provided enough support and input?

7. What was the overall reaction of having all the related services personnel available to Ms. Angie?

8. What were your thoughts when Mitch's mother suggested that since all 3rd graders were receiving aquatics, her son should too? Do you think this was a reasonable request?

9. Would you have included Mr. Pang and some of his pool staff as part of the IEP team? What are the advantages and disadvantages of doing so?

Children with Disabilities on the Playground

anny is a 10-year-old 5th grader at Sojourner Truth Elementary School who has a congenital double leg amputation. Both his legs did not develop below the knee, although the cause is not known because he was adopted. He grew up walking everywhere on his hands and is very proficient in getting around this way. When Danny became school age he started using a wheelchair. He is extremely strong and can even push it by himself almost anywhere. His parents' insurance company eventually agreed to cover a double prosthesis. Danny and his parents went to Shriner's Hospital, where two prosthetic legs were custom made for him. He tried to use them but hated everything about them. They inhibited his movement and he didn't feel like himself. Danny's parents kept the prosthetic legs just in case he might change his mind about using them, but he never did.

In school Danny excels. He has been with the same group of children since kindergarten. They are great friends and include him in many things. He goes to birthday parties, plays on the swings and monkey bars at recess, and has made many friends in his Boy Scout troop. His GPE teacher, Ms. Beatie, has good intentions but often is at a loss about how to include Danny. Most units he sits on the sidelines and keeps score, holds the net for volleyball, or goes to the library. He is included in parachute exercises, gymnastics, and swimming and helps swing the rope for jump rope. Danny's classroom teacher, Ms. Callahan, is aware of his limited involvement and truly believes he cannot do any more than he is already doing. Danny's parents are not aware of his exclusion in GPE. They think he is very social and intelligent and that that's enough. They have four other adopted children at home with disabilities and two of their own. In their mind Danny is independent, outspoken, and well adjusted.

The exclusion and limited opportunities in GPE didn't bother Danny until one day during recess the children on the playground ask him to play soccer. He is thrilled! He has dreamed of playing with the other boys, but he has never been invited, so he has always contented himself with swinging on the swings and playing on the monkey bars. As he begins to play soccer with the other boys, he feels more mobile on the grass, so during the game he walks on his hands and when the ball comes to him he kicks it with one of his stumps. He can defend for short periods of time and is even involved in a few offensive plays.

Danny continues to be involved in recess for about a week. Then one day Ms. Callahan wanders over to the field and sees him playing soccer. She is extremely alarmed and tells Danny to "stop playing this instant and get out of harm's way." Danny is crushed. He had finally been fully integrated in something, and it was suddenly being taken away for no reason. He is even more embarrassed about the other kids seeing him being reprimanded for something as "normal" as playing soccer at recess. Danny becomes withdrawn, depressed, and doesn't do anything at recess. The other kids don't want Danny to get into trouble again so they don't even ask him to play after the incident. He feels that to go back to the monkey bars and the swings would be taking a step backward and be giving up. He has no idea what to do, so he does nothing. When he goes home, he goes straight to his room and doesn't even do his homework.

One of Danny's friends, Matt, doesn't think this is fair and tells his mother about the situation. Matt's mother decides to call Danny's parents. When Danny's parents confront him, he tells them all about it and cries all night. It bothers Danny so much that it affects everything he is doing. His parents subsequently call the school and set up a meeting with Ms. Beatie; Ms. Callahan; Mr. Harrison, the principal; and Danny. Danny is nervous, but he knows he is capable of playing with the other children and probably wouldn't get hurt any more often than they would. The meeting is productive and it turns out that the concern is that Danny may get kicked in the head or body and that he may trip the other children. Danny expresses his ability to move and says he wants to participate in any aspect of the game. After much discussion, they come up with a wonderful solution. Danny can play goalie on his hands, and the ball will have to be lower than his hands outstretched above his head in order to score. Danny will wear a hockey helmet and goalie gloves. Playing goalie will involve a lot of movement, inclusion, and participation on Danny's part. To make it fair to everyone, the goalie on the other team will play on his knees and the ball also will have to be lower than the top of his hands to score. Danny is thrilled, and when the boys ask about playing touch football, the teachers, parents, and Danny come up with modifications to include him safely in touch football as well.

When Ms. Beatie sees that Danny is being included so successfully at recess she starts including Danny more and more in his GPE classes by making modifications. Danny tells Ms. Beatie what he thinks he can do, and

Danny's peers also brainstorm about ways he could successfully be included. Before, at recess, some days Danny did want to play on the monkey bars, swing on the swings, or play four-square, but now he has choices. That's all he ever wanted—to have the same choices as his peers. Danny feels so empowered and "normal" that he signs up for modified swimming the next year. The coach isn't too sure that Danny can swim independently, but when Danny swims the crawl stroke and makes a decent time, the coach includes him on the team. Now Danny believes he can do anything! His success on the playground and in the gym have had a greater effect than he could ever have imagined.

The next year Danny will be attending middle school, which has four PE teachers. They are very nice yet have had little experience working with students like Danny, and he realizes that he will have to help them find ways to include him in the various PE activities.

Resources and References

Block, M. E. (2000). *A teacher's guide to including children with disabilities in regular physical education.* Baltimore: Paul H. Brookes.

I CAN Playground Activities. Pro Ed Publishers, Austin, TX, www.proedinc.com.

NOTES

QUESTIONS

Preparing for Learning & Teaching

SUMMARY OF PARTICIPANTS

Danny, 10-year-old student with congenital double leg amputation

Ms. Beatie, GPE teacher

Ms. Callahan, classroom teacher

Matt, Danny's friend

Mr. Harrison, principal

Danny's parents

1. What is the primary issue in this case?

2. Are there related issues? If so, what are they?

3. What are some of the specific elements that contributed to these issues?

4. What role did the characters play in creating/resolving these issues?

5. Were the adaptations made for soccer appropriate? Why or why not?

6. When Danny is included in touch football, what adaptations may need to be made? What about basketball?

7. What does the law say about inclusion in recess?

8. What accommodations are required during recess, if any?

9. Will Danny need to have anything written in his IEP about modifications for recess? Why or why not?

10. What appropriate future sports opportunities are there for Danny?

11. What websites or list serves would be appropriate to find information about including Danny?

Celia Joins Her High School Swim Team

elia is a freshman at Truman High School. She is very enthusiastic, energetic, and tries very hard. Celia has mild hemiplegic spastic cerebral palsy[1] concomitant with mild mental retardation. She is being included in her general education high school classes. Her district uses the "blended" model in which there is a core subject general teacher and a special education teacher in each class. The district has been using this model since Celia was in 7th grade. Before that she was in a 12:1:1 self-contained class.[2] Celia likes the blended model better because she has more friends and receives more attention because there are only two to four students with special needs in any of her classes.

In PE class, Celia is included with her typically developing peers, and her teacher, Mr. Ramsey, is very creative. He consistently makes slight modifications, rule changes, and instructional changes according to her needs. He consults with Mrs. Jennings, the APE specialist, when he starts a new unit or he needs to address a new issue. For example, when the class was playing soccer, Mr. Ramsey created a scooter soccer game (soccer played on scooters) so that the teams would be moving at Celia's pace. When they played hockey, they used a large Frisbee. There was a 10-second rule in which the defenders could not hit the Frisbee for 10 seconds when Celia had possession. And during the step aerobics unit, Celia participated with a low step, and sometimes no step. This enabled her to keep up better and have fewer balance issues.

Although Celia always has a hard time with her academics because of her mental retardation, one thing Celia excels in is swimming. Although she has balance problems and walks with a distinct limp, she swims very well. There is a pool at the apartment complex where she lives with her mother and brother, and during the summer she spends hours swimming with her friends. Celia tried out for the swim team at her middle school, but because the pool is small and only has four lanes, only 14 students were selected. Celia was one of the ones who were cut. This infuriated Celia, but her mother has taught her never to give up.

Truman High School holds tryouts for the swim team in August, and the swim season runs from September to the end of November. Celia desperately wants to make the team. Mr. Duffy, the coach, suggests that she practice less popular strokes, namely the backstroke and butterfly. Her APE consultant, Mrs. Jennings, also points out that she may have less of a problem with the bilateral movement on these two strokes. Celia practices and practices throughout the summer and her brother times her. Although the pool at their apartment is shorter than the high school's, she believes she is faster than the year before.

Tryouts are held the week before school starts, and Celia's mother has to work. Her mother drops her off early in the morning and Celia has to wait until 9:00 A.M. for the try outs to begin. Her mother can't pick her up until her lunch break at 1:00. The first two days go well. Celia feels like she is keeping up with her peers and is confident about her times for the backstroke and butterfly. When the real tryouts start, 11 people try out for backstroke and 9 for butterfly. Celia's heart sinks, but when Coach Duffy asks which ones are seniors, most of them raise their hands. This means Celia will have a good shot at making the junior varsity team. For the backstroke she feels great and finishes seventh. For the butterfly, she realizes that they have to dive from the starting block. It's hard for her to stand by herself on the slant of the starting block, and she is embarrassed when she has to ask for help. Amanda, her friend from 8th grade, who was also cut in middle school, helps her. Celia has a difficult time with the dive and gets off to a slow start, but her determination pays off—she finishes sixth.

As the week goes on, Celia feels more confident. The extra time she has spent at her new school has allowed her to meet some of the teachers and her special education "blended" teacher, Ms. Armstrong. Ms. Armstrong is a swimmer herself and is anxious to hear about Celia's swim tryouts. Friday is the last day of tryouts, and the names of the girls who made the team will be posted on Monday, also the first day of school. Celia is so nervous over the weekend that she can barely sleep.

On Monday Celia is overwhelmed by the excitement of her first day of high school and finding out if she made the swim team. She goes to Coach Duffy's office and reads the 2000–2001 Golden Eagles swim roster. There on the top of the junior varsity list is Celia's name. Amanda's name is also on the list. Celia thinks to herself, "I can't wait to tell Ms. Armstrong! She'll be so pleased."

At 3:00 P.M. sharp the team starts its grueling practices. One thing that Coach Duffy notices is that Celia needs help balancing on the starting block. He tells her either they can put two kickboards under her left foot or a peer can hold her steady. Celia prefers having a peer hold her because the peer can also tell her when to start. Coach Duffy knows that the rule-book doesn't permit this, so he will have to get permission from the other team coaches in order for this to be legal with the officials. In addition, Coach Duffy has overlooked the fact that Celia uses only one hand for the touch finish and the rulebook states that in both her events the swimmer must use a two-hand touch for a finish. He will have to get permission from the other coaches to modify this rule as well. Coach Duffy speaks with his friend, Mrs. Donovan, who has been an official for more than 25 years. She had seen such modifications at the Special Olympics and tells Coach Duffy that he will have to write a letter to the other coaches for permission. Mrs. Donovan also tells him that he will have to show that there is no "unfair advantage" by the rule modifications. In fact, if he can prove this the case for the change will be stronger. Celia is very concerned that the other coaches won't accept the modifications.

Coach Duffy decides to ask Celia to try a start with no support in an intersquad scrimmage. She agrees to try her best. She is able to stand on the block for a short amount of time unassisted, but then she false starts twice. Celia is embarrassed and frustrated and wishes she could have just a little support from Amanda. She then tries the two-kickboard method and doesn't false start—she is right on target. Coach Duffy tells Celia not to worry.

Coach Duffy writes a letter to the other coaches explaining that he has a swimmer who has talent, yet needs a few small modifications in order to compete equally with her peers. He requests that she be allowed to use two kickboards taped together for her starts on the butterfly and the medley, and a one-hand touch finish. One coach from the rival school, Mr. Sabatini, expresses concern in a phone call. He asks about the unfair advantage because he thinks Celia could use the kickboards to gain a faster start time. Coach Duffy explains the effects of Celia's cerebral palsy and that her ability to swim is not affected, but that her balance on land, especially on a small starting block, is affected.

The next week the officials have a meeting before the season starts. They unanimously decide to allow the modifications for Celia. She is thrilled and can't wait until the competitions begin. The team is very supportive and everyone takes turns assisting her at the start. Celia becomes an active team member who participates in every meet.

Endnotes

1. Mild hemiplegic spastic cerebral palsy refers to uncontrolled flexion of the muscles on one side of the body. In Celia's case, this causes a scissor gait on one side and flexion of the arm on the same side.

2. A 12:1:1 class refers to the ratio of students to teacher and teacher aides. In this case it means 12 students to 1 teacher and 1 teacher aide. For Celia it means that she needs a ratio of 6:1 and in a 12:1:1 situation she would receive that amount of attention.

Resources and References

Adapted Physical Activity Council. (1991). *Sport instruction for individuals with disabilities: The best of practical pointers.* Reston, VA: American Alliance for Health, Physical Education, Recreation and Dance.

Lepore, M., Gayle, W. G., & Stevens, S. (1998). *Adapted aquatic programming: A professional guide.* Champaign, IL: Human Kinetics.

United States Cerebral Palsy Athletic Association. (1997). *Classification and sports rule manual* (5th ed.). Newport, RI: Author.

QUESTIONS

Preparing for Learning & Teaching

SUMMARY OF PARTICIPANTS

Celia, 9th-grade student with mild hemiplegic spastic cerebral palsy concomitant with mild mental retardation

Mr. Ramsey, GPE teacher

Mr. Duffy, swim coach

Mrs. Jennings, APE consultant

Amanda, Celia's friend from 8th grade

Ms. Armstrong, special education "blended" teacher

Mrs. Donovan, swim official and friend of Coach Duffy

Mr. Sabatini, swim coach of rival school

1. What is the primary issue in this case? Are there related issues? If so, what are they?

2. What are some of the specific elements that contributed to these issues?

3. What role did the characters play in creating/resolving these issues?

4. Who helped create the most appropriate solution? In what ways? What would you have done differently?

5. In addition to the combination of peer support or use of two kickboards for the start and a one-hand touch finish, what else could have been done and why?

6. What does the Americans with Disabilities Act (ADA) say about services for individuals with disabilities as far as after school sports participation?

7. Under the ADA what accommodations are required of a coach for such a student as Celia? Of the school? Of the athletic facility?

8. Was Celia prepared for this situation? Why or why not?

9. What are three appropriate future goals for Celia on the team? What about after school age? Community based?

10. Why was Celia so self-determined? What was the family's role? How can the school help her be more self-determined?

11. What websites or list serves would be appropriate to find information about helping Celia?

12. What additional information would the coach need to know in order to accommodate Celia?

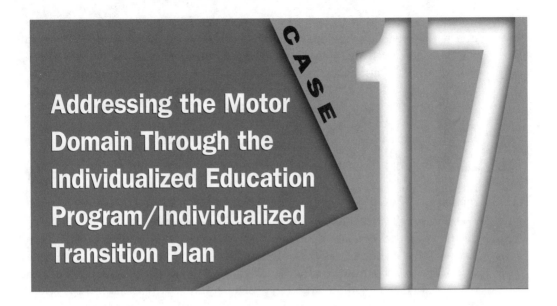

Addressing the Motor Domain Through the Individualized Education Program/Individualized Transition Plan

acob is a 19-year-old with severe cerebral palsy who uses a manual wheelchair with limited range of motion in his right arm but greater control and mobility in his left arm. Jacob can push himself around but is usually assisted by a caregiver at home or paraprofessional at school. He smiles, is energetic, cooperative, understands simple words and phrases, and enjoys swimming and watching television. Unfortunately, he easily becomes aggressive and strikes anyone within reach—usually without any provocation.

Because of Jacob's current aggressive behavior, the individualized education program/individualized transition plan (IEP/ITP)[1] team recommends that Jacob be home schooled until his behavior can be curbed or controlled. Clearly, the question of safety for other students and staff is an issue. Jacob receives home schooling from a tutor that includes math, English, science, and social studies. Physical therapy and occupational therapy are on a consult basis with monthly visitations by professionals providing these related services. Although required by Public Law 105-17, the Individuals with Disabilities Education Act Amendments of 1997,[2] Jacob does not receive instruction in physical education.

Jacob's parents want him to be more socially and physically active by getting more exercise, swimming, and recreating with others instead of watching television. During the next IEP/ITP meeting, his parents ask about physical education. Ms. Roberts, the special education teacher, indicates that Mr. Wayne, the school district adapted physical educator, knows about Jacob and is willing to follow up with a formal assessment, program recommendation, and evaluation. During her discussions with Mr. Wayne, he acknowledges that Jacob's aggressive behavior (swinging and hitting anyone within reach of his left side), which usually occurs without any warning, is a concern. Mr. Wayne suggests that other teachers at Varsity High School didn't want Jacob in class because they fear for the safety of the other students. This is partly the reason why Jacob is being home schooled. With such concern over Jacob's behavior and his parents' interest in physical education, Ms. Roberts, along with Mr. Wayne, decides to reconvene the IEP/ITP team in order to address physical education.

Because of Jacob's age, a statement on transition is warranted. This statement needs to address Jacob's educational programming with respect to interagency linkages, vocational education, and recreation leisure. The IEP/ITP team feels that Jacob should participate in a physical activity program with peers his own age. Concern for the safety of the other students deems that the IEP/ITP team will not be able to arrange a program at Varsity High School. It is therefore suggested that the local university be contacted to determine whether Jacob fulfills the transitional portion of his IEP/ITP that specifically relates to physical activity. Still, the larger question remains, "What specifically can Jacob do with regard to exercise and physical activity?" Before any formal placement can be made, the team requests that Mr. Wayne conduct a physical activity assessment of Jacob.

One morning, Mr. Wayne arranges to have the physical assessment done. He obtains permission from the recreation director across the street from Varsity High School to use the fitness center's weight machines and aquatics facilities and implements the Movement Opportunities for Building Independence and Leisure Interests through Training Educators and Exceptional Learners[3] (MOBILITEE) test. MOBILITEE is a criterion-referenced test that is suitable for assessment, planning, and teaching purposes. Mr. Wayne notes the following results from the assessment:

1. With assistance from a paraprofessional and sitting in his wheelchair, Jacob can military press one plate (approximately 10 pounds) twice on the fitness center weight machine.

2. With assistance from a paraprofessional and seated in his wheelchair, Jacob can complete two repetitions of triceps press on the fitness center weight machine.

3. Using the fitness center weight machine and a wrist strap to support and stabilize his right hand and while seated, Jacob can complete one chest press and extension with assistance five times.

4. When asked to throw a ball, Jacob can perform a level 3 on MOBILITEE. This means that he throws from one side with his predominate hand (left hand), has good extension, releases, and follows through.

5. When asked to catch a thrown ball, Jacob can perform a level 1 on MOBILITEE. This infers that he can stretch his arm out but can't make eye contact when the ball is thrown. He doesn't demonstrate any movements with his right hand. His eyes are closed, he turns his head away, and he "traps" the ball against his body. This might be considered a defense mechanism when any object is being thrown toward him.

6. When asked to strike a ball with a bat, Jacob can perform at a level 1 on MOBILITEE. Although this might be interpreted as low, he does have good extension and grip and can make direct contact with a softball-size whiffle ball placed on a tee.

7. When asked to dribble a basketball, Jacob appears to know what to do, but his movements are restricted. He can't dribble the basketball more than once. This may be attributed to the spasticity in his movements.

8. With a flotation device, Jacob can maintain a horizontal (supine) position while moving his legs and arms (as if treading water) for 10 minutes.

Upon completing the assessment, Mr. Wayne contacts the local university to see if some of the college students might be able to work with Jacob. Mr. Wayne's rationale for approaching the university is twofold: (a) it can provide exercise facilities to work on specific IEP/ITP goals; and (b) it can provide interaction with chronological age–appropriate peers. The university has a collaborative working relationship with Varsity High School and other schools within the adjoining area and is willing to include Jacob with other students his age in a specially designed physical activity class. Varsity High School will provide transportation.

In addition to the motor and fitness assessment, Jacob's parents will need to complete a needs evaluation in order to assist the IEP/ITP team with setting goals and objectives for Jacob. They are asked to complete the "Physical Activities Menu for Pupils with IEP Transition Content" tool (Murata & Jansma, 1999). This menu of physical activities offers students with special needs and IEP team members the opportunity to examine and select physical activities that are meaningful and practical with the potential for preemployment relevancy. The "Physical Activity Justification Checklist" (Murata & Jansma, 1999) was then used to verify the activity selection. Jacob's age requires a transition statement to be addressed as part of the IEP process, and to be aligned with educational content standards and benchmarks. Specifically, the "Physical Education Hawaii Content and Performance Standards"[4] are used to develop performance outcomes for Jacob. The standards addressed are: Content Standard 3, "students exhibit a physically active lifestyle"; Content Standard 4, "students demonstrate ways to achieve and maintain a health-enhancing level of physical fitness"; and Content Standard 7, "students understand that physical activity provides opportunities for enjoyment, challenge, self-expression, and social interaction."

As a result of the assessments (physical and parental needs) and to be aligned with content standards, the IEP/ITP team recommends that the best option for reaching Jacob's physical activity annual goals and objectives is to have him participate at the local university. Jacob's transitional statement is rewritten to reflect his participation with chronological age–appropriate peers (freshmen college students), while working on his physical activity goals and objectives. As required, Mr. Wayne writes Jacob's goals and objectives:

ANNUAL GOALS

1. With assistance from a paraprofessional, Jacob will use the local university's fitness center weight machines to control eccentric contractions twice a week for one semester (Content Standards 3 and 7).

2. With assistance from a paraprofessional, Jacob will participate in an aquatics program at the local university once a week with a university student (Content Standard 7).

OBJECTIVES

1. With assistance from a paraprofessional or university student and a visual chart for seating, Jacob will do three sets of seated presses with both hands with 10 pounds of weight (Content Standards 3 and 4).

2. With assistance from a paraprofessional or university student, Jacob will do three sets of seated station flies with both arms with 10 pounds to increase horizontal flexion at the shoulder joint (Content Standards 3 and 4).

3. With assistance from a paraprofessional or university student, Jacob will do three sets of seated leg extensions with 10 pounds to increase flexion in the hip region (Content Standards 3 and 4).

4. With a flotation device and assistance from a university student, Jacob will swim the short length of the pool (approximately 30 yards) using his arms and kicking with his legs twice (Content Standards 4 and 7).

Within a few days of receiving confirmation from the bus company that transportation will be provided, Mr. Wayne contacts Ms. Roberts about the initial start date for Jacob's program. Mr. Wayne is grateful that he has the support of community resources, especially the local university. Yet, he knows that Jacob's aggressive behavior might become an issue even with the university. He is reassured during the IEP/ITP meeting that the university students are willing to work with Jacob's disability, demeanor, and tendency toward aggressiveness.

On the bus ride to Jacob's first day at the university, Mr. Robb, the bus driver; the bus aide; and paraprofessional Mr. Keene, who accompanies Jacob, notice that Jacob appears agitated. Although Jacob isn't hitting or swinging at anyone, he isn't smiling and rocks in his seat back and forth during the ride. Mr. Keene wonders if this "rocking behavior" usually precedes the aggressive behavior or if it is just from the excitement of the bus ride. Mr. Keene passes on this information to Mr. Wayne as soon as they arrive at the university. Sensing a potential volatile situation, Mr. Wayne sits with Jacob and Mr. Keene outside the wellness center for a few minutes. Mr. Wayne talks to Jacob about why he is there, what he will be doing, and all the people whom he will be meeting. Jacob soon appears relaxed and nods that he is ready to work out.

It is 10:00 and the wellness center is open only to a university class. This time is set a priori in order to limit the amount of university students working out; too many individuals in one place at one time might be overwhelming for Jacob. Stopping in an open area near the center's weight machines, Mr. Wayne, with the assistance of Mr. Keene, leads Jacob through a variety of stretches for warm-up. Ten minutes later, Mr. Wayne brings Jacob over to the weight machines. Since this is day one, Mr. Wayne feels that Jacob should be given an introduction about what to do and shown how to work the machines. Mr. Keene takes notes about the various exercises and machines that Jacob will be using. Jacob is attentive and eager to try. Sensing this, Mr. Wayne allows Jacob to do a few lifts, while Mr. Keene stands within a few feet to assist whenever needed. Through this brief introduction Mr. Wayne is able to demonstrate to Jacob how each lift is done without dropping the weights, the need to practice safety during the lifts, and the importance of Jacob waiting for his turn. After 50 minutes, the session ends.

The next day, Jacob returns for his swimming goals. The pool attendant is helpful and supportive. The pool lift is already set up with flotation devices available on deck. Mr. Wayne has Rick, a university student athlete, work with Jacob in the water. Initially, Jacob is slowly introduced to the environment; he is shown the showers, lockers, and changing areas, all of which are easily accessible. This first swimming session goes well. Rick assists Jacob with showering, changing, and getting him ready for the bus ride home.

As the week passes, Mr. Wayne feels good about what Jacob is accomplishing and how well he is interacting with the university personnel. He believes that Jacob's goals and objectives can be met within the semester. Mr. Wayne knows that he needs to collect accurate assessment data during Jacob's sessions, so he creates a chart and scoring sheet to chart progress.

Endnotes

1. IEP/ITP denotes that a statement on transition should be part of the IEP document and not a separate document.

2. Individuals with Disabilities Education Act (IDEA) Amendments of 1997, Public Law No. 105-17, Sec. 601, 111 Stat. 40-41 (June 4, 1997) mandates educational service delivery including physical education for all children/youth with disabilities.

3. Rudolph, D. A., & Arnold, R. W. (1981). Project MOBILITEE. In P. Jansma (Ed.), *Psychomotor domain training and serious disabilities.* Baltimore: University Press of America. Project MOBILITEE criterion-referenced assessment test manual and curriculum guide may be secured at no charge from Adapted Physical Education Consultant, Ohio Department Building, Room 1109, 65 South Front Street, Columbus, OH 43226.

4. The Physical Education Hawaii Content and Performance Standards (1999) may be secured from the Department of Education, State of Hawaii, Office of Accountability and School Instructional Support/School Renewal Group, 189 Lunalilo Home Rd., 2nd Floor, Honolulu, HI 96825, http://doek/2.hi.us/standards/index.htm.

Resources and References

Murata, N. M., & Jansma, P. (1999a). Physical activities menu for pupils with IEP transition content. In P. Jansma (Ed.), *Psychomotor domain training and serious disabilities* (pp. 361–369). Baltimore: University Press of America.

QUESTIONS
Preparing for Learning & Teaching

CASE 17

SUMMARY OF PARTICIPANTS

Jacob, 19-year-old with severe cerebral palsy

Ms. Roberts, special education teacher

Mr. Wayne, school district adapted physical educator

Mr. Robb, bus driver

Mr. Keene, paraprofessional

Rick, university student athlete

1. What is the primary issue in this case? Are there related issues? If so, what are they?

2. What are some of the specific elements that contribute to these issues?

3. What role did the characters play in creating/resolving these issues?

4. Create your own transitional statement for Jacob. To what extent does your transitional statement address physical activity?

5. Explain what is meant by the IEP/ITP meeting. Are you able to ascertain that the ITP needs to be part of the IEP document?

6. Given this situation, what would you recommend for Jacob regarding his IEP/ITP goals and objectives?

7. How would you prepare yourself for a student who is potentially violent?

8. How should Mr. Wayne determine the possible reasons or triggers for Jacob's aggression?

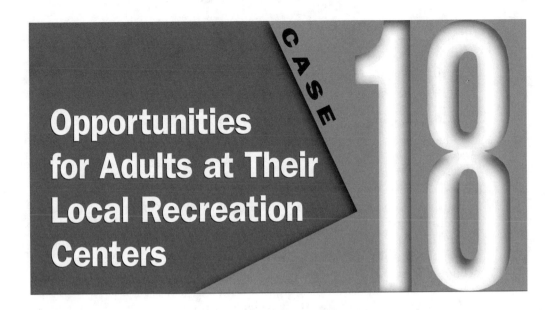

Opportunities for Adults at Their Local Recreation Centers

Javier is 17 years old and has Williams syndrome,[1] which affects his academic skills so significantly that he spends a large portion of his school day in a self-contained classroom for children with mild mental retardation. Although he doesn't play on any of East Mesa's sport teams, doesn't play in the marching band, and has never acted in any school production, Javier is one of the most popular students at East Mesa High School. The only time most students see Javier is during home room, lunch, choir, physical education, or between classes. Yet, there is something about Javier that makes other students want to hang out with him. Perhaps it is the fact that Javier has such a wonderful, outgoing personality. He is always very polite and engaging to talk to. He looks you right in the eye, always has a smile on his face, and is always interested in what you are doing.

Javier also is a favorite during physical education. This is remarkable because he is not very good at most sports and physical activities. But Javier tries hard, and he cheers loudly for his teammates during games. He is the first to give high fives to a teammate who scores a point, and he is the first to console a teammate who might have made a mistake. Yes, everyone wants Javier on their team.

Although Javier is very popular at school, he really doesn't have many friends to do things with after school. Many students at East Mesa play on sport teams or belong to clubs, but Javier misses out on these opportunities. Most days Javier simply rides the school bus home, says goodbye to neighborhood friends, and then watches TV and talks to his mother and younger sister. This after-school routine doesn't make Javier sad, though, because he really enjoys the company of his mother and sister. He never complains about being home with them in the afternoon and evening, and he never asks if he can go out and do other things with friends. Yet, Javier's mother, Mrs. Gonzales, is concerned that when Javier graduates in a few years and lives in a group home, he will not have any leisure skills to fill his afternoon and evening hours. The thought of Javier sitting home watching TV day after day has bothered Mrs. Gonzales for a long time, but she has yet to voice this concern to Javier's teachers. However, Mrs. Gonzales has decided that it is time to bring up some after-school activities at Javier's next individual transition plan (ITP) meeting in two weeks.

At the ITP meeting, which Javier also attends, Mrs. Gonzales voices her concerns about Javier's lack of after-school activities and friends. She tells members of the ITP team—Mrs. Herndon, Javier's special education teacher; Mr. Billings, his PE teacher; his choir teacher; an assistant principal from East Mesa; and Mrs. Winters, a representative from the county mental retardation and mental health agency (MRMH)—what Javier does every afternoon after school. She expresses her concern for Javier now as well as for his future as a young, semi-independent adult. She asks the members of the ITP team, "Do you have any suggestions for Javier's leisure time?" Mrs. Winters looks at Javier and asks him, "What sort of things would you like to do after school?" Javier smiles at her and thinks for a few seconds. He then says, "I like all the sports and games that Mr. Billings plays in PE, and I would like to do more of those types of activities." Mrs. Winters looks to Mr. Billings and says, "Tell us about the types of activities and games that are played in your class." Mr. Billings replies, "I run a fairly typical high school PE program with a mix of fitness programs such as aerobics and strength training; instruction in lifetime leisure sports such as golf and tennis; and some team instruction and team play in sports such as soccer, basketball, softball, and volleyball. Javier really tries hard and enjoys all these activities, but he isn't very good at any of them. He really has the most trouble understanding where he is supposed to go and what he is supposed to do. His peers have learned to give him extra cues to know where to go. Javier doesn't seem to get frustrated; he just seems to enjoy being out with his teammates and playing regardless of his skills and understanding of the games."

The team sits quietly trying to think of ways to get Javier involved in sport and recreational activities in the community. Finally, Mrs. Gonzales breaks the silence: "A few weeks ago, I attended the open house of a new Jewish Community Center not far from my house. The center has lots of activities that would be perfect for Javier. There are an indoor track and weight room; an outdoor pool; and a big basketball court, where the JCC plans to have basketball and volleyball leagues. There also is a teen center with air hockey, foosball, pool tables, a snack bar, and popular music. After the meeting, I will find out if it's open to the general public. Javier, what do you think about going to the JCC to work out and play with friends in the afternoon?" Javier smiles broadly and replies, "That sounds like a great idea. Can I go tomorrow?"

Mrs. Herndon then suggests that they need to decide (a) what needs to be done to make this recreation program happen, and (b) which team members will take on which roles. She is very excited about the prospect of adding this recreation component to Javier's ITP, and she wants to make sure that this program becomes a reality for him. To start the discussion, Mrs. Herndon lists the following things that need to be done:

1. Visit the JCC to see what programs are available.
2. Determine the times and costs for various programs.
3. Determine who will provide transportation to and from Mrs. Gonzales's house and the JCC.
4. Determine which program Javier would enjoy most and have the most opportunity for success.
5. Determine what ITP goals and objectives under the recreation domain should be written for Javier.
6. Determine other skills Javier will need to be successful at the JCC (e.g., entering the building, finding the locker room, using a locker, changing clothes, finding the weight room or basketball court) and who will teach these skills.
7. Determine what type of ongoing support Javier will need to be successful in selected activities at the JCC.
8. Once activities have been selected, determine who will teach Javier key recreation skills so that he will have a greater chance of success.

Mrs. Winters thinks the list is a good start but notes that there is another issue that needs to be discussed. There is a special recreation program offered by the county for children and adults with disabilities at this new center. The program is run by a certified therapeutic recreation specialist, there is a smaller student-to-teacher ratio, and the activities are modified to meet participants' needs. So which type of program would Javier benefit from and enjoy most—a special recreation program or a regular recreation program?

Deciding between a regular and special recreation program adds an interesting twist to the situation. Mrs. Herndon suggests that everyone take a 10-minute break, think about some of the issues that have been brought up, and be prepared to discuss them when the meeting reconvenes. Everyone wants Javier to have a new recreation program to go to in the afternoons, but it is going to take a lot more work than Mrs. Gonzales had anticipated. However, Javier's ITP team is very supportive, and Mrs. Gonzales feels that soon Javier will be doing more than watching TV after school.

Endnote

1. Williams syndrome is a rare genetic disorder that causes medical and developmental problems. It is characterized by unique facial features, small stature, mild mental retardation or learning disabilities, and attention problems. Individuals with Williams syndrome often have very good speech and long-term memory as well as exceptional social skills. For more information on Williams syndrome, go to www.williams-syndrome.org.

NOTES

QUESTIONS

Preparing for Learning & Teaching

1. What is the primary issue in this case?

SUMMARY OF PARTICIPANTS

Javier, 17-year-old student with Williams syndrome

Mrs. Gonzales, Javier's mother

Mrs. Herndon, special education teacher

Mrs. Winters, representative from MRMH

Mr. Billings, PE teacher

2. Do you think Mrs. Gonzales should have simply taken Javier to the recreation center herself and enrolled him in classes, or was she correct in making this an issue for Javier's ITP team? Why?

3. What does IDEA say about transition planning?

4. What other things need to be considered to help Javier make a successful transition to the recreation center?

5. What type of assessment tool could you create that would help determine all the skills needed (motor, physical, self-help, cognitive, social, academic) for Javier to be successful at the recreation center? How could this assessment tool be used to measure Javier's present level of performance?

6. What role do you think the physical educator should take in this process? Why?

7. Would you recommend this special program for Javier or would you recommend that he participate in a regular recreation program with support? Why? Under what circumstances would you change your mind? How would you determine which program—special or regular—Javier would enjoy more?

8. Can this after-school recreation program replace Javier's physical education? What does IDEA say about recreation compared to physical education?

Taking Advantage of Membership at a Local Health Club

Mr. Wickstrom looks around the classroom at his students and thinks to himself, "Boy, these kids are really getting fat." Mr. Wickstrom is a special education teacher at Southern High School in charge of a self-contained class of eight students with moderate to severe mental retardation. He has been teaching at Southern for 5 years, and the students he has this year have been in his class for the past 3 years. He would be the first to admit that he is getting a little burned out with teaching in general and with this group of students in particular. It's not that Mr. Wickstrom doesn't like teaching or his students, but having the same group for 3 straight years is getting a little monotonous.

Even though Mr. Wickstrom feels like he's in a rut, he runs a very good program. His students are integrated in many activities at Southern such as physical education, drama, woodworking, and lunch. Students and teachers alike are generally receptive to having Mr. Wickstrom's students in their classes and around the school. In addition to attending classes during the school day, some of Mr. Wickstrom's students are active in after-school activities at Southern. For example, two of his students are comanagers of the baseball team, two others are active members in the key club, and two others are working as stage hands for the upcoming school play.

All of Mr. Wickstrom's students have jobs around the school depending on their ability. These jobs include helping Mr. Tracey, the custodian; Mrs. Smithers, one of the secretaries; or Mrs. Stanford, one of the cafeteria staff. There also is a community partnership with the local mall that Mr. Wickstrom helped create in which his students sample jobs at various places of employment at the mall. Workers at various mall stores train and supervise Mr. Wickstrom's students with occasional support from him and his two teaching assistants. The program is quite successful, with two of Mr. Wickstrom's former students working full-time jobs at the mall, and two of his current students working part-time.

Mr. Wickstrom also has access to a school car, which he uses to take his students out into the community to learn skills such as shopping at a grocery store, using a bank, purchasing items at a convenience store or food at fast-food and sit-down restaurants, using a Laundromat, and going to the movies or bowling. This is a particularly fun part of the program for Mr. Wickstrom and his teacher assistants, as well as the students. These daily outings involve no more than two to three students with one staff member, and the students often combine activities, such as going to the bank followed by a quick snack at McDonald's.

Mr. Wickstrom again looks around the room at his students and notes that they are overweight. He realizes that through his program his students are getting fast food or a convenience store snack almost every day. Also, Mrs. Stanford, the big-hearted cafeteria worker who helps supervise his students when they help set up the cafeteria, enjoys giving his students fresh-baked cookies and other treats.

Mr. Wickstrom thinks about what his students do for exercise. Southern High School, like the other high schools in the district, requires only one year of physical education, and many of his students opt not to continue with physical education as an elective. Mr. Wickstrom is sure that none of his students belong to any community teams or recreation programs, not even Special Olympics. He pictures his students sitting at home every evening watching TV and eating microwave popcorn. He then thinks about the types of physical activity he offers his students during the school day. The only recreation program he provides is occasional bowling and miniature golf outings, and neither of these activities can really be considered exercise. Mr. Wickstrom suddenly realizes that he is probably contributing to his students' obesity.

During his planning period, Mr. Wickstrom goes to the gym to talk to Mrs. Lacey, one of the PE teachers at Southern. He explains his concern about his students and asks her if she has any thoughts. Mrs. Lacey suggests creating a special aerobics and weight-training program for Mr. Wickstrom's class the last period of the day when she has a planning period. This idea sounds good at first, but as the two of them discuss it in more detail, they realize that such a program would not have much carryover when the students graduate next year. Mrs. Lacey then mentions the therapeutic recreation program offered by the county. She is sure that it offers some type of exercise program. Mr. Wickstrom ponders this option, but he really wants to get his students in a regular program where they can interact with young adults without disabilities rather than in a special program where everyone has a disability. Mrs. Lacey, getting a little frustrated, sarcastically remarks that the class should go to the health club where she works out. At first, Mr. Wickstrom laughs, but then he thinks that Mrs. Lacey might actually have a great idea. He tells her that the health club will be perfect. First, it is a place where his students could go now as well as in the future when they graduate and move into the community. Second, the health club has equipment that would be relatively easy for his students to learn how to work, such as stationary bikes and weight machines that are easy to program. Third, the health club has staff who supervise the aerobic and weight rooms and who could help his students as needed. Finally, there are several beginner-level classes that his students could join. Even if they aren't able to do all the steps correctly, they would be having fun moving to the music and would get a workout as well. Yes, the health club would be perfect.

Mrs. Lacey is surprised that Mr. Wickstrom actually likes her pseudo suggestion. She tells him that she was only joking about his students going to her health club and then points out several reasons why it isn't a good idea. The health club is very expensive to join, and it is like a maze with the aerobic rooms, basketball courts, swimming pool, and locker rooms placed almost haphazardly. It would be difficult for his students to figure out where to go. Also, the health club could be a dangerous place, especially in the weight room. Mrs. Lacey questions whether the health club would even allow Mr. Wickstrom's students access. Who would be liable if one of the students got hurt? Finally, she notes that many of Mr. Wickstrom's students need help in some basic skills including dressing and undressing and using the bathroom.

Mr. Wickstrom had not realized that there would be so many problems. However, he really feels that this is a great opportunity to get his students to work out and be involved in a regular community program. He had success with a school–community partnership before with the mall, so he is sure he can make this health club program work too. Mr. Wickstrom thanks Mrs. Lacey for her help and tells her that he will be back in touch with her to discuss some details about the health club. As he walks down the hall, more excited about teaching than he has been for some time, he begins to outline what needs to be done to make this idea work.

NOTES

122

QUESTIONS

Preparing for Learning & Teaching

1. What is the primary issue in this case?

SUMMARY OF PARTICIPANTS

Mr. Wickstrom, special education teacher

Mr. Tracey, custodian

Mrs. Smithers, secretary

Mrs. Stanford, cafeteria staff

Mrs. Lacey, PE teacher

2. Do you think using a local health club is a good idea for children with disabilities? Why or why not?

3. Mrs. Lacey outlined several potential problems with the health club idea. What are some possible solutions to these problems? What are some other potential problems with accessing the health club? What could be done to solve these problems?

4. What does the Americans with Disabilities Act say about public access to places like private health clubs?

5. What are some of the things that Mr. Wickstrom will need to do to make this program a reality?

6. What role do you think Mrs. Lacey should play in this process? Why?

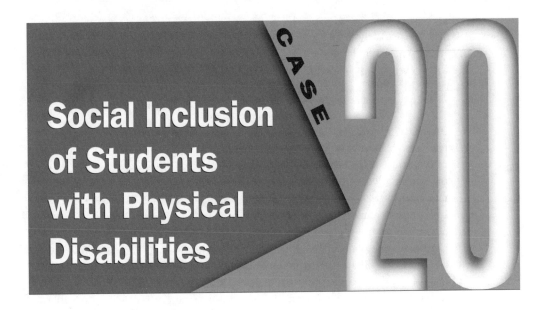

Social Inclusion of Students with Physical Disabilities

CASE 20

L arry Washington is completing his master's degree requirements for K–12 certification in physical education. He was recently notified of his final student teaching placement and is enthusiastic about the opportunity to teach physical education in a diverse, urban school setting. Moreover, Larry has no reservations about teaching students with disabilities who are to be included in his classes. Larry considers the inclusion of students with disabilities in his classes a challenge and an opportunity to put to work what he has learned within his physical education–teacher education (PETE) program at the local university. In fact, during his PETE elementary-level student teaching experience, Larry had a girl with mild mental retardation and a boy with juvenile scoliosis in his 2nd grade class. He recalls the rewards of that experience as well as reading that the inclusion of students with disabilities in GPE classes is a fast and growing trend in American education. Larry agrees with those who argue that inclusion should be considered a philosophical approach to implementing social justice in PE classes so that all students are valued. In support of that argument, he has decided to write his final paper on social inclusion[1] at the secondary level. He knows that his secondary internship placement at Southview Middle School will provide an excellent context for this project.

Larry asks Mrs. Lewis, his cooperating teacher at Southview, if he can observe several of her classes to collect data for his final paper. Mrs. Lewis agrees and tells him that her 3rd-period class includes several students with physical disabilities and 27 other students without disabilities. The students with physical disabilities are Shareef, Val, and Anna. Larry decides to study this group of students to determine their level of social interaction[2] as an indication of the social benefits of inclusion. His first act is to review these students' school records. He finds that Shareef and Val's categorical label is spastic cerebral palsy and that Anna has had a left leg amputation. In addition, just before observing Mrs. Lewis's classes, and more specifically her students, he talks briefly with Shareef, Val, and Anna to get a feel for their personalities and gain more background information. In his paper, Larry describes them as follows:

> Shareef is an African American boy with spastic cerebral palsy, who lives a few blocks from Southview Middle School. In his school records Shareef's condition (i.e., spastic cerebral palsy) is defined as a chronic neurological disorder that adversely limits his movement and posture. He also has abnormal muscle tightness and stiffness. Further, Shareef has difficulty with balancing and movement but is ambulatory with his walker. Mrs. Lewis describes Shareef as an intelligent boy who can get "rowdy" at times, but she is in support of his inclusion in her GPE classes. Mrs. Lewis and his classroom teachers state that Shareef exhibits an assertive, yet delightfully vivacious personality and that he enjoys socializing with others.
>
> Val, an African American girl, also has spastic cerebral palsy. She lives a mile or so from Southview and rides the school bus. Val's condition makes it difficult for her to walk, so she uses a powered wheelchair. Val does have full range of motion in her upper body. She is included in general education classes throughout the school day. Val is outgoing and personable. In fact, she will initiate a conversation with just about anyone.
>
> Anna is a White girl with a single-limb (left leg) congenital amputation resulting from a genetic birth defect. She lives about 4 or 5 miles from Southview. Anna typically uses a standard walker, but she also uses a wheelchair while participating in some class activities (e.g., basketball). She is a very shy girl, at least in the presence of her classmates. By contrast, she does not hesitate to talk with Mrs. Lewis or other teachers at Southview.

In his paper, Larry also provides background about Southview. He describes it as an urban middle school located in a large public school district. In this school district, students with disabilities are often bused to designated schools based on their categorical disability. Southview is one such school selected for serving students with physical and developmental disabilities. However, Larry notices that no teacher assistants or other support personnel accompany the students with disabilities to the gym for their PE classes. This doesn't seem to concern Mrs. Lewis, as she puts it, "I have a master's degree in physical education, and I've taught PE at Southview for 15 years now. A few kids with disabilities is not a problem."

Larry decides to use several different methods for collecting data for his paper over a 3-day period: Monday, Wednesday, and Friday. These are the days that Shareef, Val, and Anna have their GPE classes. The week before he is to teach at Southview, Larry videotapes the targeted lessons and later codes students' behavioral interactions using an observational instrument designed for such purposes. He also codes "academic learning time variables."[3] He recalls practicing how to do this in his PETE supervision class on campus. He understands that academic learning time in physical education (ALT-PE) is an observation system that uses time intervals for coding key student behaviors, such as waiting, off-task, activity, and instruction. In addition to coding student interactions and other key behaviors, Larry drafts notes using nonparticipant observations. Using these methods, he codes students' behaviors from the videotapes and analyzes the data regarding the individual interactions among Shareef, Val, and Anna and their peers without disabilities as well as Shareef, Val, and Anna's interactions with each other. He averages and reports the data as percentages of behavioral interactions (e.g., talking, physical assistance, feedback) and ALT-PE variables (transition, off-task behaviors, management, knowledge, activity, and waiting time). Larry also writes field notes that focus on the format of the lessons (including time components) and the type of interactions that occur among and between Shareef, Val, and Anna and their peers without disabilities. These field notes focus on behavioral interactions between and among the students with regard to who initiated social and other behavioral contacts, with whom, and the nature of such interactions.

Larry wants to determine the degree to which social inclusion occurs between and among students with physical disabilities (i.e., Shareef, Val, and Anna) and their peers without disabilities. Much to his surprise, he finds mostly that no social interaction occurs in the classes that he observes. Larry determines that most of the "noninteraction" time involves Shareef, Val, and Anna and their peers without disabilities listening to instructions from Mrs. Lewis, high levels of transition time, class management, and other noninteractive behaviors coded for students participating in the lesson-directed activities void of interaction.

In fact, the most frequent category coded across the three lessons is no interaction. This lack of behavioral interaction is true for Shareef, Val, and Anna and ranges from 83 percent to 95 percent of the total observed time across the three lessons. For example on Monday, during the first lesson, although Shareef talks to and receives praise and feedback from Val and Anna (his peers with physical disabilities), there are no interactions with his peers without disabilities. Larry writes in his field notes:

> At the start of class today, the students seem a bit more restless. However, all students are at their self-space spots and separated by about 3 or 4 feet. Shareef, Val, and Anna are not talking as instructed by Mrs. Lewis, with no interactions during this time. Many of the students without disabilities are very talkative and do not follow Mrs. Lewis's instructions. Most students are off-task and not fully cooperating. Mrs. Lewis has to reprimand them and she threatens them with additional laps and time-out warnings. Deliberately, on Mrs. Lewis's verbal command, all of the students transition into a semicircle formation at the front of the gym. While in this formation no interaction occurs between Shareef, Val, and Anna and their peers without disabilities. Those students without disabilities are grouped close to each other but are far from Shareef, Val, and Anna.
>
> As they transition outside to the soccer field Shareef, Val, and Anna travel through the hallway while the other students go through the locker room and interact with one another. Some of the students without disabilities engage in horseplay with each other, joking and laughing. All of the students are very slow at transitioning. Many ignore Mrs. Lewis's warnings

and continue to talk. Once on the soccer field the students without disabilities are organized into groups of three or four including Shareef, Val, and Anna, who, however, are some distance away from the other groups. Mrs. Lewis yells out additional instructions. No interactions between Shareef, Val, and Anna and their peers occur.

Shareef, Val, and Anna are now in a group far away from their peers, who are kicking and dribbling soccer balls with one another. Mrs. Lewis calls out corrections regarding the critical elements of the dribbling task they are supposed to do; she also talks to several students about their inappropriate behaviors. At this time Shareef, Val, and Anna remain far away from their peers without disabilities as they pass a soccer ball back and forth and talk with one another. This continues throughout the lesson. (Field notes, Lesson 1)

Larry observes that whenever behavioral interactions did occur, the largest category coded is talking. In fact, for lessons 1, 2, and 3, Shareef, Val, and Anna mostly talked to one another and rarely talked with their peers without disabilities. The exception to this was when Anna had a higher talking percentage with her peers without disabilities than with either Shareef or Val, on Friday, the third lesson. This was because Anna had been injured and the students (without disabilities) were asking questions about whether or not she was "hurt badly." Larry's field notes illustrate this incident with Anna:

Shareef, Val, and Anna are again positioned away from the other students and passing the soccer ball to one another. The rest of the students are playing 3 vs. 3 lead-up games with one another and they are far away from Shareef, Val, and Anna again as with Monday's and Wednesday's lessons. Mrs. Lewis is giving lots of information to the students without disabilities, whereas it seems that Shareef, Val, and Anna are left to do as they please. A soccer ball rolls off course in the direction of Shareef, Val, and Anna's group. While retrieving the ball a student kicks it in Anna's direction and accidentally strikes her in the face. Many students run over and ask if she is "hurt badly." Val and Shareef engage in small talk. Anna is escorted back to the building to seek medical attention because her nose is bleeding. (Field notes, Lesson 3)

The next most frequent type of interaction that Larry observes is assistance or physical contact. On average, Shareef, Val, and Anna and their peers without disabilities engaged in various types of contact with one another 2 percent, 1 percent, and 5 percent of the time across lessons 1, 2, and 3, respectively. Larry determines that these data are similar across all lessons for students without disabilities in their efforts to assist or engage in physical contact with a peer with a physical disability. In his notes he writes: "Limited appropriate physical contact occurred between Shareef, Val, and Anna and their peers without disabilities."

Larry wonders what typically happened in those situations in which interactions did occur. He takes a closer look at all the data he has gathered and finds that most of those interactions involved Shareef, Val, and Anna interacting among themselves, or the same few students without disabilities assisting either Shareef, Val, or Anna in a skill or task performance, such as dribbling or passing the soccer ball. Such interactions (e.g., talking, praising, giving feedback, engaging in physical contact) were apparent in both the systematic observations and field notes. In addition, other types of assistance included getting equipment, holding a door open, or a peer placing a hand on Val or Anna's wheelchair. Moreover, at times talking consisted of students without disabilities stating their willingness to "help" Shareef, Val, or Anna in skill execution.

Larry also notices that on average across lessons, talking occurred mostly among Shareef, Val, and Anna (more than 87%), and to a lesser degree (13%) among their peers without disabilities. It was also obvious that Shareef and Val talked with one another the most, and that Anna would often be left out of many interactions. Most often talking occurred during transitions, waiting, or activity times. Larry writes:

> While transitioning outside to the soccer field playing area, Shareef and Val talk with one another. Anna transitions without talking to anyone. These students leave to go outside by way of the hall while their peers without disabilities get additional instructions from Mrs. Lewis and then go through the locker room. (Field notes, Lesson 3)

Using the ALT-PE data, Larry finds that on average across the three lessons Shareef, Val, and Anna engaged in transitions (17%), off-task (2%), management (9%), knowledge (10%), activity (32%), and waiting (30%) behaviors during their PE classes. Similarly, the students without disabilities engaged in transitions (24%), off-task (5%), management (6%), knowledge (21%), activity (35%), and waiting (9%) behaviors across the same three lessons. These data (and his field notes), lead Larry to ask himself, "Does Mrs. Lewis's planning and/or lesson implementation limit or enhance opportunities for Shareef, Val, and Anna to socialize with their peers without disabilities?"

In his final paper, Larry writes:

> In the broader context, limited interaction occurred between and among students with and without disabilities in this physical education class. In those situations in which social interaction did occur, Shareef, Val, and Anna tended to initiate and sustain interactions with one another more so than they engaged in social interactions with their peers without disabilities. Obviously the grouping of Shareef, Val, and Anna together and separate from their peers without disabilities had an adverse effect on their opportunity and willingness to socialize "outside" their group.

Larry has more questions now regarding inclusion than before he started his secondary internship at Southview.

Endnotes

1. The reader is encouraged to consult the literature on social inclusion (e.g., Chamberlin, 1999; Place & Hodge, 2001).

2. The reader is encouraged to consult the literature on social interaction (e.g., Chamberlin, 1999; Goodwin, 2001; Goodwin & Watkinson, 2000; Place & Hodge, 2001).

3. For more information on the use of ALT-PE in physical education, consult Siedentop, Tousignant, and Parker (1982) and relevant published reports (e.g., Place & Hodge, 2001; Vogler, Koranda, & Romance, 2000).

4. The reader is encouraged to consult the physical education literature on the importance and development of equal-status relationships and attitude change (e.g., Sherrill, 1998; Sherrill, Heikinaro-Johansson, & Slininger, 1994; Slininger, Sherrill, & Jankowski, 2000).

Resources and References

Chamberlin, J. L. (1999). *Inclusion in physical education: The student's voice.* Unpublished master's thesis, The Ohio State University, Columbus.

Goodwin, D. L. (2001). The meaning of help in PE: Perceptions of students with physical disabilities. *Adapted Physical Activity Quarterly, 18,* 289–303.

Goodwin, D. L., & Watkinson, E. J. (2000). Inclusive physical education from the perspective of students with physical disabilities. *Adapted Physical Activity Quarterly, 17,* 144–160.

Place, K., & Hodge, S. R. (2001). Social inclusion of students with physical disabilities in general physical education: A behavioral analysis. *Adapted Physical Activity Quarterly, 18,* 389–404.

Sherrill, C. (1998). *Adapted physical activity, recreation and sports: Crossdisciplinary and lifespan* (5th ed.). Dubuque, IA: Brown.

Sherrill, C., Heikinaro-Johansson, P. M., & Slininger, D. (1994). Equal-status relationships in the gym. *Journal of Physical Education, Recreation and Dance,* 65(1), 27–31, 56.

Siedentop, D., Tousignant, M., & Parker, M. (1982). *Academic learning time—physical education 1982 revised coding manual.* Unpublished manuscript, The Ohio State University, Columbus.

Slininger, D., Sherrill, C., & Jankowski, C. M. (2000). Children's attitudes toward peers with severe disabilities: Revisiting contact theory. *Adapted Physical Activity Quarterly, 17,* 176–196.

Vogler, E. W., Koranda, P., & Romance, T. (2000). Including a child with severe cerebral palsy in physical education: A case study. *Adapted Physical Activity Quarterly, 17,* 161–175.

Acknowledgment

The authors wish to express our appreciation to Kimberly Place for her input in this case. Kimberly is an APE teacher at the Franklin County Board of Mental Retardation and Developmental Disabilities in the greater Columbus, Ohio, area.

QUESTIONS

Preparing for Learning & Teaching

SUMMARY OF PARTICIPANTS

Larry Washington, physical education teacher

Mrs. Lewis, Larry's cooperating teacher

Shareef, middle-school student with spastic cerebral palsy

Val, middle-school student with spastic cerebral palsy

Anna, middle-school student with congenital leg amputation

1. What is the primary issue in this case? Are there related issues? If so, what are they?

2. What concerns do Larry's findings present?

3. Should Larry share his observational findings with Mrs. Lewis? Why or why not? How might he go about presenting his findings to her?

4. What teacher effectiveness issues do you see as critical in this case?

5. What can be learned from the (a) behavioral interaction data, (b) ALT-PE data, and (c) field notes?

6. What social inclusion benefits, if any, are revealed in Larry's project for Shareef, Val, and Anna and their peers without disabilities?

7. What impact will Mrs. Lewis's choices about student groups and formations have on learning outcomes?

8. In what ways was Anna included or excluded from both her peers with disabilities and peers without disabilities?

9. Given what Larry's data reveal, what changes should Mrs. Lewis make in her classes? What would be possible positive outcomes of these changes? What might be the negative outcomes?

10. How can teachers implement PE classes that provide opportunities for frequent, meaningful, pleasurable, long-lasting, and equal-status[4] interactions between students with and without disabilities that foster the attainment of effective outcomes for all students?

Proactive and Preventive Strategies

Max Johannes is an induction (first year) GPE teacher at a private elementary and middle school. His typical workday starts around 7:00 A.M. He exits a city bus on 72nd Street and 3rd Avenue and begins his walk past high-rise buildings on both sides of the street. As he approaches the school, he can see the students arriving in Lincoln Town Cars and other luxury vehicles driven by their parents.

Max enters the gym, where his office is located, sits down in front of his computer, reviews his class schedule, and plans the lessons for the day. German Village Academy is a private coeducational elementary and middle school located in New York City that was established in the early 1900s. The academy provides instruction to a wide range of age levels from prekindergarten through 8th grade. Teachers at the academy have the freedom to introduce new teaching styles and pedagogy practices. The academy has a population of more than 350 students along with more than 80 faculty and staff members. The student population comprises 90 percent White Americans, 7 percent African Americans, and 3 percent other backgrounds. The community is made up of middle- to upper-class families and is known for its generous alumni and parental support to the academy. German Village Academy offers scholarship programs for ethnic "minorities" along with a financial aid assistance incentive program. In addition, children who have various disabilities including asthma, diabetes, hyperactivity and attention deficit disorder, left arm and eye paralysis, and birth defects are included in the physical education program.

Each morning, 48 to 50 7th and 8th graders come to the gym for physical education. The first 45 minutes of class consists of Max and his teaching partner, Mr. Tycho, working with the boys on the current unit of basketball. They want to help each child develop his skills and attitude toward the

133

sport. Max believes, however, that Mr. Tycho is a lackadaisical type of teacher. He thinks that for a job that requires the teacher to be neat, organized, and persistent, Mr. Tycho lacks most of these essential qualities. Mr. Tycho sometimes loses dates and phone numbers and lacks the commitment to get things done. Mr. Tycho's disorganization makes it difficult for them to work together to maximize the time they have in the gym. Further, Max feels that they have two completely different teaching styles, which makes coteaching challenging. Max strives to create a unit with progression, whereas Mr. Tycho does not focus on the fundamentals of the game. He seems to try to find drills or activities just to pass the time.

Moreover, Max insists that some of the students (with and without disabilities) at the academy frequently misbehave by talking back to the teacher in a negative or sarcastic tone, failing to listen, and not following simple directions and rules. Such behavior management problems occur during class routines and important listening times, making the teaching of games and skills difficult.

As an educator, Max takes pride in focusing on how to make the most of every class period and how to increase academic learning time for his students. Recently he has established a simple routine for his students. After they change into their PE uniforms, they are allowed free time in the gym to run, play basketball or group games, or do whatever they like. When he blows the whistle two times everyone must stop what they are doing, put away the equipment, and have a seat in the middle of the gym. This is the time when everyone should be quiet, focused, and ready to listen to Max as he introduces a drill, skill, or game. This routine works well aside from the fact that not all of the children get quiet. Too many times several students continue to talk, whisper, and move restlessly, which is frustrating to Max. Although he discusses and posts class rules on the gym walls at the beginning of the school year, he must regularly ask a child not to sit on another child's lap or repeatedly ask different children not to talk. Max wonders what other approaches he could use to get his students to listen and pay attention.

After the children finish changing and by the time Max and Mr. Tycho have everyone's full attention, there is only about 30 minutes of actual teaching and learning time available. The two teachers divide the class into three lines and run a basketball drill called "3 v 2, 2 v 1 fast-break." Max observes the three lines of children and sees them laughing and kidding around as Mr. Tycho tells a joke or says something humorous. Mr. Tycho isn't focusing on teaching and learning, but rather occupying time. To counter this, Max stops the drill and explains to the students the purpose of the activity and demonstrates where they should be when passing the ball and playing defense.

When most of the students already have trouble listening, it becomes even more difficult to manage an overcrowded classroom. What seems to work at times is dividing the class in half and putting up the curtain in the middle of the gym. Mr. Tycho gets to instruct the boys who play on the basketball team and Max instructs the other 25 boys. Using this strategy, Max feels that he is able to teach these boys the game of basketball and slowly build their knowledge and skills through challenging activities and clearly established goals. He also feels that when the class is divided in half, the students get more out of the class and there are fewer disciplinary issues. He has complete control of what goes on, and if there are any behavior problems he deals with them quickly and firmly, while trying not to disrupt the lesson flow.

In terms of inclusion practice, Max is most concerned about Lester, a 5th grader who was born with a benign blood-filled tumor around his trachea. Lester has had numerous surgeries that have left him scarred from skin grafts taken from his shoulder, and he has loss of sensation in half of his face and an artificial eye. Moreover, he is considered developmentally delayed. Lester presents a challenge in PE class as he often refuses to participate in activities because he is very susceptible to injury; is overweight; has poor balance and coordination, which limits his ability to move well; and exhibits immature fundamental locomotor and object control skills. Because Lester can see out of only one eye and has no sensation in his chin and the left side of his face, he needs to be very careful not to get hit in the face while involved in any physical activities. A facial injury could cause skin complications. When Lester is in class, Max encourages him to do everything all the other children do but perhaps in a modified fashion. He often refuses to participate, but when he does, it is at a slower pace than his classmates and the teachers pay close attention to the activities he performs. For example, if Lester is engaged in an activity that could lead to an injury or a movement problem, Max will either modify the activity or explain that he may need to be very careful and perhaps stop. However, neither Max nor his colleagues do much else to include Lester or any of the other students with disabilities in the physical education program. Max wonders, "How best can I include Lester and the other students with disabilities in my classes?"

At the end of the day, Max reflects on his teaching and realizes that he must become more proactive and focused on creating a positive learning environment to prevent or at least better address the disciplinary problems he faces with some of the students as well as ensure the inclusion of students with disabilities in his classes. Over the weekend, he decides to consult the literature on behavior management strategies[1] and is reminded that it is important for him to be aware of what is going on during his classes at all times. He should develop his "with-it-ness" (class awareness) and "back-to-the-wall" strategies. He also must show enthusiasm in his teaching; plan ahead and modify his lessons to match the needs, abilities, and interests of all students; and allow his engaging personality to help build trusting relationships with his students. Max learns that it is important to use students' names regularly and seek to catch them behaving positively and then to offer positive reinforcement immediately, such as praise, an approving nod, or a pat on the back. He also learns about the importance of consistency in dealing with inappropriate behaviors and how to use positive approaches effectively such as public posting, a token economy system, and the Premack principle[2] in his classes to promote appropriate behaviors. Finally, he learns about avoiding negative approaches such as making idle threats to students or being sarcastic with them.

Max has always understood that effective communication and taking time out to consult with his students, one-on-one whenever possible, is an important piece of the behavior management puzzle. Although Max had established class rules and routines at the beginning of the school year, he decides to revisit these with the students come Monday morning. He will reemphasize the rules about listening to the teacher during instruction and following directions. In other words, he and his colleagues must establish specific rules that identify the behaviors that they expect students to display, and then they must be consistent in their application of the rules and consequences. He knows that a positive learning environment for all students will also facilitate the inclusion of students with disabilities. At the same time, Max wonders whether creating a positive learning environment and using the "textbook" behavior management strategies will work in the days to come. Max is also concerned about the inconsistencies between him and Mr. Tycho in their teaching behaviors.

Endnotes

1. See the Resources and References section for several excellent APE resources that address inclusion pedagogy for students with disabilities and behavior management strategies.

2. A *token economy system* allows teachers to delay administering reinforcement for successful performance of the targeted desired behavior; awarded tokens are later exchanged for desired reinforcers (Lavay, French, & Henderson, 1997; McKenzie, 1990). *Public posting* occurs when the teacher publicly displays in some manner (e.g., bulletin board, writes student's name on the chalkboard) a student's name or performance results as a means to recognition for accomplishments. *Premack principle* is a strategy used for which activities in which students prefer to engage can be used as positive consequences or reinforcers for activities that are less desirable (Lavay et al., 1997).

Resources and References

Block, M. E. (2000). *A teacher's guide to including children with disabilities in regular physical education* (2nd ed.). Baltimore: Brookes.

Lavay, B. W., French, R., & Henderson, H. L. (1997). *Positive behavior management strategies for physical educators.* Champaign, IL: Human Kinetics.

Loovis, E. M. (2000). Behavior management. In J. P. Winnick (Ed.), *Adapted physical education and sport* (3rd ed.) (pp. 93–107). Champaign, IL: Human Kinetics.

McKenzie, T. L. (1990). Token economy research: A review for the physical educator. In R. French and B. Lavay (Eds.), *A manual of behavior management methods for physical educators and recreators* (pp. 102–123). Kearney, NE: Educational Systems.

Sherrill, C. (1998). *Adapted physical activity, recreation and sports: Crossdisciplinary and lifespan* (5th ed.). Dubuque, IA: Brown.

Acknowledgment

The authors wish to express our gratitude to Jeffery Nurenberg for his insightful contribution to this case. Jeff is a GPE teacher at the Town School in Manhattan, New York.

QUESTIONS

Preparing for Learning & Teaching

1. What is the primary issue in this case? What are the related issues?

SUMMARY OF PARTICIPANTS

Max Johannes, GPE teacher

Mr. Tycho, teaching partner

Lester, 5th-grade student born with a benign blood-filled tumor around trachea

2. What are some of the specific elements that contribute to these issues?

3. What role did the characters play in creating/resolving these issues?

4. How might Max's assumptions about the ethnic, cultural, and socioeconomic backgrounds of the children in his classes impact his decision making and actions toward them?

137

5. What would you do to address Max's concerns about inconsistencies between his and Mr. Tycho's didactic approaches and teaching styles? How might their inconsistencies as teachers impact student behavior?

6. Do you think Max's classes were overcrowded? How would you deal with the issue of overcrowded classrooms?

7. What would you do to address the disciplinary concerns in this case? What were the specific inappropriate behaviors? What behavior management strategies are you aware of for handling children who frequently misbehave?

8. What is your understanding of the terms *positive reinforcement, token economy system, Premack principle,* and *public posting*? What other strategies have you used or would consider using in your classes?

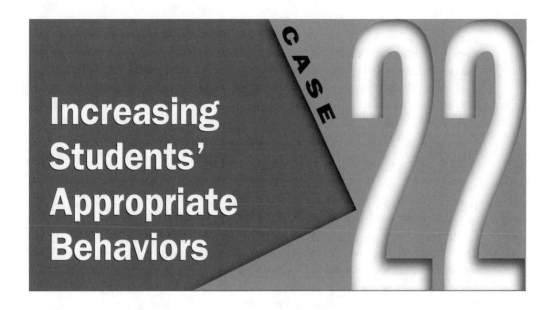

Increasing Students' Appropriate Behaviors

Amuary Perez is a veteran APE specialist at Everglades High School within the Collier County Public School District located on the southwest coast of Florida near Naples. A typical school day starts around 7:15 A.M. for Amuary. Each morning, after he parks his Jeep in the school parking lot he enters the physical education office and sits down at the computer to make a few edits to his lesson plans and quickly check his e-mail messages. Like clockwork, at 8:07 each morning Ms. Marjorie, the teacher assistant who works with Amuary throughout the school day, peeks her head in his office door to talk and offer a smile. She is attending evening classes at the local university to earn her K–12 physical education teaching certification.

Everglades High School first opened in the late 1990s. If you were to spend some time there, you would notice how the teachers demonstrate consistent teamwork and collaboration across subject areas. This environment of community and teamwork is primarily the result of the excellent motivational and leadership skills of the school principal, Mr. Holmes. The school has a culturally diverse student body, faculty, and staff. The student population comprises 12 percent African Americans; 3 percent Asian Americans; 14 percent Hispanics, non-Whites, and Latin Americans; 68 percent White Americans; and 3 percent other backgrounds. The community is made up of mostly low- to middle-class families and has a dependable parental support base with regard to the school's academic mission and athletics.

Under Mr. Holmes's leadership, Everglades High has established several community-focused after-school programs, such as the popular English courses designed for adults for whom English is a second language. In addition, Mr. Holmes has convinced the faculty and staff of the benefits and importance of including students with disabilities in the general education curriculum. Ms. Pity, the school's GPE teacher, is supportive of inclusion and depends heavily on Amuary's expertise in teaching the children with disabilities. In fact, Amuary was hired to help ensure that effective inclusion practice takes place in the GPE classes. Amuary usually divides the classes by gender, with Ms. Pity taking responsibility for the girls, and Amuary the boys. The students in Ms. Pity's and Amuary's combined 9th-grade class have a variety of disability types: asthma, autism, diabetes, attention deficit disorder and hyperactivity, learning disabilities, and cerebral palsy. In addition to the assistance of Ms. Marjorie, Amuary receives periodic visits from Mrs. Miller, the speech pathologist.

Amuary is very organized and motivated, and his knowledge of sports and fitness is impressive. His enthusiasm and charming personality show when he teaches. He enjoys talking and interacting with the students and highly praises students who behave in appropriate ways. However, if a student does misbehave, Amuary quickly intervenes using a firm voice and expressions of genuine disappointment. But he is careful never to criticize the student; rather, he identifies very explicitly what the inappropriate behavior is and what the student should do as an alternative. Although Amuary seldom raises his voice in class, he is the dominant force. He uses his professional training, knowledge, and charm to get the most out of his students. He is always in charge and has remarkable self-control. At times he is direct and assertive, while at other times he can be caring and sensitive to the needs, interests, and abilities of his students.

Although Amuary leads the class sessions, he invites Ms. Marjorie's input and comments. She is willing to assist in any way that she can, but for the most part, she gathers the equipment to set up for the lesson, assists those students with disabilities who need hands-on help, and helps train and direct the peer tutors in their roles. Amuary and Ms. Marjorie work well together.

Before class begins, Amuary's students change into their PE uniforms in the locker room. Changing clothes can be a very difficult time for the boys with disabilities. For example, Shawn has cerebral palsy and sometimes needs help unbuttoning his shirt. Carl, who has autism, sits and stares at the wall while the other boys without disabilities yell as they gear up for the sports games that they hope to play. When class is over and it is time for everyone to change back into their regular school clothes, the locker room experience can get even more hectic. The boys often argue about being bad sports or even about a particular sequence of events that occurred in one of the games that they were playing.

Amuary knows that the daily arguments, teasing, and chatter in the locker room must be handled in an effective and thoughtful manner. So he decides to have an awareness talk[1] with all of the 9th-grade boys. He tells them, "Your locker room behavior is completely unacceptable. Since many of you are not listening to my warnings, I will implement the 'quick change and no talking rule.' There are seven stipulations to this rule for which you earn points. They are as follows:

1. No talking in the locker room, unless it is to help a peer. If you do help a peer you can earn 1 point on the tally sheet.

2. If you talk, then you lose at least 1 point from the tally sheet. However, if you do not talk while changing in the locker room you can earn 1 point.

3. If you quickly change your clothes and find your position on home base within 3 to 5 minutes, you earn 1 point.

4. If you show enthusiasm and team spirit by cheering and demonstrating good sportsmanship throughout the class period, you can earn up to 3 points.

5. If you participate fully in the planned activities without a warning from me or Ms. Marjorie for any type of inappropriate behaviors throughout the class period, you can earn up to 3 points.

6. If you have earned less than 5 points by the end of the week, you will visit the talking bench[2] with me or Ms. Marjorie for a one-on-one conference; students earning less than 3 points will have a conference with me, and I will call their parents to discuss any inappropriate behaviors and/or lack of participation, enthusiasm, or other concerns.

7. If you have earned 10 or more points by the end of the week, you earn a chance to get one item out of the prize bag. Prize bag items include gift certificates to the local bowling alley and fast food restaurants, movie passes, and other things you will like.

Now, with a little effort, I think you all can become better students."

Amuary randomly monitors the locker room during changing times and records each student's behaviors on a tally sheet. The tally sheet consists of several categories: quick change and no talking, helping others, enthusiasm, participation, team spirit (such as cheering for a peer), and good sportsmanship. The students all know how they can receive and lose points, and most of them are anxious to earn a prize by the end of the week.

This token economy system[3] combined with response cost strategy has worked very well over the past couple of weeks. There are now fewer arguments and more time for actual game play. In the days ahead, Amuary plans to make fewer and fewer random checks contingent on the 9th grade boys continuing to show that they can behave appropriately while in the locker room and change their clothes quickly and quietly.

Endnotes

1. *Awareness talk* represents one of six general strategies Hellison (1995) identified to facilitate use of his Personal and Social Responsibility Model: (a) awareness talks, (b) levels in action, (c) reflection time, (d) individual decision making, (e) group meetings, and (f) counseling time. During awareness talk the responsibility levels are explained and students can engage in sharing sessions (Hellison, 1995; Lavay, French, & Henderson, 1997).

2. The *talking bench* is an easy-to-use psychodynamic behavior management approach that facilitates conflict resolution in which students who are in conflict with one another are asked to sit down together and talk until they can resolve their misunderstandings or misgivings (Horrocks, 1978; Lavay et al., 1997).

3. A *token economy system* allows teachers to delay administering reinforcement for successful performance of the targeted desired behavior; awarded tokens are later exchanged for desired reinforcers (Lavay et al., 1997; McKenzie, 1990). *Response cost* is a punishment strategy whereby the teacher takes away a reinforcer from a student who has misbehaved (Lavay et al., 1997). *Premack principle* is a strategy used for which activities in which students prefer to engage can be used as positive consequences or reinforcers for activities that are less desirable (Lavay et al., 1997).

Resources and References

Hellison, D. R. (1995). *Teaching responsibility through physical activity.* Champaign, IL: Human Kinetics.

Horrocks, R. N. (1978). Resolving conflict in the classroom. *Journal of Physical Education and Recreation, 48* (9), 20–21.

Lavay, B. W., French, R., & Henderson, H. L. (1997). *Positive behavior management strategies for physical educators.* Champaign, IL: Human Kinetics.

Loovis, E. M. (2000). Behavior management. In J. P. Winnick (Ed.), *Adapted physical education and sport* (3rd ed.) (pp. 93–107). Champaign, IL: Human Kinetics.

McKenzie, T. L. (1990). Token economy research: A review for the physical educator. In R. French and B. Lavay (Eds.), *A manual of behavior management methods for physical educators and recreators* (pp. 102–123). Kearney, NE: Educational Systems.

QUESTIONS

Preparing for Learning & Teaching

1. What is the primary issue in this case? What are the related issues?

2. What are some of the specific elements that contribute to these issues?

3. What role did the characters play in creating/resolving these issues?

4. How would you deal with the issues that Amuary identified in this case?

5. What would you do to address the locker room concerns? What were the specific inappropriate behaviors? What strategies would you have used?

6. Why is it important to create a positive relationship with students as well as coworkers? How might Amuary's relationship with Ms. Marjorie impact his inclusion pedagogy and behavior management strategies?

7. How would you go about creating positive relationships with students and coworkers? Would this be more or less difficult to do with those who may be viewed as similar or different from yourself (i.e., students with disabilities; ethnically, culturally, or linguistically diverse groups)?

8. What behavior management strategies were used or considered in this case? What are the advantages and disadvantages of these strategies?

9. What additional behavior management strategies can you identify for increasing students' appropriate behaviors?

10. What additional behavior management strategies can you identify for decreasing students' inappropriate behaviors?

11. What types of punishment would you use or consider using in this case?

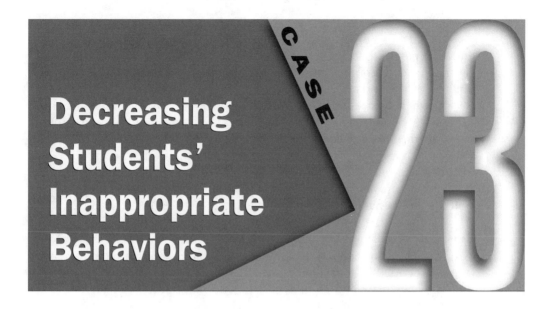

Decreasing Students' Inappropriate Behaviors

CASE 23

ackson Stivrens is a general physical education teacher at Sojourner Truth Elementary School, located in a large urban public school district in the midwestern United States. The community is made up of mostly African American families. In fact, Sojourner Truth has a student body comprising 97 percent African Americans and 3 percent Asian and European Americans. These children come from mostly low-income families, and some live in governmental housing.

Jackson teaches prekindergarten through 5th grade, and his average class size is 18 students. Although no students with physical disabilities are included in the PE program, 24 students at the school have asthma; one has sickle-cell anemia (a condition resulting from defective hemoglobin, which causes red blood cells to have a sickle shape), one has a hereditary bleeding disorder known as hemophilia, 8 are currently on medication for ADD, and 6 are classified with speech and language impairments (e.g., stuttering).

Prior to teaching at Sojourner Truth Elementary School, Jackson taught elementary PE classes at King Afrocentric Academy, which is in the heart of the city. While at the academy, Jackson began to appreciate the values of an Afrocentric educational system.[1] First he learned that an Afrocentric curriculum provides students with an awareness of African and African American contributions to the world's history. He realized that such an educational system provides students with a historically accurate awareness of their place in the world and American society in particular. Moreover, he realized that an Afrocentric educational system seeks to empower students through a sense of cultural location and self-worth. Jackson was also impressed that most parents consistently showed their support for the educational mission of the academy. While at the academy, Jackson became accustomed to an environment in which teachers had high expectations of students, parental support was evident, and teachers and parents worked together in concert to facilitate learning and to promote appropriate student behaviors and respect.

By contrast, Jackson's first year at Sojourner Truth Elementary School has been a big adjustment for him because of a lack of parental support and daily disciplinary concerns because some of the children in his classes frequently misbehave. The task of getting these children to change their attitudes and behaviors and to listen has become a daily source of frustration for Jackson because they believe that their behaviors are not inappropriate. These behavioral issues mainly concern three to four children within each class; the other students typically behave in appropriate and respectful ways. The negative influence and time spent with the children who misbehave takes away from all of the students' learning experiences. These students who misbehave include both those with and without disabilities. They tease and argue with one another, talk excessively, fail to listen, and show a lack of respect toward Jackson.

Jackson thinks that most of these children don't feel threatened when they choose to misbehave, don't listen, or overstep their boundaries as students. There are no serious consequences to their actions if they do choose to misbehave. Jackson is a firm believer that students should show self-discipline and respect toward others. Therefore, the challenge of trying to get every child to behave appropriately is both exhausting and frustrating for him. He feels as if his verbal reprimands directed toward those children who misbehave have had no lasting effect on their behavior. These children appear to have difficulty listening and following instructions.

After much thought, Jackson decides it is time to meet with Ms. Lewis, the school principal. They sit down in her office and discuss the problems that he is having, particularly with the 5th grade boys. Jackson explains that the lack of respect these boys demonstrate toward him is unacceptable and how hard it has become to teach in this particular setting. He tells Ms. Lewis, "Students with disciplinary problems are in every class. I can't really give a number, but there are many who don't seem to understand two words: *listen* and *respect*. I have talked to some of the students' parents, but they seem to be the main reason the children are having problems with discipline. There have been a few times when the parents have made an appointment to meet with their child and me, but they never show up for the scheduled meetings."

Jackson recites an exhaustive list of concerns as Ms. Lewis listens. But before he can finish, Ms. Lewis intervenes and states that she will support him in his efforts to address each of his concerns. Ms. Lewis also suggests that he look into the Consistency Management and Cooperative Discipline (CMCD) program.[2] CMCD is a research-based, classroom and school reform model that advocates joint responsibility for learning through cooperation and building community between teachers and students. The program works with local schools, which includes all students (from prekindergarten through 12th grade), teachers, and administrators in various urban areas. CMCD emphasizes self-discipline and espouses five themes—(a) prevention, (b) caring, (c) cooperation, (d) organization, and (e) community—to promote resilience with youth in inner-city schools. Each theme includes strategies and activities that allow students to feel like they are valued members of their classes.

Jackson also decides to try a few of his own ideas. These include regularly calling the parents of children who misbehave, and talking with those children on an individualized, one-on-one basis. He believes that these ideas will work but that it will take time before positive results will be seen, and that talking, sharing, and working with as many students as he can on an individual basis is a critical step toward reducing inappropriate behaviors. Jackson decides to record which students misbehave, and what their specific misbehaviors are. With this information, he can later confront individual students to have a private discussion, and if he feels that it's necessary he can draw up a behavioral contract[3] with the student. Jackson hopes that relating to and communicating with the children at a personal level will help produce recognizable changes in their willingness to listen and show respect. Also, in drawing upon his previous years' experiences at King Afrocentric Academy, he decides to use affirming messages frequently to help the children feel valued, thus promoting their self-worth.

Ms. Lewis and Jackson also decide to have a group meeting to have an "awareness talk"[4] with the students to help address the ongoing disciplinary problem. Ms. Lewis will meet with the 5th-grade students to express how disappointed she is in them. She will also explain to them that their behavior is unacceptable and discuss the consequences of their misbehaviors.

Afterward, in a separate meeting, Jackson will have a brief talk with the same group of students about his expectations. He will also point out that he is readily available to talk with any student on an individual basis. Jackson takes this opportunity to introduce the "behavior chart" to the students. This chart has everyone's name on it and is designed so that when a behavior problem arises, he will place a check mark next to that student's name. If a student obtains two check marks within a week, that student will be obligated to serve a Friday afternoon detention. If a student makes it through the entire week without a check mark, he or she will be able to vote on what game he or she will play during "game day."

Jackson feels that these strategies will help to shape the attitudes and behaviors of most of his students. He is committed to working on these problem areas, and optimistically expects to see improvements as he uses the resources available to him and the school community.

Endnotes

1. Visit the following websites for excellent discussions regarding Afrocentric educational systems: www.nbufront.org/html/FRONTalView/ArticlesPapers/AfroCentricCurriculum and www.nbufront.org/html/FRONTalView/ArticlesPapers/asa1.html.

2. Information about CMCD appearing in this case was taken from the CMCD website: www.ed.gov/pubs/ToolsforSchools/cmcd.html.

3. A *behavioral contract* refers to a verbal or written agreement between the teacher and student regarding the student's improvement in behavior or performance over an identified time frame in exchange for a desired reinforcer (Lavay et al., 1997).

4. Hellison's (1995) Personal and Social Responsibility Model is designed to help students take on personal and social responsibilities. The model has six responsibility levels—irresponsibility, respect, participation, self-direction, caring, and outside the gym—and six general strategies to put the levels into practice—awareness talks, levels in action, reflection time, individual decision making, group meetings, and counseling time. During awareness talk, the responsibility levels are explained and students can engage in a sharing session (Hellison, 1995; Lavay, French, & Henderson, 1997).

Resources and References

Hellison, D. R. (1995). *Teaching responsibility through physical activity.* Champaign, IL: Human Kinetics.

Hilliard, A. G., III, & Martin, L. (2001). The education of African people: Contemporary imperatives [On-line]. Available: www.nbufront.org/html/FRONTalView/ArticlesPapers/asa1.html.

Iyewarun, S. A. (2000). A new look at Afrocentric curriculum [On-line]. Available: www.nbufront.org/html/FRONTalView/ArticlesPapers/AfroCentricCurriculm.html.

Lavay, B. W., French, R., & Henderson, H. L. (1997). *Positive behavior management strategies for physical educators.* Champaign, IL: Human Kinetics.

Loovis, E. M. (2000). Behavior management. In J. P. Winnick (Ed.), *Adapted physical education and sport* (3rd ed.) (pp. 93–107). Champaign, IL: Human Kinetics.

Acknowledgment

The authors wish to express our gratitude to Scott A. Butler for his insightful contributions to this case. Scott is a physical education teacher at Windsor Elementary School within the Columbus Public School District in Columbus, Ohio.

QUESTIONS

Preparing for Learning & Teaching

SUMMARY OF PARTICIPANTS

Jackson Stivrens, physical education teacher

Ms. Lewis, principal

1. What is the primary issue in this case? What are the related issues?

2. What are some of the specific elements that contribute to these issues?

3. What role did the characters play in creating/resolving these issues?

4. How would you deal with the many issues that Jackson identified in this case? Why is Ms. Lewis's encouragement and support important?

5. What would you do to address the disciplinary concerns that Jackson described? What behavior management strategies are you aware of for handling children who frequently misbehave?

6. Why is it important to create a positive relationship with parents and students?

7. How would you go about creating positive relationships with parents and students? Would this be more or less difficult to do with those who may be viewed as similar or different from yourself (i.e., students with disabilities; ethnically, linguistically, and culturally diverse groups)?

8. What behavior management strategies were used or considered in this case? What are the advantages and disadvantages of these strategies?

9. What additional behavior management strategies can you identify for increasing students' appropriate behaviors?

10. What additional behavior management strategies can you identify for decreasing students' inappropriate behaviors?

11. What types of punishment would you use or consider using in this case?

Southern Side High School, located in Hope Mills, North Carolina, has a large, diverse student population. The surrounding community is made up of mostly low- to middle-class families. Jacques, a physical education teacher and coach, has taught and coached baseball and soccer at the school for 3 years now. He has aspirations of coaching basketball following Coach Sandburg's retirement in a few years. Since arriving Jacques has received guidance and mentoring from Coach Sandburg, and Jacques has helped with scheduling games and other duties.

However, Jacques was hired primarily to teach 9th- through 12th-grade physical education. He has a wide range of knowledge and understanding of many sports, which he uses to his advantage in teaching with the sport education model.[1] He tries to maximize his teaching capabilities with all students, including students with disabilities. Currently, students with disabilities who are included in Jacques's PE classes are Laila, who has Rett disorder, a pervasive developmental disorder (PDD) affecting only females concomitant with mental retardation; Phil, who has Asperger disorder (a PDD affecting primarily males) and also exhibits clumsiness; Craig, Rodney, Harold, and José, who have learning disabilities and attention deficits; and Ebony, who has asthma and is excessively obese with a low fitness level.

Jacques is thankful that he has reliable support from Ms. Washington, a teacher assistant. Support is also provided by several seniors who volunteer as peer tutors. Jacques helps train these peer tutors to work with students with disabilities in physical education.

Jacques is a very friendly person who gets along well with his colleagues and most of the students at the school. He shares an office with Marcus, who also teaches PE and is the school's head football coach. The two of them often talk about sports. They have common hobbies and interests and enjoy participating in competitive sports. The differences between Jacques and Marcus stem primarily from their teaching styles. For example, Jacques starts out by developing a friendly and respectful relationship with students (e.g., he greets the students as they enter the gym; frequently uses students' first names; asks the students for input on class rules, routines, and expectations; and points out the consequences of misbehaving) as he establishes his role as a teacher with them. He has great communication skills and is apt at resolving student conflicts. He frequently uses positive and negative reinforcement strategies throughout each class session, and as various situations arise he doesn't hesitate to hold a one-on-one counseling session with a student.

Marcus, on the other hand, starts out disciplined and demanding. He makes sure that the students understand what is considered acceptable and unacceptable behavior. As the academic year progresses, he focuses more on establishing a personable relationship with the students. He feels that a teacher must be very conscious of his or her students and learn to discipline them when they misbehave or disobey authority. His approach to resolving student conflicts is to separate the students who are in conflict with one another and put them in time-out until they can rejoin the group without misbehaving.

By comparison, Jacques's favorite approach to resolving conflicts is using the talking bench[2] approach. He hopes that by using this approach with his students, interpersonal communication and conflict resolution skills will improve. For example, José and Ebony are arguing with each other. Immediately, Jacques intervenes and tells them that they must resolve their problem before they can rejoin the group activities and before they will be permitted to go to their next class. He directs them to sit on the "talking bench" and to discuss the situation that led to the argument. They should talk with each other until they have both agreed on the cause of and a solution to the conflict. In addition, they must apologize to each other. Apparently, José felt that Ebony had made fun of his pronunciation of a few words (English is a second language for José and he has difficulty pronouncing some words), and, in turn, José had made some derogatory comments about Ebony's weight.

After a few minutes, Jacques approaches the two students and asks them, "How did you resolve the conflict?" José responds, "We talked about our misunderstandings and apologized to one another." Jacques then asks a few questions to determine whether or not José and Ebony had truly resolved their differences. Ebony says, "I'll help José with his pronunciation of those difficult words." José quickly adds, "I won't tease Ebony about her weight anymore." In fact, José encourages Ebony and points out that she could exercise progressively by taking longer walks through their neighborhood after school. Jacques is soon convinced, and after they apologize to each other in front of him, José and Ebony are allowed to return to the class's activities.

Although Jacques and Marcus have different didactic approaches to teaching and behavior management, both approaches seem to work. Most likely this is because they consistently send the message to their students that inappropriate behaviors are not acceptable in their PE classes and that there are always consequences for one's actions.

Endnotes

1. Siedentop's (1994) sport education model is "a curriculum and instruction model developed for school physical education programs" (p. 3) and is used to promote positive sport experiences for students at various age levels.

2. The *talking bench* is an easy-to-use psychodynamic behavior management approach that facilitates conflict resolution in which students who are in conflict with one another are asked to sit down together and talk until they can resolve their misunderstandings or misgivings (Horrocks, 1978; Lavay, French, & Henderson, 1997).

Resources and References

Craft, D. H. (2000). Learning disabilities and attentional deficits. In J. P. Winnick (Ed.), *Adapted physical education and sport* (3rd ed.) (pp. 127–141). Champaign, IL: Human Kinetics.

Horrocks, R. N. (1978). Resolving conflict in the classroom. *Journal of Physical Education and Recreation, 48*(9), 20–21.

Lavay, B. W., French, R., & Henderson, H. L. (1997). *Positive behavior management strategies for physical educators.* Champaign, IL: Human Kinetics.

Loovis, E. M. (2000). Behavior disorders. In J. P. Winnick (Ed.), *Adapted physical education and sport* (3rd ed.) (pp. 143–157). Champaign, IL: Human Kinetics.

Loovis, E. M. (2000). Behavior management. In J. P. Winnick (Ed.), *Adapted physical education and sport* (3rd ed.) (pp. 93–107). Champaign, IL: Human Kinetics.

Siedentop, D. (Ed.). (1994). *Sport education: Quality PE through positive sport experience.* Champaign, IL: Human Kinetics.

QUESTIONS
Preparing for Learning & Teaching

1. What is the primary issue in this case? What are the related issues?

2. What are some of the specific elements that contribute to these issues?

3. What role did the characters play in creating/resolving these issues?

CASE 24
SUMMARY OF PARTICIPANTS

Jacques, physical education teacher and coach

Coach Sandburg, basketball coach

Marcus, physical education teacher and head football coach

Laila, high school student with Rett disorder

Phil, high school student with Asperger disorder

Craig, high school student with learning disability and attention deficits

Rodney, high school student with learning disability and attention deficits

Harold, high school student with learning disability and attention deficits

José, high school student with learning disability and attention deficits

Ebony, high school student with asthma and obesity

Ms. Washington, teacher assistant

4. Were Jacques's and Marcus's approaches to teaching and managing behaviors equally effective? If not, which approach do you think would be most effective for controlling student behaviors? Why?

5. What would you do to address the conflict between José and Ebony? What was the conflict or specific inappropriate behaviors? What other strategies might you use to address this conflict?

6. How would you go about creating positive relationships with parents, students, and coworkers? Would this be more or less difficult to do with those who may be viewed as similar or different from yourself (i.e., students with disabilities; ethnically, culturally, or linguistically diverse groups)? Why?

7. What behavior management strategies were used or considered in this case? What is your understanding of these strategies? What are their advantages and disadvantages?

8. What additional behavior management strategies can you identify for increasing students' appropriate behaviors?

9. What additional behavior management strategies can you identify for decreasing students' inappropriate behaviors?

10. What types of punishment would you use or consider using in this case?

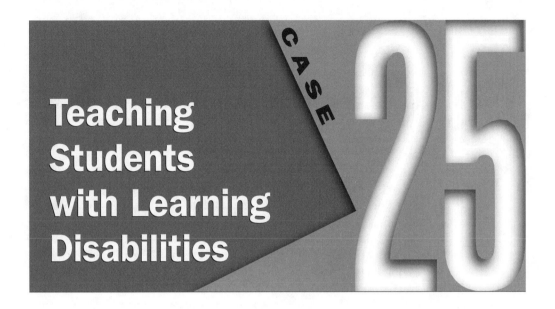

Teaching Students with Learning Disabilities

CASE 25

Northwest High School is located within a large school district in central Ohio. There has been a great deal of growth and expansion over the years. This has lent itself to an ethnically and culturally diverse student body. In terms of their socioeconomic backgrounds, some of the students are from wealthy homes and others come from very modest circumstances. At Northwest the students with city/urban backgrounds mix with those with rural and small-town experiences. Most students at the school are White Americans, but with the growth of the district, the school's demographics are slowly changing.

Renee Moore is an induction (first year) GPE teacher at Northwest High School. She is motivated and feels that she is making a difference in the lives of her students. Renee says, "This is my first year teaching, so I have yet a long road to travel. So far, I absolutely enjoy teaching. I am in a great school system, with plenty of opportunities. My goal is to provide physical activity opportunities to students. I feel as though I have begun to do so in my first year." Two new teachers joined the physical education faculty this year, and as a result, class sizes have decreased. Currently, Renee has a range of 15 to 25 students per class, several of whom have disabilities. Most of these students have learning disabilities. Renee also has several students with and without disabilities who present her with behavior management problems.

Recently, Renee was concerned about one student in particular, D'Angelo, who has a learning disability concomitant with attention deficit hyperactivity disorder (ADHD). In addition to D'Angelo's tendency to exhibit inattentiveness and hyperactive-impulsive behaviors, he is a very aggressive teenager who is quite competitive. An excellent athlete, D'Angelo plays football at Northwest, and his on-the-field aggressiveness is often praised and rewarded. However, Renee is concerned about D'Angelo's aggressiveness in her classes toward his classmates. Regularly during class activities, D'Angelo will go as hard and fast as he can to win at all costs. He has a tough time understanding that the activities in class require self-control and even finesse in certain situations. It also appears that D'Angelo can't quite comprehend that rules and routines, safety awareness, and task structures are necessary in physical education.

D'Angelo is very "football" minded and every move he makes seems to be associated with football. He chases after classmates by starting in a football player's three-point stance. His lack of self-control and aggressiveness around classmates causes them to fear, make fun of, or encourage his aggressive behaviors. Many of D'Angelo's classmates also present Renee with behavioral issues, and some of these students' general lack of motivation to participate in activities and their constant teasing seem to fuel the fire for D'Angelo and his aggressive tendencies. D'Angelo isn't out to hurt a classmate intentionally; rather, he is overaggressive in showing his competitiveness. Renee knows that D'Angelo will require some extra effort on her part.

Early one morning, Renee meets with Ms. Lattimore, a special education teacher at the school, to discuss D'Angelo's case. Ms. Lattimore points out some of the tendencies that children with learning disabilities and ADHD may exhibit. She suggests that D'Angelo might respond best to visual stimulation, demonstrations, and verbal cues rather than written information. Renee agrees and states that she will keep Ms. Lattimore's suggestions in mind during her planning and teaching. Next, Renee decides to talk with Coach Chestnut, the head football coach, to get additional insight regarding D'Angelo's tendency to be aggressive with classmates. Coach Chestnut is very helpful and has several ideas about how to help deal with D'Angelo's problem. Coach Chestnut even agrees to talk with the entire football team about what he defines as an athlete's appropriate display of aggressiveness on the football field versus inappropriate aggressive behaviors off the playing field.

The next day, Renee has an opportunity to speak with D'Angelo after class and express her concerns regarding his aggressiveness toward classmates. She also tells D'Angelo that she is impressed with his athletic skillfulness and that she wants him to take more of a leadership role in her PE classes. She further explains that his opportunities for leadership in class are contingent upon him not acting overly aggressive toward his classmates. D'Angelo is very receptive to these comments and says that he will try to control himself better.

Using her textbooks and the World Wide Web, Renee reads up on behavior management methods and about strategies for teaching students with learning disabilities and ADHD. She soon feels prepared to implement some specific behavior management strategies. Her method of choice is positive reinforcement. Renee reads that positive reinforcement means the "offering of something valued (e.g., praise) after a desired behavior had been emitted, resulting in an increased likelihood that the behavior would be exhibited again in the future."[1] Her strategy is to introduce a skill or task during class and afterward call upon D'Angelo to take on a leadership role (e.g., demonstrating a skill or helping a classmate one-on-one to execute the skill/task) and then provide him with positive reinforcement (i.e., if he cooperates and performs the skill/task appropriately). Renee is aware that D'Angelo cherishes praise and seeks approval from others, so she uses an abundance of social reinforcers (i.e., approving smiles, an affirming nod, a high five, a hand on his shoulder) plus she always makes a statement about his actual skill performance and/or appropriate cooperative behaviors. She also calls D'Angelo's parents and talks with them about his tendency toward aggressiveness. She tells them about her use of various social reinforcers and encourages them to use these same types of strategies with him at home.

Next, Renee decides to reemphasize to the entire class the need for self-control and focuses attention on the task of successful skill/task execution. She also groups the students so that those who enjoy getting D'Angelo "worked up" are separated from him as much as possible. During tournament and game play, she reminds the students of the game rules and boundaries and frequently uses praise and other positive reinforcement strategies to promote D'Angelo's as well as his classmates' appropriate behaviors, effort, and performances.

Renee also uses planned ignoring[2] with those students who tease each other, unless the teasing becomes excessive or leads to additional inappropriate behaviors. After a verbal warning, she uses a time-out[3] strategy of removing the student who continues to misbehave from active participation for a brief period of time. She talks with the student while in time-out and occasionally verbally reprimands[4] the student about his or her inappropriate behaviors. In using verbal reprimands, Renee understands that she must point out to the student what specific behavior is expected, and that the verbal reprimand should immediately follow the inappropriate behavior with a stern look and firm voice indicating why she is disappointed in the student's inappropriate actions. For example, she might say, "D'Angelo, I'm disappointed in your overaggressiveness with your classmates. You must play more cooperatively."

As the semester progresses, D'Angelo still has trouble comprehending most written information, including rules and routines. However, he responds extremely well to verbal cues, enjoys demonstrations, and does a better job of listening to instructions. In addition, he continues to make progress in not being overly aggressive toward classmates. Still, each new unit seems to prompt the question of how D'Angelo and his classmates will handle themselves. Things start to work out with D'Angelo and his classmates as they begin to interact in friendly and cooperative ways. Not surprisingly, D'Angelo ends up doing very well in physical education that year. He definitely progresses throughout the year. He still has his "football" attitude, but he has started to adjust that attitude to make it more conducive to class activities and interacting appropriately with classmates.

Endnotes

1. The description given for positive reinforcement in this case was taken from Lavay, French, and Henderson (1997) and Loovis (2000).

2. *Planned ignoring*, or *extinction*, is a method of punishment used to decrease and eventually eliminate inappropriate behaviors. Planned ignoring requires that the teacher, peers, and others withhold reinforcement when an inappropriate behavior is exhibited, to increase the likelihood that the specific behavior will decrease or be eliminated in the future (Lavay et al., 1997).

3. The description given for time-out in this case was taken from Lavay et al. (1997) and Loovis (2000).

4. *Verbal reprimand* is a method of punishment used to decrease inappropriate behaviors in which the teacher tells the student that the behavior she or he is exhibiting is unacceptable and why it is unacceptable (Lavay et al., 1997).

Resources and References

ADHD: Inclusive instruction and collaborative practices, videocassette. (1995). Paul H. Brookes, P.O. Box 10624, Baltimore, MD 21285-0624; telephone: 800-638-3775; fax: 410-337-8539; website: www.pbrookes.com.

Bishop, P., & Beyer, R. (1995). Attention deficit hyperactivity disorder (ADHD): Implications for physical educators. *Palaestra*, 11(4), 39–46.

Craft, D. H. (2000). Learning disabilities and attentional deficits. In J. P. Winnick (Ed.), *Adapted physical education and sport* (3rd ed.) (pp. 128–141). Champaign, IL: Human Kinetics.

Lavay, B. W., French, R., & Henderson, H. L. (1997). *Positive behavior management strategies for physical educators.* Champaign, IL: Human Kinetics.

Learning Disabilities Association of America (LDA), 4156 Library Road, Pittsburgh, PA 15234-1349; telephone: 412-341-1515; fax: 412-344-0224; website www.ldanatl.org.

Loovis, E. M. (2000). Behavior management. In J. P. Winnick (Ed.), *Adapted physical education and sport* (3rd ed.) (pp. 93–107). Champaign, IL: Human Kinetics.

Sherrill, C., & Pyfer, J. L. (1985). Learning disabled students in physical education. *Adapted Physical Activity Quarterly*, 2, 283–291.

Acknowledgment

The authors wish to thank Jennifer Clark for her input on this case. Jennifer is a GPE teacher within the Columbus Public School District in the greater Columbus, Ohio, area.

QUESTIONS

Preparing for Learning & Teaching

SUMMARY OF PARTICIPANTS

Renee Moore, induction GPE teacher

D'Angelo, high school student with a learning disability concomitant with ADHD

Ms. Lattimore, special education teacher

Coach Chestnut, head football coach

1. What is the primary issue in this case? Are there related issues? If so, what are they?

2. What are some of the specific elements that contribute to these issues?

3. What role did the characters play in creating/resolving these issues?

4. What is your understanding of learning disabilities? What is your understanding of ADHD?

5. What behavioral tendencies do individuals with learning disabilities and/or ADHD typically exhibit?

6. What behavior management strategies were implemented in this case?

7. Which of the strategies that you have identified are most appropriate for increasing students' appropriate behaviors?

8. Which of the strategies that you have identified are most appropriate for decreasing students' inappropriate behaviors?

9. Do you agree with the use of social reinforcers in this case? Why or why not?

10. Why did Renee feel it was important that D'Angelo desire praise and social approval from others in using social reinforcement?

11. What types of punishment strategies did Renee use or consider using in this case?

12. What pedagogical and/or behavior management strategies would you use to provide greater opportunities for D'Angelo to interact with his classmates in appropriate ways?

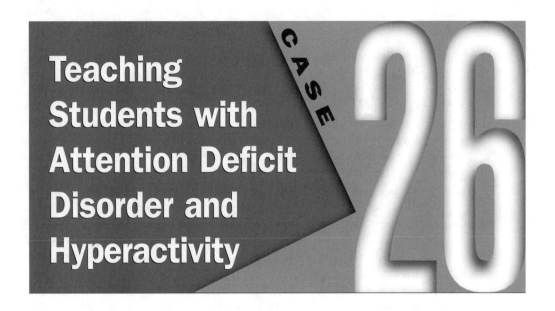

Teaching Students with Attention Deficit Disorder and Hyperactivity

N avajo Middle and High School is located near Indian Wells, Arizona. The school has a small population of students comprising predominantly Native American children from the Navajo Indian Reservation. Na Ah' has been a dance instructor and physical education teacher at the school for more than 15 years. She loves sports and dancing. In fact, Na Ah' began dancing and choreographing dance routines when she was only 13 years old. In recent years, she has had experiences teaching dance and basic sports skills at summer sport camps for children ages 12 to 16. She received both her undergraduate and master's degrees in dance and physical education from Northern Arizona University in Flagstaff.

Na Ah' is well respected as a teacher in her community. Her classes range from 13 to 22 students, with an average class size of 17, including 1 to 3 students with disabilities per class. Na Ah' believes that dance programs (i.e., adapted dance and dance therapy[1]) and physical activity are beneficial for her students with disabilities. She feels that this is particularly important for those students with behavioral disorders (e.g., autism), learning disabilities, ADD, and ADHD. She therefore regularly incorporates her knowledge of physical activity, sports, and dance into her lessons. Na Ah' firmly believes that children with and without disabilities must have an awareness and appreciation for their bodies and their capacities for movement before they can cope with the world around them.[2]

Na Ah' teaches a third-period 6th-grade class with 17 students including Alston. Alston is a Native American boy who has ADHD. He tends to be inattentive, impulsive, and is always moving (i.e., overactive). Alston has been included in GPE classes since kindergarten and participates with few modifications required. He loves playing basketball or baseball with his cousins after school and on the weekends. The biggest struggle for Na Ah' with Alston is keeping him focused on a particular task for more than a minute.

Alston's PE class is from 10:15 to 11:27 A.M. Mondays through Fridays. A typical class session consists of Alston and his peers starting their routine warm-up for about 5 minutes on the gym floor, and then Na Ah' introducing the day's lesson. Afterward, the students are led in a closure activity. For class on this particular day, following warm-ups, the students are led outside to an area adjacent to the school building, which consists of a large playing field and blacktop area with tennis courts and basketball goals.

Na Ah' pairs the students with peer partners for tennis skill development. Alston is paired with Nathaniel on court number 3. The doubles teams will rotate to the next court if they win and stay if they lose; there are a total of six courts available. Tennis is a favorite of Alston's, and he gets excited whenever the ball flies over the metal fence or rolls off the court and needs to be retrieved. Although there are plenty of extra tennis balls, Alston takes off running after the balls every time. Throughout the tennis games Alston is verbally interactive with his peer partner and other classmates. He talks to them either about how he is going to hit the ball if it comes to him or about how he is going to serve. Na Ah' praises Alston for his serving technique, but as soon as she can get the words out of her mouth he runs off to retrieve another ball. Each time that Alston serves successfully, Nathaniel says, "Nice serve, Alston!" In turn, whenever Nathaniel serves successfully, Alston runs over to give him a high five. Clearly, Alston enjoys playing tennis—or at least he enjoys chasing the tennis ball. After all this play, Alston and his classmates are excited, sweating, and in no mood to sit at a desk to read, write, or do whatever their next class requires, so Na Ah' decides to take them back into the gym for class closure.

After taking a quick drink of cool fountain water, the students return to their home bases on the gym floor. Na Ah' has the students match up with their peer partners, take one end of a long, soft, tubular nylon fabric, and perform "spin-abounds," rhythmic dance and movement exploration activities, while holding onto opposite ends of the fabric. The students enjoy moving rhythmically to the music playing in the background. They begin to relax as they enjoy the experience and continue to move quietly to the music. For the final "cool down" activity, Na Ah' has the students participate in a deep body awareness relaxation activity[3] for about 5 minutes. By now, Alston and his classmates are ready to transition from the excitement of PE class to their next class.

Endnotes

1. Sherrill (1998, pp. 410–419) provides an excellent discussion of the benefits and application of adapted dance and dance therapy for use in physical education with students with disabilities.

2. This paraphrased statement was taken from Sherrill (1998, p. 411).

3. Sherrill (1998, p. 407) provides an excellent discussion of the benefits and application of deep body awareness relaxation as a "cool-down" activity.

Resources and References

American Dance Therapy Association. National Office. Telephone: 410-997-4040; fax: 410-997-4048; website: www.ADTA.org.

Craft, D. H. (2000). Learning disabilities and attentional deficits. In J. P. Winnick (Ed.), *Adapted physical education and sport* (3rd ed.) (pp. 127–141). Champaign, IL: Human Kinetics.

Learning Disabilities Association. National, nonprofit organization. Website: www.ldanatl.org.

Sherrill, C. (1998). *Adapted physical activity, recreation and sport: Cross-disciplinary and lifespan* (5th ed.). Dubuque, IA: WCB McGraw-Hill.

NOTES

QUESTIONS
Preparing for Learning & Teaching

SUMMARY OF PARTICIPANTS

Na Ah', dance instructor and PE teacher

Alston, 6th-grade student with ADHD

Nathaniel, Alston's classmate

1. What is the primary issue in this case? Are there related issues? If so, what are they?

2. What are some of the specific elements that contribute to these issues?

3. What role did the characters play in creating/resolving these issues?

4. Do you agree with the "peer partner" strategy Na Ah' used with the tennis lesson? How might this strategy benefit Alston and his classmates in terms of skill development and opportunity to interact with each other?

5. Was Alston successfully included in this physical education program? Why or why not?

6. What is your reaction to Alston's repeatedly running off to retrieve tennis balls? What actions would you take to desist this behavior, if any?

7. Why did Na Ah' take the students back into the gymnasium for rhythmic dance and movement and deep body awareness activities? Why were these closure activities particularly important for Alston?

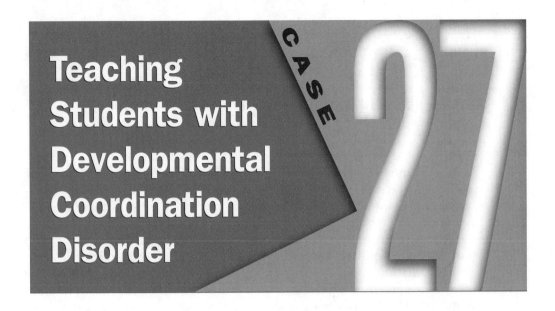

Teaching Students with Developmental Coordination Disorder

CASE 27

St. Louis Elementary School is a coeducational parochial school for kindergarten through 6th grade. The school is located in a rural (considered up-country) area where the nearest city is a 45-minute drive away. Sonny and Les are 5th graders at St. Louis Elementary School. These two boys are always getting into trouble, such as fighting, stealing, and teasing. On several occasions, teachers at the school have tried to have Sonny and Les expelled, but they come from very influential families and often are given only a hand slap for doing something wrong. One can imagine how stressful and frustrating being a teacher at St. Louis Elementary might be. However, the teachers are concerned about these boys teasing and taunting other children, especially during PE classes.

Sitting on the stone wall before school one morning, Sonny and Les listen to their portable CD player. At the same time, Jared, who has a developmental coordination disorder (DCD), walks by with his oversize backpack, hunching over to maintain balance. Sonny taps Les on the leg and says "Hey, its Jared. He's the one who can't walk and chew gum at the same time." Both students start yelling out to Jared, calling him names. At that very moment, Jared trips over some loose rocks. Sonny and Les bellow with laughter. Les says, "Sonny, you're right. He *can't* walk and chew gum at the same time." Jared continues to class despite the taunting.

Jared is a bright young boy with the desire to please everyone, be accepted, and most of all, be well liked by his teachers and peers. He is above average in all his courses, except physical education, and loves to read. In PE class Jared has always had difficulties performing motor tasks. This makes him clumsy and awkward. He has difficulties with throwing in opposition, he runs with his arms swinging uncontrollably, his knees knock, he has difficulty catching and dribbling a basketball, and he cannot make contact with an underhand-thrown softball. Yet, Jared refuses to have the activities modified for his sake alone. The social anxiety and peer pressure that he feels is overwhelming. Although Jared dislikes PE class and anything associated with motor performance, he enjoys having Ms. Pang as his PE teacher.

Teaching physical education at St. Louis Elementary is Ms. Pang's first teaching job. She has been at the school for only two years, but she commands the respect and cooperation from her colleagues and students as if she were a veteran teacher. Ms. Pang knows about the problems with Sonny and Les and also is well aware of Jared and others like him who have difficulty with physical education. She tries to accommodate all her students without having them feel isolated or given preferential treatment that may have negative consequences. For instance, in her softball lesson, she could have used a batting tee for all students, but everyone wanted to go with a pitcher, so she obliged. Ms. Pang feels that an APE specialist might be able to assist with such modifications; however, that isn't an option because the district doesn't have one available. She remembers her APE practicum experiences, in which she taught students with physical and emotional disabilities. "How difficult could teaching students who have DCDs be?" she wonders.

As Ms. Pang prepares her field hockey lesson, she ponders, "What can I do to ensure that all the students are benefiting from physical education, make students like Jared excel and enjoy physical education, without students like Sonny and Les creating an unpleasant environment for everyone?" She decides that it would be wise to treat this unit like a typical unit with minimal changes. As the students arrived for PE class, Ms. Pang overhears Sonny and Les teasing and laughing at Jared while waiting in line for roll call. She confronts them and speaks about how inappropriate it is to tease and taunt other students. The boys become quiet, but she senses that they are still amused.

Organizing the class for warm-ups, Ms. Pang asks Jared and Aimee, a classmate, to lead the exercises. Jared is apprehensive at first but obliges. Fortunately, the exercises had been routinely performed since the beginning of the school year, so he feels comfortable about leading the class because he knows that he can do each exercise. After 7 minutes, it is time to begin the lesson activities, which consist of field hockey skills. Ms. Pang has the class form two lines facing each other 30 yards apart. She instructs them to dribble the ball, using the hockey stick, across the field to the other person. She demonstrates this skill, gives teaching cues, and has them practice. As she watches, she notices that some students are skilled and others are not. Jared is one of the unskilled ones. He consistently misses the ball, trips over his feet, and when he does make contact, the ball rolls diagonally to the others. At one point, the hockey stick even flies out of his hands, almost hitting another student. Of course, Sonny and Les are laughing boisterously.

Ms. Pang senses that she might be losing control of the lesson, so she blows her whistle and has everyone stop. She has to think quick on her feet—she decides to set up two stations: one for shooting into the goal and one for passing with a partner. She tries to make sure that the skilled and unskilled are homogeneously grouped, but unfortunately, given time constraints this isn't the case. As a result, the taunting and teasing become even more unbearable for Jared. Aligning himself directly in front of the goal, Jared attempts to score. In his first attempt he completely misses the ball; on his second, the ball dribbles about two feet; and on the third, the ball misses the goal by 10 yards. Ms. Pang is at the other station and can't see the students in Jared's group, but she hears Sonny and Les laughing loudly much too often. By the time she gets to Jared's station to see how the students are performing, it is time to end the class.

Jared walks over to the sideline and places his hockey stick in the cart. He feels depressed, angry, and ashamed. He knows deep down that he isn't able to do motor skills proficiently. The way Sonny and Les tease and laugh at him makes him despise physical education even more. Furthermore, he wonders "How could Ms. Pang put me in a group with Sonny and Les? I thought she was cool. Maybe Sonny and Les were right about me being a klutz."

As class ends, Ms. Pang feels that she has further humiliated Jared and some of the others with this lesson. She acknowledges that it is important to maintain and promote self-esteem with all students, especially those with DCDs. Feeling guilty, Ms. Pang seeks the advice of Ms. Boon, the school counselor, at the end of the day. She thinks to herself, "Perhaps Ms. Boon could help with building Jared's self-esteem while I work on his motor skills." Ms. Pang asks Ms. Boon, "What are your thought about students who have DCD?" Ms. Boon replies, "Students like Jared may be more successful in an individualized sports activity instead of team sports. I believe that most children who are clumsy tend to retain their motor clumsiness even as they get older. It's the social anxiety and peer pressure that make it difficult." "Can anything be done to help this situation?" asks Ms. Pang. Ms. Boon casually responds, "Students like Sonny and Les will always be around, and there will be many more students like Jared." Ms. Boon's response is of no help to Ms. Pang, but she acknowledges that Ms. Boon is probably right. As Ms. Pang walks back to her office, she trips and almost falls. She can almost hear Sonny and Les laughing. Now she has an idea what class must be like for Jared and some of the other students. This makes Ms. Pang even more determined to create a positive learning environment in her PE class.

NOTES

QUESTIONS

Preparing for Learning & Teaching

SUMMARY OF PARTICIPANTS

Sonny, 5th-grade student who taunts others

Les, 5th-grade student who taunts others

Jared, 5th-grade student with DCD

Ms. Pang, PE teacher

Aimee, Jared's classmate

Ms. Boon, school counselor

1. What is the primary issue in this case?

2. What are some of the factors that contributed to this case?

3. How might Sonny and Les's behavior affect Jared's self-esteem and clumsiness?

4. What actions did Ms. Pang take when she heard the boys taunting and teasing Jared? What other actions could she have taken?

5. What would you do with students like Sonny and Les in your classes?

6. Did Ms. Pang employ any specific behavior and/or teaching strategies to address the situation?

7. Do you think that by quickly changing her lesson, Ms. Pang did more or less harm to Jared's self-concept?

8. What supports or accommodations could Ms. Pang have used?

9. Can you think of other pedagogy strategies that she might have tried?

10. Do you think Ms. Boon's advice to Ms. Pang was appropriate and helpful? Why or why not?

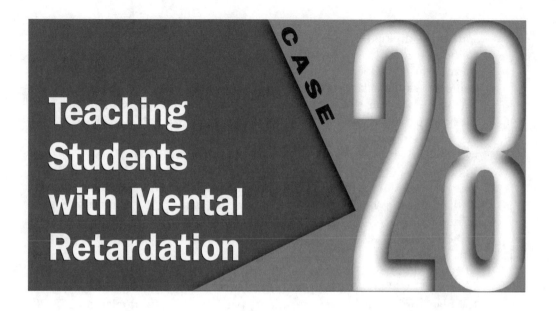

Teaching Students with Mental Retardation

harity is a 13-year-old Native American girl who attends Black Hills Middle School. Charity and her parents live in a small southwestern community outside of Buffalo Gap, South Dakota. Charity has Down syndrome concomitant with mild mental retardation. She has been included in GPE since kindergarten and participates in regular physical activities. She mostly enjoys running, jumping rope, soccer, parachute activities, lacrosse, volleyball, singing, and especially dancing. It is no surprise that Charity's teacher, Ms. Calhoun, describes her as a very social and outgoing child. In fact, Charity engages in soccer and horseback riding on the weekends.

Mr. Wovoka and Ms. Calhoun team teach GPE classes at Black Hills. Mr. Wovoka is a certified physical education teacher in his first year at this rural middle school. Although she does teach GPE classes, Ms. Calhoun was trained and still teaches within a special education unit at the school. She does not yet have certification in physical education. However, Ms. Calhoun's experiences teaching students with disabilities are extensive.

Charity's PE class lasts from 9:30 to 10:47 A.M. Mondays through Fridays. A typical class consists of Charity and her peers changing into their "Sioux Savages" (the school's mascot name) PE uniforms in the locker room—that is, whenever the students do get dressed for class. On more than one occasion, Charity has told Ms. Calhoun that she does not like wearing a tee shirt with the name "Sioux Savages" on it, because as Charity explains, her relatives are not "savages." Ms. Calhoun tells her that she must wear her PE uniform, and usually she complies. Changing into their PE uniforms prior to class usually takes the students between 3 and 5 minutes, followed by a routine warm-up for about 5 minutes on the gym floor. Then the class is sometimes divided by gender, with Mr. Wovoka taking all the boys and Ms. Calhoun the girls. They engage them in physical activities for nearly 55 minutes of the allocated time. A few minutes before the bell rings the students are sent back to the locker room to change. For their classes, these teachers use either the gym or an area outside of the building, which consists of a playing field and blacktop area with basketball goals.

Some students in this GPE class exhibit positive attitudes and behaviors toward Charity. For example, when Ms. Calhoun asks, "If we are playing a team sport such as basketball, would it be okay to have Charity on your team?" Mary Beth replies, "Yes, I like playing with her." Chris agrees: "I like helping her practice and play the games." By contrast, Steven responds, "Charity can't shoot the ball right. She's a klutz." In fact, several of her peers express little confidence in Charity's ability to perform specific sport-related skills.

One Monday, Charity doesn't participate with her peers in any of the station work—basketball (knockout), floor hockey, or kickball—outside on the blacktop. At each station students participate in sport-related activities for about 15 minutes and then they rotate to the next station. Ms. Calhoun leads a kickball game at station 3. However, since Charity isn't dressed for class that day, Ms. Calhoun asks her to walk laps around the blacktop area, but she doesn't follow Ms. Calhoun's directions. Instead, for the entire class, Charity sits singing on some benches adjacent to the playing area. From time to time, she stands up and dances around by herself. At no time during this class period does Ms. Calhoun desist Charity's off-task behaviors. Moreover, since Charity is separated from her classmates she doesn't interact with any of them. On this day, Charity has no opportunity to participate with her peers in meaningful, interactive, and pleasant ways while focused on common GPE objectives. Fortunately, this is not always the case.

On Wednesday of that same week, Charity's interactions with her peers are mostly positive and appropriate. Ms. Calhoun and Mr. Wovoka coteach this particular class and don't divide the students based on gender; instead, they randomly choose the teams for volleyball. Charity is on the blue team with all girls and only one boy. The teams rotate to the next court if they win and stay if they lose. A total of four nets are set up.

Volleyball is a favorite of Charity's and she really seems to enjoy playing. Throughout the games, she is verbally interactive with her classmates, telling them how she is going to hit the ball if it comes to her or how she is going to serve. Charity's team members praise her serves, but when she attempts to reach the ball when it is hit back by the opposing team in her direction, her teammates quickly intercept the shot. When Charity serves successfully, Keon says, "Nice serve, Charity," and gives her a high five. A few times Charity's classmates physically go through hitting the ball with her so that she will be prepared the next time it comes her way. But Charity doesn't hit many of the balls headed toward her; instead, she just stands there. Most of her peers are excited when she hits the ball or helps block a ball coming over the net. However, when she misses the ball on a particular attempt, Mark criticizes Charity and asks, "Why can't you hit the ball?"

Yet, overall Charity seems to enjoy playing volleyball with her classmates. Moreover, in this lesson, Charity and her peers had multiple opportunities for structured contacts (i.e., organized volleyball play with classmates) that were focused on common goals (i.e., hitting the ball over the net), interactive, pleasant, mostly respectful, and meaningful. These interactions were mostly equal-status[1] in nature between Charity and her peers. It appears that positive attitudes and friendly relationships are being developed between Charity and her classmates during this volleyball lesson. Although Ms. Calhoun stands by to monitor the volleyball games and frequently give encouragement, she doesn't provide any of the students with specific feedback about how best to hit the ball.

The following day, Charity plays dodgeball, a game that she doesn't like very much. She expresses this to Ms. Calhoun, who is leading that activity for the day. For much of this class period, Charity's interactions with her classmates are unidirectional with her as the recipient (as opposed to equal-status). For example, Mary Beth yells to Charity, "Move to the right, Charity!" or "Watch out!" when dodging the balls. Charity's interactions during this activity are mostly accidental, that is, running into other classmates in an effort to dodge the ball. Some of the boys yell at her and call her names. Otherwise, Charity doesn't interact with her peers. This may be partly because she doesn't like dodgeball, and if given a chance will stand off to the side, not interacting in the game. Yet, Ms. Calhoun does nothing to hold Charity accountable for her off-task behaviors.

At home that evening, Charity tells her mother about the "boys in PE." Mrs. Keller, Charity's mother, learns that Charity really enjoys GPE and has developed several friendships in her classes, but feels uncomfortable with some of the boys in the class. Mrs. Keller decides to question her in greater detail:

Mrs. Keller: *Charity, you first said that most of the time you enjoy playing with your classmates in PE. Tell me more about why you feel this way.*

Charity: *Because I make friends and I get along with everyone. I have fun.*

Mrs. Keller: *But now you say that your classmates make you feel uncomfortable.*

Charity: *(laughing) Yeah, sometimes the boys make me feel uncomfortable.*

Mrs. Keller: *Why?*

Charity: *Because they can be real . . . rough sometimes.*

Mrs. Keller: *What do they do to make you feel uncomfortable in class?*

Charity: *If I miss the ball they call me names and put me down.*

Mrs. Keller: *Oh, they do . . . So, let's say you're hitting the volleyball incorrectly. No one will come and help you?*

Charity: *No. If I'm like having a hard time, or having trouble thinking, my friends will help me do my work . . . in gym.*

Mrs. Keller: *So, people help you in PE class. Do they help you outside of class?*

Charity: *Yeah, in reading. My favorite classes are gym and reading.*

Mrs. Keller: *What do you like about gym so much?*

Charity: *We play fun games and my friends are there. I like volleyball.*

Mrs. Keller: *So PE is one of your favorite classes? What activities do you like to do?*

Charity: *I like to sing, and my favorite thing about gym is playing soccer and basketball.*

Mrs. Keller: *Why?*

Charity: *Because one time in 5th grade I scored 6 or 7 points.*

Mrs. Keller: *What else do you like?*

Charity: *I like running, volleyball, line soccer, parachute . . . dancing, kickball, basketball, jump rope, relays, lacrosse, and . . . stuff.*

Mrs. Keller: *Does your PE teacher include you in most of the activities?*

Charity: *Yes. I can play everything everyone else plays.*

Mrs. Keller: *Do you think everyone is the same? Does your teacher treat you the same?*

Charity: *Yes, but I can do some things better than the others. I can do things better than some of the girls.*

Endnote

1. The reader is encouraged to consult the physical education literature on the importance and development of equal-status relationships and attitude change (e.g., Sherrill, 1998; Sherrill, Heikinaro-Johansson, & Slininger, 1994; Slininger, Sherrill, & Jankowski, 2000).

2. Attitudinal theory (see p. 182) refers to theories put forward to better understand and predict behaviors in association with attitudes. One such theory is found in the theoretical framework of contact theory (Allport, 1954; Slininger, Sherrill, & Jankowski, 2000). In physical education, contact theory has been used as a framework in which to influence the attitudes and behaviors of PETE students toward teaching/interacting with children/youth with and without disabilities from culturally diverse backgrounds. Second, contact theory's structured contact variables (i.e., frequent, interactive, pleasant, cooperative, focused on common goals, meaningful, respectful, equal status, and long term) are used to guide program objectives (Sherrill, Heikinaro-Johansson, & Slininger, 1994; Slininger et al., 2000).

Resources and References

Allport, G. W. (1954). *The nature of prejudice.* Cambridge, MA: Addison-Wesley.

Block, M. E. (1998). Don't forget about the social aspects of inclusion. *Strategies, 12*(2), 30–34.

Block, M. E. (2000). *A teacher's guide to including children with disabilities in regular physical education* (2nd ed.). Baltimore: Brookes.

Block, M. E., & Zeman, R. (1996). Including students with disabilities in regular physical education: Effects on nondisabled children. *Adapted Physical Activity Quarterly, 13,* 38–49.

Block, M. E., & Zeman, R. (1997). "Pass the ball to Jimmy!" A success story in inclusive physical education. *Palaestra, 13*(3), 37–41.

Murata, N. M., Hodge, S. R., & Little, J. R. (2000). Students' attitudes, experiences, and perspectives on their peers with disabilities. *Clinical Kinesiology, 54*(3), 59–66.

Sherrill, C. (1998). *Adapted physical activity, recreation and sports: Cross-disciplinary and lifespan* (5th ed.). Dubuque, IA: WCB McGraw-Hill.

Sherrill, C., Heikinaro-Johansson, P. M., & Slininger, D. (1994). Equal-status relationships in the gym. *Journal of Physical Education, Recreation and Dance, 65*(1), 27–31, 56.

Slininger, D., Sherrill, C., & Jankowski, C. M. (2000). Children's attitudes toward peers with severe disabilities: Revisiting contact theory. *Adapted Physical Activity Quarterly, 17,* 176–196.

Acknowledgment

The authors wish to thank Rhea S. Butler for her input on this case. Rhea is an adapted physical education specialist at F. C. Hammond Middle School within the Alexandria, Virginia, area.

NOTES

QUESTIONS

Preparing for Learning & Teaching

CASE 28

SUMMARY OF PARTICIPANTS

Charity, 13-year-old student with Down syndrome concomitant with mild mental retardation

Ms. Calhoun, GPE teacher and special education unit teacher

Mr. Wovoka, physical education teacher

Mary Beth, Chris, Steven, Keon, Mark, all classmates

Mrs. Keller, Charity's mother

1. What is the primary issue in this case? Are there related issues? If so, what are they?

2. What are some of the specific elements that contribute to these issues?

3. What role did the characters play in creating/resolving these issues?

4. How effective was Ms. Calhoun's physical education pedagogy? What concerns do you have regarding her lack of physical education certification?

5. Do you agree with the "grouping" strategies of gender-separate activities and random selection of teams? Why or why not?

6. What should Ms. Calhoun have done to address Charity's failure to change into her PE uniform for class?

7. What affect might the school's mascot "Sioux Savages" have had on Charity's unwillingness to change into her PE uniform? What other issues might this raise?

8. What could Ms. Calhoun have done to hold Charity accountable for her off-task behaviors?

9. What strategies would have provided greater opportunities for Charity to interact with her classmates?

10. Was Charity successfully included in this GPE program? Why or why not?

11. What is your understanding of unidirectional and equal-status relationships?

12. Why is it important that Charity and her peers had opportunities to engage in structured contacts that involved them working toward focused common goals and exhibiting behaviors that were interactive, meaningful, pleasant, and frequent?

13. What attitudinal theory[2] posits that these variables (e.g., structured contacts) are important to attitude development or change?

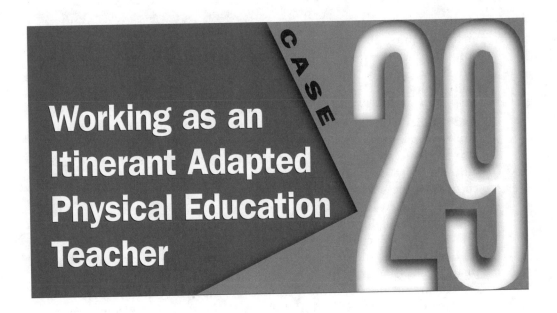

Working as an Itinerant Adapted Physical Education Teacher

Toni Richardson is an itinerant teacher entering her second year of teaching APE in central Ohio. As an itinerant teacher, she must travel to various schools within the district to provide direct APE instruction. In fact, on a weekly basis she teaches a diverse group of students with disabilities at seven different schools. All of these schools, with one exception (a preschool daycare center affiliated with the local university), are within the same large urban school district. Toni has a wide range of diverse learners across these multiple school sites. She provides APE instruction to preschoolers through high school seniors. More specifically, she has students with disabilities within three preschool units (one of these preschool units is housed within the same school building as one of the elementary units she teaches), eight elementary units, five middle school units, and four high school units. It stands to reason that as an itinerant teacher Toni encounters more unique instructional and administrative problems[1] compared with other APE teachers who teach within just one school site.

Toni is delighted that her classes are composed of students with varied disabilities from culturally and ethnically diverse backgrounds. More specifically, her classes comprise students with varied disability types (e.g., developmental disabilities, visual impairments, autism) who are African American, Cuban American, East Indian natives, White American, as well as students from Spanish-speaking countries including those with English as a second language, and many other ethnic groups. Although some of these students come from middle-class families, most come from families who are of low socioeconomic status. Toni's average class size is eight students per class, and classes are held 30 minutes twice a week for the elementary units, 45 minutes twice a week for the secondary units, and 30 minutes once per week for preschool units. However, in four of her class settings (one preschool unit, one elementary unit, all five middle school units, and all four high school units), she teaches combined classes. Therefore, she is responsible for a range of 15 students in the elementary combined class to 28 students in the middle and high school combined classes. All of the students in Toni's classes have varied developmental disabilities, including two students who are wheelchair users. Usually, she has enough teacher aides to assist her with the instructional and behavior management concerns with these students.

When asked about involving all students in class activities and learning experiences, Toni says that there is one student who comes to mind. This student is Roc, who has severe mental retardation coexisting with cerebral palsy. Roc is included in the elementary combined class with approximately 14 other students who have disabilities. According to Toni, Roc scored extremely low on the Test of Gross Motor Development[2] (TGMD-2); he was unable to meet the TGMD-2 criteria for throwing, kicking, catching, running (or walking for a distance), dribbling, jumping, hopping, and skipping. Further, while in PE class, Roc often sits off to the side of the gym while his peers are involved in motor activities. The only time Roc is included in activities is when Toni interrupts the class and provides him with one-on-one assistance.

Toni is frustrated because she feels that she should be doing more for Roc, yet she also understands the need to keep the "flow of the class going." Therefore, interrupting the whole class to provide one-on-one assistance with Roc is problematic. Toni believes that Roc benefits most from one-on-one assistance while engaged in sensory-motor activities. However, she feels that she doesn't have enough time to teach a lesson to the rest of the class, then come back to work with Roc. Further, Toni feels that she could work with Roc after class, but that would require taking him away from his academic work. This situation has left her searching for answers.

In addition to pedagogical concerns regarding providing effective instruction for Roc, Toni has several students who present behavior management problems. Most of these students have autism and/or emotional-behavioral disorders. Toni is concerned that these students don't participate in planned adapted activities unless they are constantly verbally and/or physically prompted. These students will only focus on a particular activity for a short block of time (about 3 to 4 minutes), then must be given a minute or two for a break. Then, during the break, they usually run around the gym, spin, engage in hand-flapping, and so on, so she must desist them and bring them back into planned activities. Toni is quick to point out that she also teaches an entire elementary class comprising only students with autism and emotional-behavioral disorders. She must enlist the assistance of peer tutors, which greatly cuts down on behavior management. These peer tutors are from the 4th-grade gifted and talented class and seem to enjoy working with the students. These same peer tutors must still engage in their own GPE classes.

Toni describes her other classes as being composed of students who will stay on task most of the class period. The one or two students out of the eight who need the little breaks can do so with little to no interruption to the flow of the class. Yet, Toni still has questions about teaching such students. In addition to using peer tutors, what other behavior management and instructional strategies should she consider for teaching students with autism and/or emotional-behavioral disorders in physical education? What resources[3] might she consult for guidance?

Despite her concerns relative to behavior management, Toni believes that her main issue as an itinerant APE teacher is simply a lack of quality equipment. And since she must travel each day from one school to another, her car trunk and backseat have become "storage closets." She explains: "We have ball bags that have holes so large in them that we must tie the hole so the equipment doesn't fall out. We have other people who work in our office building who like to 'borrow' the equipment—our equipment is kept in the basement storage area, which doesn't have a lock. Often, I will utilize the equipment at the particular school where I am teaching because it is in better shape than ours."

Another critical issue that Toni encounters as a teacher without her own office and instructional spaces is the limited availability of adequate space to work relative to planning, team meetings, and teaching. She states that when she and her APE colleagues sit down at the beginning of the year to schedule their respective class times, they have to work around the GPE teachers' schedules at each of the different school sites and around these respective school lunchtimes. To compound this issue, at the beginning of the school year while at one of the elementary schools where she teaches, Toni discovered that the occupational therapist, Ms. Lacy, had scheduled her time in the gym during what was supposed to be her APE class time. She attempted to work this matter out with Ms. Lacy directly, by suggesting that they team teach this particular group of students or share the gym, but Ms. Lacy was unwilling to do either. Toni had no alternative but to take her concern to the school principal, and later to her supervisor. As a result, Ms. Lacy was asked to provide her services in the classroom or on the stage, which she now does. Nonetheless, Toni was told that *she* had to reschedule around GPE times, lunch, and the elementary classes' afternoon reading blocks. Although, she ended up "getting" a designated time in the gym, she feels like she really had to fight for it.

Toni has similar concerns at the high school where she teaches APE classes. She explains: "Half the gym is blocked off so that typically developing students can enjoy playing basketball during their lunch hour. I really don't mind it, though, because, somehow, having a smaller space to work in keeps more of my students on task more of the time."

Toni completes another day. Later, while journaling[4] at home, she reflects on the many issues she encounters in part because she is an itinerant APE teacher. She realizes that her situation calls for skillfulness in human relations and that she must be flexible and open to change, exhibit high energy for the work demands, and have an ability to befriend teachers and principals at the various school buildings. To make her job easier, she also decides that she needs to communicate via cell phone while traveling from school to school and establish a professional mentoring relationship with a veteran APE teacher for guidance and support. The good news is that Toni has the opportunity to teach a diverse group of students[5] across multiple school sites, and at these different sites, the principals and staff members are very supportive of her APE program. Moreover, her colleagues and teacher aides are very helpful. Toni says, "Not all of my teachers will stay in the gym during APE, but the aides always do and work really hard. It's a real comfort knowing that they will always be there to support me."

Endnotes

1. French, Lavay, and Montelione (1986) and Jansma and French (1994) provide a more complete discussion of potential instructional and administrative problems associated with traveling and teaching students with disabilities as an itinerant adapted physical educator. Moreover, they provide strategies that can be used by such a teacher to function more efficiently and effectively within such a service delivery model (French et al., 1986; Jansma & French, 1994).

2. Ulrich's (2000) TGMD-2 is an assessment tool designed to measure ability in 12 gross motor areas divided into locomotor and object control skills and has both norm- and criterion-referenced standards. The TGMD-2 may be purchased from Pro-Ed, 8700 Shoal Creek Boulevard, Austin, TX 78757. Website: www.proedinc.com/store.

3. A number of excellent physical education resources are available that provide guidance for teaching students with autism and/or emotional-behavioral disorders. These resources include Block (2000); Jansma and French (1994); Lavay, French, and Henderson (1997); Loovis (2000); and Sherrill (1998).

4. The reader is encouraged to consult the physical education literature on the importance and process of reflective teaching (e.g., Graham, Holt/Hale, & Parker, 2001).

5. The reader is encouraged to consult the physical education literature on the issue of teaching diverse learners (e.g., Sparks, 1994; Sutherland & Hodge, 2001).

Resources and References

Block, M. E. (2000). *A teacher's guide to including children with disabilities in regular physical education* (2nd ed.). Baltimore: Brookes.

French, R., Lavay, B., & Montelione, T. (1986). Survival strategies: Itinerant special physical educators. *Journal of Physical Education, Recreation and Dance, 57*(8), 84–86.

Graham, G., Holt/Hale, S. A., & Parker, M. (2001). *Children moving: A reflective approach to teaching physical education* (5th ed.). Mountain View, CA: Mayfield.

Jansma, P., & French, R. (1994). *Special physical education: Physical activity, sports, and recreation.* Englewood Cliffs, NJ: Prentice Hall.

Lavay, B. W., French, R., & Henderson, H. L. (1997). *Positive behavior management strategies for physical educators.* Champaign, IL: Human Kinetics.

Loovis, E. M. (2000). Behavioral disorders. In J. P. Winnick (Ed.), *Adapted physical education and sport* (3rd ed.) (pp. 148–157). Champaign, IL: Human Kinetics.

Sherrill, C. (1998). *Adapted physical activity, recreation and sports: Crossdisciplinary and lifespan* (5th ed.). Dubuque, IA: Brown.

Sparks, W. G., III. (1994). Culturally responsive pedagogy: A framework for addressing multicultural issues. *Journal of Physical Education, Recreation and Dance, 65*(1), 24–26.

Sutherland, S. L., & Hodge, S. R. (2001). Inclusion of a diverse population. *Teaching Elementary Physical Education, 12*(2), 15–17.

Ulrich, D. A. (1988). Children with special needs—Assessing the quality of movement competence. *Journal of Physical Education, Recreation and Dance, 59*(91), 43–47.

Acknowledgment

The authors wish to thank Jennifer Kinkela for her input on this case. Jennifer is an itinerant APE specialist. She has a master's degree in both APE and GPE with K–12 certification and teaches within the greater Columbus, Ohio, area.

NOTES

QUESTIONS

Preparing for Learning & Teaching

SUMMARY OF PARTICIPANTS

Toni Richardson, itinerant APE teacher

Roc, student with severe mental retardation coexisting with cerebral palsy

Ms. Lacy, occupational therapist

1. What is the primary issue in this case? Are there related issues? If so, what are they?

2. What role did the characters play in creating/resolving these issues?

3. How can Toni resolve some of the issues that she encounters as an itinerant teacher relative to teaching in a large urban school district, traveling and teaching at multiple school sites, lack of quality and disrepair of equipment, and limited space availability?

4. What were the pedagogical issues that Toni struggled with in her classes? What suggestions can you offer to help resolve such issues?

5. What were the behavior management issues that Toni struggled with in her classes? What suggestions can you offer to help resolve such issues?

6. What should Toni do or have done differently to ensure cooperation between herself and her professional colleagues, such as related service providers (e.g., Ms. Lacy) and others?

7. What issues might arise relative to the diversity of students[5] Toni is responsible for providing APE instruction to in terms of varied disability types, cultural and ethnic differences, English as a second language, and socioeconomic dissimilarities?

8. What might be the similarities and differences between a self-contained adapted PE class and an inclusive GPE class? How might these similarities and differences affect the students?

9. What guidelines are you aware of for including a diverse group of students with varied disability types into your PE program? What resources are available for such guidance?

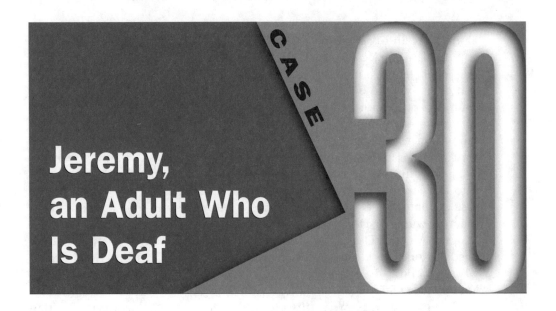

Jeremy, an Adult Who Is Deaf

Jeremy is a 22-year-old young man who is profoundly Deaf.[1] He was born Deaf and has used sign language since he was 4 years old. He grew up in New Mexico and attended the New Mexico School for the Deaf (NMSD) in Albuquerque for his entire schooling. He loved the school and played basketball and soccer in high school. He excelled at basketball and played varsity since 8th grade and later played for the Rochester Institute of Technology (RIT) in New York, while attending college.

Jeremy grew up with his grandmother Maria Fernandez because his father left his mother at a young age and his mother was too young when he was born to care for him. He has been in his grandmother's custody since birth, and during school he spent all his weekends and holidays with her. She has learned some sign language and can finger spell and sign about a dozen words. Grandma Fernandez practices, but because she has arthritis and really doesn't see Jeremy for long periods of time, she has a hard time with finger spelling. In addition, English is her second language, which makes it even harder for her to use American finger spelling. Jeremy and his grandmother love each other, so they communicate the best that they can.

Leaving for college isn't easy for Jeremy because it means that he will be so far away from Grandma Fernandez, but she knows it is the best thing because the National Technical Institute for the Deaf, a technical school specifically for Deaf students, is a part of RIT. Although Jeremy majors in applied computer technology through RIT, the services, Deaf peers, and appropriate support for sports are there. He loves his 4 years at RIT and is a star on the school's basketball team. There are three other Deaf players on his team, and one player, Frank, is even from Jeremy's high school. They get along great and become best friends. Throughout his college years, Jeremy goes to New Mexico to visit his grandmother as much as he can.

When Jeremy graduates, he looks for a job close to home. He has several offers but the best and closest one is in Hobbs, New Mexico, which is southeast of Albuquerque and about a half-day's drive. The company that hired him has some great perks as well as paid vacation time, training, and salary increases. It will be hard to be so far from his grandmother, but at least it is closer than RIT.

Jeremy finds a nice apartment 10 minutes from work, but his integration into the community is not easy. He misses his friends, basketball, and the ease of communication. He does drive to Albuquerque several weekends to practice with his Deaf basketball team for tournaments with the United States of America Deaf Sports Federation,[2] but the commute is tough and he needs to practice closer to his new "home." Jeremy calls his friend Frank, who is working in Washington, D.C., and he suggests that Jeremy join a Young Men's Christian Association (YMCA) or Community Recreation Club.

Jeremy is thrilled with this idea; he is now 22 and has to start initiating his own recreation and sport activities. He calls the local community recreation center on his telecommunicative device for the Deaf (TDD).[3] The center hangs up on him three times. After Jeremy calms down he calls again through the relay system.[4] He finally "speaks" with a day manager and asks about membership. The manager seems reluctant to provide information and tells Jeremy that he may want to join a local community college gym because such a facility would better meet his needs. This is not what Jeremy wants. He wants to join sports teams and a fitness club with adults, and this club has all of that—basketball teams, softball teams, martial arts, and a huge fitness center. He decides to go to the club and set up a meeting with the manager. Jeremy asks his interpreter from work to go with him to ensure that his needs are clarified and that the manager clearly understands him.

The evening manager, Mrs. Pappas, is very interested in how she can meet Jeremy's needs so that he can become a member at the center. Jeremy starts off by telling her that he is concerned about the lack of communication because the center does not have a TDD. He explains what a TDD is and that he needs it to communicate on the phone. He explains that the receiver of the phone is placed on the top of the keyboard and emits different signals for each letter. The information Jeremy wants to say is then displayed on the screen of the person receiving the call. He points out to her that according to the Americans with Disabilities Act[5] the club should have one and all staff should know how to use it. This surprises Mrs. Pappas because Jeremy is the first Deaf person who has applied for membership. However, she understands his need for the TDD and agrees to spend $200 to $300 for the device. She asks Jeremy if he could come in and teach the staff how to use it, and he is thrilled by the opportunity.

The next concern Jeremy expresses is the availability of an interpreter for his orientation into the club, personal training, and initial communication with the basketball team that he wants to join. He definitely will need an interpreter for orientation and personal training, which is part of the new membership. In addition, because he has never been integrated into a totally hearing team and he is nervous about this, he would like someone to be available to assist him in communication and interactions at the beginning. Mrs. Pappas is sympathetic but uncomfortable about the cost. She is not unwilling, but she is concerned that the club won't be able to afford ongoing interpreting. Jeremy assures her that the interpreter needs to be hired only for the amount of time it will take for the initial training and orientation, and for the initial communication with the basketball team.

Mrs. Pappas ends the meeting positively, saying that she will have to go to the board of trustees to get permission for all the "extra" costs and will get back to him soon. On his way out, Jeremy picks up some pamphlets. He is excited about joining the club yet nervous about how other members will feel about him. He just wants to join a club and be part of something now that he is independent; he doesn't want to be a spokesperson or a "poster child." Jeremy patiently waits and is just starting to get anxious when he receives a call from Mrs. Pappas on a TDD. She thanks him for his visit two weeks earlier and tells him that the trustees approved the TDD and an interpreter for orientation and training as well as for the first two practices and two games of the basketball season. Jeremy is thrilled to know that the center has made an investment in him as a member and that he can start participating in the center's activities soon. The only concern Mrs. Pappas has is where to hire an interpreter, so Jeremy gives her the number of the interpreting service for his interpreter at work.

Mrs. Pappas calls the interpreting service and sets up the initial meeting with an interpreter, Joanna Colgan, and the club's staff. Joanna is an active person herself, so she is looking forward to the assignment. Joanna and Jeremy meet the first day and discuss how they will educate the staff about his needs. They teach the staff the following techniques:

1. To get Jeremy's attention, tap his shoulder lightly and say his name out loud. Do not shout to get his attention.

2. Use basic signs for *hello, thank you, good, fine,* and *help* and finger spelling so that you don't always need to use pen and paper.

3. When the interpreter is not available, it is okay to use a pen and paper to communicate.

4. When communicating with Jeremy and an interpreter, face and speak to Jeremy, not the interpreter.

5. When Jeremy is in the middle of a game and the coach needs his attention, the coach should either wave his arms or flick the lights on and off.

The orientation goes well and helps dispel some myths about Deaf people. Jeremy looks forward to going to the center every day and starts making friends on the basketball team. At first, some of his teammates are skeptical and think that he is not only Deaf but also mentally retarded and has limited skills. They won't pass the ball to him unless they have to. But after a few games, Jeremy's demonstration of skill proves their perceptions wrong, and they gain respect for him.

One of Jeremy's teammates asks him if he knows Andy Spiecker, a Deaf man from Albuquerque. Jeremy knows his younger brother Alex well and has played basketball with him for three years. He remembers that Andy played basketball for NMSD too. After contacting him, Jeremy discovers that Andy still wishes to play basketball and had tried to join the recreation center five years earlier but had such difficulty that he gave up. With Jeremy's encouragement, Andy joins the club and Jeremy's team the next season. The understanding staff, the TDD, and the use of interpreters when necessary make joining the center much easier, and Andy's whole family even joins. Although the process of joining the center was not easy for Jeremy, he realizes that he has made a difference and is happy with his independence.

Endnotes

1. The Deaf community prefers the use of the word *Deaf* with a capital *D. Deaf* refers to a culture and a linguistic minority as opposed to *deaf*, which the Deaf community perceives as a medical perspective on Deafness.

2. The United States of America Deaf Sports Federation is the national governing body of Deaf Sport (see www.usadsf.org).

3. The TDD looks like a typewriter keyboard with a small screen. People who are Deaf and cannot functionally use a telephone use this device with a phone to communicate.

4. A relay service is a service used by Deaf and hearing people when the hearing person does not have a TDD. (Each state either establishes an 800 number or uses the numbers 711 to access the relay service.) One party dials 711 or the 800 number and the relay operator relays information from the spoken word to text on their TDD, or from text on the TDD to voice so that the two parties can communicate.

5. Americans with Disabilities Act Public Law 101-336 stipulates civil rights protection for individuals with disabilities in all areas of American life. Provisions include employment, public accommodation and services, public transportation, and telecommunications.

Resources and References

Craft, D. H., & Lieberman, L. (2000). Visual impairments and deafness. In J. P. Winnick (Ed.), *Adapted physical education and sport* (3rd ed.) (pp. 171–178). Champaign, IL: Human Kinetics.

Lieberman, L. J., & Cowart, J. F. (1996). *Games for people with sensory impairments.* Champaign, IL: Human Kinetics.

Stewart, D. A. (1991). *Deaf sport: The impact of sports within the deaf community.* Washington, DC: Gallaudet University.

QUESTIONS

Preparing for Learning & Teaching

CASE 30

SUMMARY OF PARTICIPANTS

Jeremy, 22-year-old who is Deaf

Maria Fernandez, Jeremy's grandmother

Frank, Jeremy's friend who is Deaf and plays basketball

Mrs. Pappas, evening manager at community recreation center

Joanna Colgan, interpreter

Andy Spiecker, Deaf basketball player

1. What is the primary issue in this case? Are there related issues? If so, what are they?

2. What are some of the specific elements that contribute to these issues? Social? Educational? Legal?

3. What role did the characters play in creating/resolving these issues?

4. Did Mrs. Pappas, Joanna Colgan, and Jeremy create the must appropriate solution? Why or why not? What would you have done differently?

5. The combination of purchasing a TDD and hiring an interpreter was helpful. What else could have been done and why?

6. Regarding community recreation facilities, what does the Americans with Disabilities Act say about services for individuals with disabilities?

7. What accommodations are required in recreation facilities, if any?

8. Was Jeremy prepared for this situation? Why or why not?

9. What are three appropriate future goals for the recreation club?

10. What websites or list serves would be appropriate for Jeremy to find information?

11. What additional information would Mrs. Pappas need to know in order to accommodate Jeremy?

12. Are there any related topics for discussion?

P urdue Elementary School is located in a rural/suburban area outside of Buffalo, New York. Mrs. Delaney is a veteran physical education teacher and has taught at Purdue Elementary for 18 years. Mr. Angelo also teaches physical education at this school, and over the past 6 years twice a week has cotaught double classes with Mrs. Delaney. This year Mr. Angelo is working with Mrs. Delaney to effectively include Bobby Green, a 5th grader with a visual impairment, in their GPE program.

Bobby has Stargardt disease, which causes the degeneration of the macula. This disease has left Bobby with little central vision, only peripheral vision. Until recently Bobby never received physical education at any grade level because his teachers did not know how to include him effectively in the physical education program. In fact, no school in the district has an APE specialist available. To compound Bobby's problem of exclusion from physical education, his teacher, Mrs. Delaney, until recently had no idea how to include him effectively in her PE classes. In previous years, an orientation and mobility class replaced Bobby's PE classes, and at that time his parents did not complain because they were pleased that he was getting some degree of service. Moreover, Bobby's reading class was held with Mrs. Mason, the vision teacher, during his scheduled recess time 3 days a week; however, he did have recess for the other 2 days per week. On those days, during recess Bobby swung on the swings or talked to his friend Jeff. Bobby was so busy with his services that he didn't really know what he was missing until he entered the 4th grade, whereupon his reading class was moved to a different time slot (i.e., after school), allowing him to go to recess every day instead of just twice a week. At that point, Bobby really began to realize that he was being excluded from playing soccer, kickball, and football with his peers during recess.

Bobby's parents, Mr. and Mrs. Green, found out about Bobby's exclusion from recess activities. Moreover, they learned that he was in essence excluded from meaningful participation in physical education, and they became increasingly upset with this situation. In previous years Mr. and Mrs. Green had made many attempts to get Bobby involved in physical activity in the community. For instance, since he was a 3rd grader they had him join a junior bowling league to participate with his sister on Saturday afternoons. Furthermore, Bobby participated in monthly recreational activities with the Commission for the Blind,[1] such as horseback riding, canoeing, rock climbing, and goal ball. Bobby also went to a sports camp for children who are blind called Camp Abilities.[2] He participated in a wide variety of sports and recreational activities for children and youth with blindness and really enjoyed the experience in addition to making several new friends. Mr. and Mrs. Green knew that Bobby was capable of being included in sports and activities but had never pushed the issue.

Neither Bobby's parents nor Mrs. Delaney were aware of the public law mandating that schools provide all students with disabilities a free and appropriate education, including physical education with specialized services and accommodations as needed. Bobby should have been receiving such services all along no matter what his condition. Mrs. Green decides to call Mrs. Adelman, the school principal, to discuss the matter, and they agree upon a meeting time and place. Mrs. Adelman, Mrs. Delaney, Mr. Angelo, Mrs. Mason, and the Green family all attend the meeting. Mrs. Green says, "I'm not blaming anyone for the current, unacceptable situation, but I want Bobby's future to be full and normal, and in order to achieve this he should be included in GPE classes with his typically developing peers to learn and participate in all the games and activities that they do." Immediately reacting to this comment with apprehensiveness, Mrs. Delaney asks, "What can Bobby see?"

Mrs. Mason explains, "Stargardt disease is a genetic disorder that causes irreversible damage to the central part of the retina called the macula. The macula provides central vision and enables us to see images straight ahead of us. The peripheral area of the retina remains intact, which is why Bobby can distinguish those running around him. His symptoms began in kindergarten and progressed throughout the summer enough to require special services by 1st grade. The truth is that Bobby can see what is happening around him peripherally and could very well be included in GPE classes if his schedule was changed." To support her argument, Mrs. Mason proudly states, "Marla Runyan, who also has Stargardt disease, ran the 1500 meters in the 2000 Olympics and placed 8th in the world." Both Mrs. Delaney and Mr. Angelo express their sincere interest in including Bobby in physical education, yet they are concerned because they have no idea even where to start making appropriate instructional adaptations.

At that point, Mrs. Mason acknowledges that her good friend Professor Yagel is a teacher, educator, and researcher at the local university who has expertise in the area of physical education for children with visual impairments. Before the meeting, Mrs. Mason had "picked her brain" about the situation with Bobby. Mrs. Mason and Professor Yagel had agreed upon several strategies to help Mrs. Delaney and Mr. Angelo more effectively include Bobby in GPE classes:

1. Since their school district already uses the FITNESSGRAM[3] for the assessment of physical fitness levels of students without disabilities, Mrs. Delaney, through her PE department's budget, should purchase the Brockport Physical Fitness Test[4] to test and assess Bobby's physical fitness levels. This test has standards for students with visual impairments and other disabilities. This way Bobby could do all the fitness assessment items that the class does but would have standards appropriate for him.

2. Because they are just starting to include Bobby in physical education, Mrs. Delaney and Mr. Angelo should incorporate a Disability Awareness Program[5] so that his peers can learn more about what he can see, and why they make the modifications they do.

3. After the assessment and program development, Mrs. Delaney and Mr. Angelo should implement a Peer Tutor Program.[6] If Bobby were to have a trained peer tutor, he could be given individualized directions with modeling up close if necessary, specific feedback, and records could be kept of his performance and improvement. Of course, the peer tutor would need to be trained in order to work effectively with Bobby. Such a training program is simple to implement, and Mrs. Mason will provide Mrs. Delaney and Mr. Angelo the information they need to train the tutors.

4. Equipment should be adapted or changed whenever warranted; for example, replace regulation baseballs with a beep baseball. There will be times when Bobby may benefit from a bell ball, beeping ball, brighter Frisbee, or sound source at one end of the gym or at a base. There may also be times when he benefits from modified rules. For example: in hockey, soccer, or basketball there would be no defenders from the front because Bobby cannot see them, or there could be a no defender rule. Bobby may also benefit from a bounce pass in basketball to let him know where the ball is. Additionally, he could benefit in games in which other kids simulate the same visual impairment to equalize the playing field.

5. The curriculum should be modified to incorporate individual units in addition to team game units. Bobby will be able to participate in (closed-skill) units such as swimming, aerobics, archery, fitness, and line-dancing units independently. He will need some assistance in developmental team sports (open skills) such as badminton, volleyball, soccer, and basketball. If Mrs. Delaney and Mr. Angelo utilize part open- and part closed-skill units, Bobby won't have to depend on others all the time.

6. They should incorporate some units of blind sports such as goal ball and beep baseball with the entire class. This way all the students

would experience movement and a sense of blindness (of course, Bobby would be at an advantage in such situations).

7. Mrs. Delaney should consult the APE literature. The books *Games for People with Sensory Impairments: Strategies for Including Individuals of All Ages*[7] and *Adapted Physical Education Activity Guides*[8] will help her with adaptation ideas.

8. Bobby could continue to take advantage of the Commission for the Blind's activities each month and also attend Camp Abilities again during the summer.

9. Bobby should participate in the United States Association for Blind Athletes[9] (USABA) activities such as Judo, tandem cycling, track and field, and swimming in intramurals and in the community. Participating in these activities will give Bobby the skills and knowledge to compete in such sports against other youth with visual impairments if he chooses to do so.

Much to their credit and professionalism Mrs. Delaney and Mr. Angelo are very receptive to these suggestions and everyone is enthusiastic after the meeting. The first task is to reschedule Bobby's orientation and mobility class. This class is moved to mornings before school, and Bobby will take the early middle school bus (just across the street from Purdue Elementary School) twice a week so that he has time for his orientation and mobility training. Mrs. Mason is happy about this arrangement because her children are in the high school and are gone early in the morning anyway.

The first PE unit is volleyball. Bobby's good friend Jeff is his trained peer tutor, and they practice their skills together with a bright yellow volleyball trainer ball. Jeff gives a verbal cue before tossing Bobby the ball, and Bobby turns his head so that the ball is in his field of vision. For the modified game, Bobby serves the ball from anywhere he wishes and is allowed to catch the ball. He can walk with it too if he wishes, and his teammates can catch the ball and give it to him during the game. The teams decide that it is okay for the ball to bounce up to two times, and for Bobby to hit the ball more than once. During their game, some of the points continue for a long time, and everyone enjoys the unit. Most important, Bobby is now meaningfully being included in GPE with his peers. The next unit will be swimming, and Bobby is excited because he knows that he is a good swimmer and will do well.

Endnotes

1. Many states have a State Commission for the Blind. The commission provides children's educational services as well as transition services. State commissions are divided into counties, and some counties may offer recreational or summer programming.

2. Lieberman and Lepore (1998) provide an excellent discussion regarding Camp Abilities.

3. The FITNESSGRAM (Cooper Institute for Aerobics Research, 1999) is a physical fitness test with criterion-referenced standards for children and youth (ages 5 to 17+). Additional information and software regarding the FITNESSGRAM can be secured from the Cooper Institute for Aerobics Research, Dallas, Texas.

4. The Brockport Physical Fitness Test (Winnick & Short, 1999a, 1999b) may be purchased from Human Kinetics at 1-800-747-4457.

5. See Wilson and Lieberman (2000).

6. Lieberman, Dunn, van der Mars, and McCubbin (2000) provide empirical evidence for the advocacy of peer-tutoring programs. A step-by-step peer tutor program can be found in *Strategies for Inclusion* (Lieberman & Houston-Wilson, 2002; see below).

7. This book by Lieberman and Cowart (1996) can be purchased from Human Kinetics at 1-800-747-4457.

8. This book can be secured from Sporttime at 1-800-444-5700.

9. For information regarding the USABA, write to 33 North Institute Street, Colorado Springs, CO 80903; call 719-630-0422; fax 719-630-0616; e-mail at usaba@usa.net; or visit its website at www.usaba.org.

Resources and References

Barfield, J. P., Hannigan-Downs, S. B., & Lieberman, L. J. (1998). Implementing a peer tutor program: Strategies for practitioners. *The Physical Educator, 55*(4), 211–221.

Cooper Institute for Aerobics Research. (1999). *Prudential FITNESSGRAM.* Dallas, TX: Author.

Craft, D., & Lieberman, L. J. (2000). Visual impairments and deafness. In J. P. Winnick (Ed.), *Adapted physical education and sport* (3rd ed.) (pp. 159–180). Champaign, IL: Human Kinetics.

Houston-Wilson, C., Lieberman, L. J., Horton, M., & Kasser, S. (1997). Peer tutoring: An effective strategy for inclusion. *Journal of Physical Education, Recreation and Dance, 68*(6), 39–44.

Lieberman, L. (1993). Games and activities for individuals with sensory impairments. In S. Grosse & D. Thompson (Eds.), *Sports recreation and leisure for individuals with disabilities: The best of practical pointers.* Reston, VA: AAHPERD.

Lieberman, L. (1999). Including everyone in physical education and peer tutoring strategies. In B. Pettifore (Ed.), *Physical education methods for classroom teachers.* Champaign, IL: Human Kinetics.

Lieberman, L., & Cowart, J. (1996). *Games for people with sensory impairments: Strategies for including individuals of all ages.* Champaign, IL: Human Kinetics.

Lieberman, L. J. (Spring 2002). Fitness for individuals who are visually impaired or deaf-blind. *Re:View.*

Lieberman, L. J., & Houston-Wilson, C. (2002). *Strategies for inclusion: A handbook for physical educators.* Champaign, IL: Human Kinetics..

Lieberman, L. J., & Houston-Wilson, C. (1999). Overcoming barriers to including students with visual impairments and deaf blindness into physical education. *Re:View, 31*(3), 129–138.

Lieberman, L. J., & Lepore, M. (1998). Camp Abilities: A developmental sports camp for children who are blind and deafblind. *Palaestra, 14*(1), 28–31, 46–48.

Lieberman, L. J., & McHugh, B. E. (2001). Health related fitness of children with visual impairments and blindness. *Journal of Visual Impairment and Blindness, 95*(5), 272–286.

Lieberman, L. J., Butcher, M., & Moak, S. (2001). Preferred guide-running techniques for children who are blind. *Palaestra, 17*(3), 20–26, 55.

Wilson, S., & Lieberman, L. J. (2000). DisAbility awareness in physical education. *Strategies, 13*(6), 12, 29–33.

Winnick, J., & Short, F. (1999a). *The Brockport physical fitness test manual.* Champaign, IL: Human Kinetics.

Winnick, J., & Short, F. (Eds.). (1999b). *The Brockport physical fitness training guide.* Champaign, IL: Human Kinetics.

QUESTIONS

Preparing for Learning & Teaching

SUMMARY OF PARTICIPANTS

Mrs. Delaney, physical education teacher

Mr. Angelo, physical education teacher

Bobby Green, 5th-grade student with Stargardt disease

Mrs. Mason, vision teacher

Jeff, Bobby's friend

Mr. and Mrs. Green, Bobby's parents

Mrs. Adelman, school principal

Marla Runyan, famous athlete with Stargardt disease

Professor Yagel, expert in physical education for children with visual impairments

1. What is the primary issue in this case? Are there related issues? If so, what are they?

2. What role did the characters play in creating/resolving these issues?

3. Was the solution created by Mrs. Delaney, Mr. Angelo, Mrs. Mason, and Mrs. Green appropriate? Why or why not? What would you have done differently?

4. What does the law say about physical education for children with visual impairments?

5. How would you develop a program that is appropriate for Bobby?

6. How would you modify a cooperative games unit? Gymnastics?

7. Whom else could Mrs. Delaney turn to for support?

8. What websites or list serves would be appropriate to find information on developing programming for Bobby?

9. What additional information would Mrs. Delaney need to know in order to include Bobby with peers his same age? What information would she need to get him involved in competitive blind sports events?

10. Are there any related topics for discussion?

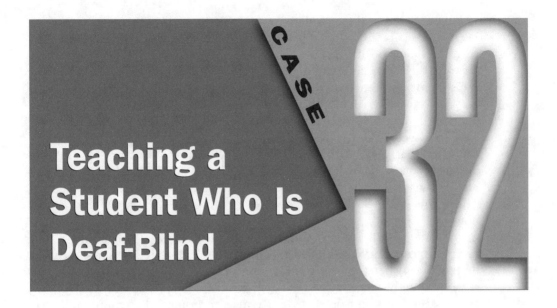

Teaching a Student Who Is Deaf-Blind

Mr. Roberts is a high school physical education teacher who has been teaching for more than 17 years. He has worked hard to keep current, attends the state conference each year, and often attends workshops and seminars. He has had several student teachers over the last few years and believes he is a good teacher. The high school where Mr. Roberts teaches is large, and there are four other full-time physical educators. The high school is also the designated school for Deaf students in the district. Over the past 5 years, Mr. Roberts has had four Deaf students in his classes. One of these students has graduated, two others are seniors, and one is a junior. Mr. Roberts was told that he will be having another Deaf student, Cory, in the fall as a freshman. He is looking forward to teaching Cory because he is becoming more skilled at using basic sign, using interpreters, and modifying activities to ensure proper inclusion. It has been a year since he has had a Deaf student, but he is very comfortable working with such students.

At the beginning of the school year, at the fall teachers' meetings, Mr. Roberts meets the new interpreters for Cory. In his conversations, he learns that Cory was recently diagnosed with Usher syndrome and is also losing his vision. Ms. Lyle, one of the interpreters, explains that Cory's type of Usher syndrome involves being born Deaf and the slow loss of vision as the result of retinitis pigmentosa. Retinitis pigmentosa is characterized by night blindness and the gradual loss of peripheral vision. In Cory's case, he does have night blindness in which he cannot see in dimly lighted areas, but so far he has lost only some peripheral vision. Upon learning this, Mr. Roberts becomes extremely concerned because he has had only two students with vision loss. One of these students was in his class 10 years ago and she had been in a separate PE class. The other student came to Mr. Roberts recently, in 11th grade, and had been in another teacher's class. The APE consultant for the district, Ms. Sullivan, had consulted with the other PE teacher when the student who was visually impaired was attending Mr. Roberts's school.

Unfortunately, Ms. Sullivan is the only APE consultant for the entire district and couldn't make an appointment with Mr. Roberts until October. She does recommend a book and gives him a few 800 numbers to call, but Mr. Roberts wants answers before Cory comes to his class. Mr. Roberts doesn't know what to do or whom to turn to for help. His wife recommends that he talk to the family since they know Cory best. Mr. Roberts thinks this is a great idea and decides to call Cory's parents for advice on how to help Cory. Mr. Roberts is so apprehensive that he almost hopes Cory's parents will say that Cory can't attend PE class at this point. When he tries to call Cory's mother, Mrs. Lufson, he finds that she is also Deaf, so he has to call her through the relay service. He is familiar with using the relay because he once had a Deaf athlete on his track team. In their phone conversation, Mrs. Lufson says that Usher syndrome is hereditary and that Cory's uncle and grandmother both were born with it. Mrs. Lufson is concerned because Cory has just found out himself. She says, "He is having a tough time dealing with it since he was looking forward to getting his driver's permit next year when his friends will get theirs, and now he has to deal with the fact that he will never drive. Cory loves basketball," she continues, "but is now having trouble receiving passes from the side and seeing opponents when he is on defense." Mr. Roberts cannot imagine how he will be able to include Cory in the units that he is currently planning, such as soccer, volleyball, and gymnastics. Mrs. Lufson mentions that Cory was recently assigned a vision teacher and a mobility teacher and that perhaps they could help with his preparation. Mr. Roberts quickly sets up a meeting with Mrs. Norment, Cory's vision teacher, to find out what to do in Cory's case. Ms. Lyle also wishes to participate so that she will know what to do for Cory during PE class and to meet Cory's vision teacher.

Mrs. Norment is very honest saying, "Retinitis pigmentosa is a difficult disability both physically and psychologically. It will not be an easy transition from reading small print, to using magnifiers, and maybe even having to learn Braille. Nor will it be easy to transition from being independent to perhaps using a cane, and being able to communicate through visual sign to needing to use tactile sign." The meeting lasts for 3 hours. In that time, Mr. Roberts learns where to stand when communicating with Cory, what type of lighting he needs, and what color of equipment he may need. He learns what size font to use when printing handouts, and how large Cory's sign space is. Mr. Roberts is now prepared to meet with Cory and ask him pertinent questions to ensure that his needs are met.

The first day of class is just a short class to get lockers and choose units for the fall semester. Mr. Roberts finally meets Cory and asks if they could discuss his future needs. Cory appears depressed and unenthusiastic about his new PE class. He tells Mr. Roberts where he can see to sign, what colors he sees best, what lighting is hard or easy for him, and how much modification he is comfortable with in game situations. Many of Cory's classmates know sign and are already used to making some accommodations for him, so a few additional accommodations don't seem like a big deal.

During the first week, Mr. Roberts sets up a disability awareness program. The other students are used to Cory's deafness, but they have no idea about what Cory can see. Mrs. Norment brings in a box of simulation glasses. These are glasses that emit an image of what Cory can currently see. For one week during the skills practice, Cory's peers take turns trying out the simulation glasses. This provides them with a much greater appreciation of what Cory can and cannot see. Many of them adapt to their partner's visual needs when they wear the glasses; this is the same type of accommodation they will need to make for Cory. Although it is clear that some of the students are uncomfortable thinking about having less vision, they ask good questions and even direct some of them to Cory. Cory is used to standing out because of his deafness, as well as educating his peers because he teaches them signs every day, so he doesn't mind their questions. This has truly been a learning experience for his peers, and they now completely understand that modifications need to be made for Cory.

The first unit is soccer. Cory chooses his position, the color of the pinnies, and a few rule modifications. He prefers to have his team pass him the ball from in front of him to ensure that he sees the ball, and that no defender can approach him from the sides. He refuses to adopt the rule of no defender because he doesn't want special treatment, but he does want the game to be fair. One difficult issue that arises is receiving information from the interpreter. Ms. Lyle stands next to the teacher as she is supposed to do, but Cory can't see her during the game. As a result, he receives important information after Mr. Roberts has finished explaining something. He misses important offensive and defensive strategies, and when there is a foul or a play has to end, Cory has trouble finding Ms. Lyle to see what is going on. Mr. Roberts is frustrated and senses Cory's frustration as well, so he decides to discuss the situation with Cory and Ms. Lyle. Cory seems discouraged and says, "I just want to keep score and not play in the games because it is too hard." Mr. Roberts is inclined to agree, but he knows that would be wrong. He remembers reading about a peer tutor program that teaches peers how to interpret, give instruction, and provide feedback. After reading a few current journal articles and textbooks, Mr. Roberts learns that it doesn't take much time to set up the program. Ms. Lyle teaches three of Cory's peers how to sign the basic physical education concepts and give feedback. The last few classes of the unit go much more smoothly now that communication is less of an issue and there is much more interaction between Cory and his peers. Cory says, "I'm glad I didn't end up keeping score. I want to go out for the soccer team next year!"

Cory later expresses to Mr. Roberts that he is looking forward to trying out for the basketball team in November. Mr. Roberts is a friend of the coach and knows it will be a tough sell to get Cory on the team. Another Deaf student wanted to be on the team, but it took a lot of convincing to get the coach to let him try out. Through collaboration, this Deaf student did make the cut and played on the varsity team for a year. Cory's desire to try out would definitely be another hurdle for the basketball coach. Mr. Roberts feels that it is his responsibility to sensitize the other teachers to Cory's needs.

Mr. Roberts is now thinking about how he is going to modify the volleyball and gymnastics units for Cory. He decides that he will have to take it one unit at a time and have Cory be his guide in this endeavor. Another thought in the back of Mr. Roberts's mind is that Cory's younger sister Sarah is in 7th grade and will be in his school in the next 2 years. Sarah is also Deaf, and there is a 50 percent chance that she will also have retinitis pigmentosa (Usher syndrome). But because of his experience with Cory, he feels confident that he will be able to include her successfully in his class.

Resources and References

Craft, D., & Lieberman, L. J. (2000). Visual impairments and deafness. In J. P. Winnick (Ed.), *Adapted physical education and sport* (3rd ed.) (pp. 159–180). Champaign, IL: Human Kinetics.

Deafblind LINK: Inquiries about anything related to Deaf-blindness. 1-800-438-9376 (voice); 1-800-854-7013 (TDD).

Lieberman, L. (1993). Games and activities for individuals with sensory impairments. In S. Grosse, & D. Thompson (Eds.), *Sports recreation and leisure for individuals with disabilities: The best of practical pointers.* Reston, VA: AAHPERD.

Lieberman, L. (1995). Recreation for individuals who are deaf-blind. In L. Alsop (Ed.), *Deaf-blind perspectives.* Monmouth, OR: D-B Link.

Lieberman, L., & Cowart, J. (1996). *Games for people with sensory impairments: Strategies for including individuals of all ages.* Champaign, IL: Human Kinetics.

Lieberman, L. J. (1996). Adapting games, sports and recreation for children and adults who are deaf-blind. *Deaf-Blind Perspectives, 3*(3).

Lieberman, L. J. (1999) Physical fitness and adapted physical education for children who are deafblind. In *Deafblind training manual.* Logan, UT: SKI-HI Institute Press.

Lieberman, L. J., & Downs, S. B. (1995). Physical education for students who are deaf-blind: A tutorial. *Brazilian International Journal of Adapted Physical Education, 2,* 125–143.

Lieberman, L. J., & Stuart, M. E. (in press). Recreation practices, preferences and barriers for adults who are deaf-blind. *Journal of Visual Impairment and Blindness.*

Lieberman, L. J., & Taule, J. (1998). Including physical fitness into the lives of individuals who are deafblind. *Deaf-Blind Perspectives, 5*(2), 6–10.

Sporttime: An equipment company with a variety of equipment that is bright and auditory; 1-800-283-5700.

QUESTIONS

Preparing for Learning & Teaching

SUMMARY OF PARTICIPANTS

Mr. Roberts, physical education teacher

Cory, 9th-grade Deaf student with Usher syndrome

Ms. Lyle, Cory's interpreter

Ms. Sullivan, district APE consultant

Mrs. Lufson, Cory's mother, who is Deaf

Mrs. Norment, Cory's vision teacher

Sarah, Cory's sister, who is in the 7th grade and also is Deaf and may have Usher syndrome

1. What is the primary issue in this case? Are there related issues? If so, what are they?

2. What are some of the specific elements that contributed to these issues?

3. What role did the characters play in creating/resolving these issues?

4. Were the adaptations Mr. Roberts made for soccer appropriate? Why or why not?

5. When Cory is included in the volleyball unit what adaptations may need to be made? What about gymnastics?

6. When setting up a peer tutor program for Cory what information in addition to signs would the students need to know?

7. What instructional accommodations are required for Cory, if any?

8. Cory did not have a specific physical education IEP in middle school because he was only Deaf. Will he need a physical education IEP now? If so, who will write it and how?

9. What appropriate future sports opportunities are there for Cory?

10. What websites or list serves would be appropriate to find information on including Cory?

11. What additional information would the teacher need to know when Sarah, Cory's sister, comes to his school?

12. Are there any related topics for discussion?

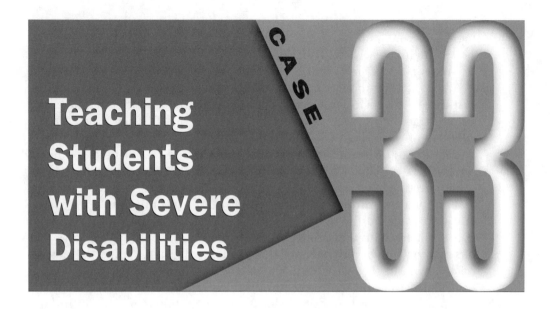

Teaching Students with Severe Disabilities

Mr. Brewer is a veteran elementary school teacher with 25 years of teaching experience at Broadwater Elementary School in southwest Virginia. He is that unusual breed of physical educator who has no interest in coaching. He truly loves teaching physical education to young children while they are still enthusiastic about movement and physical activity. He particularly enjoys the challenge of taking children who are not as skilled or confident as other children and helping them learn motor skills, improve their fitness, and in turn develop confidence and enjoyment in physical activity.

There are very few children with disabilities who live in the small town where Mr. Brewer teaches. However, over the years he has worked with his share of children with relatively mild disabilities. For example, early in his career he worked with a kindergartner who was hearing impaired. Mr. Brewer learned a few key signs and developed some simple gestures so that he was able to communicate fairly well with him. The student eventually moved to the state school for the Deaf, so Mr. Brewer didn't get a chance to follow up with him in later grades. Another year he had a student who was totally blind. He was a little apprehensive about how this student could safely participate in physical education. Yet, within a few weeks he learned how to make simple modifications to accommodate her, be more specific in the verbal cues he gave her, and use peers to help her move around the gym. By the time she moved on to middle school, Mr. Brewer felt pretty good about how she had done in physical education. And every year Mr. Brewer has a few students who have learning disabilities, mild mental retardation (including a few students with Down syndrome), behavior problems, or attention problems. Although these students need extra attention, more structure, and more modifications to be successful, Mr. Brewer manages to include each child successfully.

Yes, Mr. Brewer feels that he has seen pretty much everything, and he is feeling confident about starting his 26th year of teaching. He reports to the first day of in-services on August 28 along with the other teachers and administrators in his school district. There is the usual social time with discussions of vacations, families, who is engaged, who is pregnant, who moved away, and so on. At 10:00 A.M. Mrs. Collins, the principal, calls all the teachers together for a brief welcome-back-to-school meeting. At the end of the meeting, she asks Mrs. Brown, the special education teacher, to stick around for a few minutes. Mr. Brewer lingers for a few minutes to try to find out what is up, but he has to leave before he can find out much. He figures that a student with a disability will be attending school this year, and that Mrs. Brown will be in charge of that student. He makes a mental note to track down Mrs. Brown later in the day to find out more.

That afternoon Mr. Brewer wanders down to Mrs. Brown's special education room. He finds not only Mrs. Brown there but also Mrs. Collins and several other people whom Mr. Brewer has never met. He knocks on the door and Mrs. Collins invites him in. Mr. Brewer is then introduced to Mrs. Harrison, the mother of a 5th grader named Dwayne, who will be enrolled at Broadwater Elementary School this year. He is also introduced to Mr. Rogers, who is going to be Dwayne's full-time teacher assistant; Ms. Martin, the nurse for the school district; Mrs. Johnson, a physical therapist for the school district; and Ms. Davidson, an occupational therapist for the school district. "Steve, I'm glad you stopped by, because this concerns you as well," says Mrs. Collins. "Mrs. Harrison, why don't you explain to Mr. Brewer about Dwayne," continues Mrs. Collins. Mrs. Harrison hands Mr. Brewer a very detailed medical report, then proceeds to describe Dwayne's disabilities: severe, quadriplegic cerebral palsy (Dwayne is very stiff and has very little voluntary movement); severe mental retardation (Dwayne seems to understand basic cause and effect but not much else); and limited vision (Dwayne wears thick glasses, but his mother says that the physicians aren't sure how much Dwayne actually can see). In addition, Dwayne has some swallowing problems, so he has to be fed through a tube in his stomach. His swallowing problems also cause him to drool a lot, and he often has breathing problems. Finally, Dwayne does not have any bladder or bowel control, so he wears diapers. Mr. Brewer is amazed that any one child could have so many different and severe disabilities. He also is confused why Mrs. Collins had said that this concerned him too. Surely she didn't think that Dwayne would receive physical education. What on earth could Dwayne possibly do in physical education?

Mrs. Collins tells Mr. Brewer that Dwayne's IEP from his previous school prescribed physical education three times per week in a small group with other children with similar disabilities (Mr. Brewer thinks to himself, "There are other children with these types of disabilities!") Mrs. Collins realizes that this is not possible at Broadwater Elementary, so she explains to Mr. Brewer that he could either include Dwayne in GPE or work with him one-on-one. She notes that although Mrs. Harrison is flexible about how Mr. Brewer provides physical education to Dwayne, she does hope that Dwayne can be around his peers at least some of the time. Mrs. Collins points out that Mr. Rogers will accompany Dwayne to GPE class.

The conversation continues for a few more minutes, Mrs. Collins hands Mr. Brewer a copy of the physical education portion of Dwayne's IEP, and then Mr. Brewer leaves. As he walks down the hallway toward the gym, he feels like a prize-fighter who has just taken a few too many punches. He wonders, "What in the world do you do with a child with such severe disabilities in PE? This kid needs a physical therapist, not a physical educator. And what about his mother wanting him to be around kids without disabilities? Surely she doesn't think Dwayne can be included in GPE." Mr. Brewer arrives at his office and glances at Dwayne's IEP. There appear to be two goals for physical education: (a) to improve overall fitness, and (b) to develop lifetime leisure skills. He looks up at the ceiling and laughs to himself, "Right, this kid is going to run the mile, do 20 pull-ups, and learn how to play tennis." He looks back at the specific, short-term objectives listed under each goal:

Fitness Goal: Dwayne will demonstrate improved upper-body strength and flexibility.

Short-Term Instructional Objectives

1. While seated in his wheelchair, Dwayne will demonstrate upper-body range of motion so that he can reach for and manipulate objectives of varying size placed anywhere on his lap tray 50 percent of the time 2 consecutive days.
2. While seated in his wheelchair, Dwayne will demonstrate upper-body strength so that he can hold objects in his hand for up to 10 seconds and push objects off his lap tray or down a ramp 50 percent of the time 2 consecutive days.

Leisure Goal: Using adapted equipment and physical assistance as needed, Dwayne will demonstrate the basic skills necessary to bowl and fish.

Short-Term Instructional Objectives

1. In bowling and while seated in his wheelchair, Dwayne will develop skills necessary to independently push a ball down a ramp so that the ball rolls down the lane and strikes pins 50 percent of the time 2 consecutive days.
2. In fishing and while seated in his wheelchair, Dwayne will (with hand-over-hand assistance) cast and then reel using a modified fishing pole so that the lure lands in a 10 foot × 10 foot target 5 feet away from his wheelchair 50 percent of the time 2 consecutive days.

Well, the objectives do seem to match Dwayne's abilities, and they do seem to be in the ballpark of "physical education." Yet, Mr. Brewer still doesn't understand how he will be able to help Dwayne work on these objectives. He is not trained in APE. In fact, the more he thinks about working with Dwayne, the more nervous he gets. What if he hurts Dwayne when he is providing "hand-over-hand-assistance"? What if Dwayne begins to choke during PE class? What if he begins to cry? What if he needs his diaper changed in the middle of class? What is Mr. Rogers's role? Mr. Brewer realizes he doesn't have a clue how to even begin to answer these questions. He sits there for what seems like hours before he gets up and walks back to Mrs. Brown's room. He figures that, as the school's special education teacher, surely she will be able to help him at least get started on a plan for working with Dwayne.

When Mr. Brewer reaches Mrs. Brown's special education room, he sees her slumped with her head in her hands on the sofa in the corner of the room. "Hey, catching a few z's," he jokes. But when Mrs. Brown sits up, he can see that she has been crying. She confesses to him, "I have never worked with a child who was that severely disabled, and I don't think I can handle it." Mr. Brewer tries to console her, saying, "I don't know what to do either, but maybe we can work together and find some resources that will help us. Do you know of any other special educators in our school district or neighboring school districts who work with children like Dwayne?" Mrs. Brown thinks for a few minutes, and then says, "I can't think of any offhand. Is there an APE specialist for the school district?" He replies, "There was talk of sharing one among three school districts including ours, but nothing ever came of it. What are we going to do?"

QUESTIONS
Preparing for Learning & Teaching

SUMMARY OF PARTICIPANTS

Mr. Brewer, physical education teacher

Mrs. Collins, principal

Mrs. Brown, special education teacher

Mrs. Harrison, Dwayne's mother

Dwayne, 5th-grade student with severe, quadriplegic cerebral palsy; severe mental retardation; and limited vision

Mr. Rogers, Dwayne's full-time teacher assistant

Ms. Martin, nurse for the school district

Mrs. Johnson, physical therapist for the school district

Ms. Davidson, occupational therapist for the school district

1. What is the primary issue in this case?

2. What are some of the factors that contributed to this issue?

3. From a legal standpoint, must Dwayne receive physical education? What laws (if any) require physical education services for children with severe disabilities?

4. What is appropriate physical education for Dwayne? Do you think the IEP that was created for Dwayne at his previous school is appropriate for him? Why or why not?

5. Clearly Mr. Brewer is not prepared to provide physical education services to Dwayne. Nevertheless, is he "qualified" to provide such services according to federal and state laws or does his school district need to find a certified APE specialist?

6. Is Mr. Brewer required to include Dwayne in GPE? What does the law say about inclusion? How are decisions regarding placement made?

7. If Mr. Brewer were to include Dwayne in GPE at least once a week, should Dwayne work on his IEP objectives or should he be assisted in doing what the other children are doing? Why?

8. What other resources (i.e., people, equipment) within the school district should Mr. Brewer seek? What resources outside of the school district (i.e., people, agencies) might be helpful to him?

9. Although Mr. Rogers will accompany Dwayne to GPE, does he know what to do with Dwayne in physical education? Who is going to direct Mr. Rogers? Should Mr. Brewer work with Dwayne occasionally in GPE, or should Mr. Rogers be the only one who works with Dwayne?

10. Mr. Brewer has used peer tutoring successfully in the past. Is peer tutoring a viable option with a child who is as severely disabled as Dwayne? How might such a peer-tutoring program be created and implemented?

11. What role does Mrs. Harrison play in this entire process? Is she a good resource for information about Dwayne? If so, what types of things might Mr. Brewer ask her?

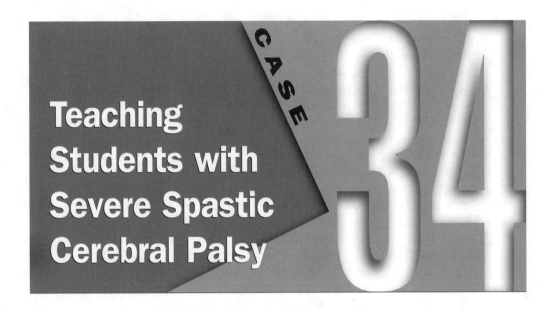

Teaching Students with Severe Spastic Cerebral Palsy

Chanh is an 8-year-old girl who attends Southside Elementary School. She has spastic cerebral palsy in all four limbs, uses a wheelchair, requires a feeding tube, and takes Tegretol™ to control her seizures. This medication helps to reduce her seizures, but she still has several seizures each week, lasting anywhere from 5 seconds to 2 minutes. Chanh has no formal mode of communication, but she can point to objects that she desires and makes specific sounds when she is frustrated, happy, or sad. She is in a separate self-contained class for most of the day but is integrated for art and music. She has physical education once a month with the APE consultant, Mr. Martinez, and then one day a week for the next 3 weeks her aid, Mrs. O'Leary, implements the lesson developed by Mr. Martinez. Most of Chanh's physical education is spent one on one, and the goals are predominantly the same as those used for physical therapy. She receives physical therapy three times a week along with occupational therapy twice a week.

Chanh's parents very much want her to work on communication with a communication board. However, when the communication specialist, Mrs. Malloy, evaluates Chanh, she determines that Chanh does not have enough head control or arm extension to work with a basic communication board. Chanh has little head control, and for some periods during the day her head is strapped to the back of her chair so that she can participate in class activities. Chanh would need to be able to hold her head up for a longer period of time, extend her arm, and control it for a few seconds. She presently cannot execute these skills, so Mrs. Malloy says she will return when Chanh can do them.

Chanh's mother, Mrs. Lu, is very troubled about how this can be accomplished and who would even be able to help her. Mr. Lu is a computer specialist and feels that if Chanh were placed in a computer class for more than one period per week she could develop the necessary skills. Mrs. Lu decides to call the special education director, Ms. Kelly, to tell her about this idea. Ms. Kelly tells Mrs. Lu that Chanh's current schedule leaves absolutely no time for her to add another class. Mrs. Lu suggests eliminating physical education to add computers, or even another physical therapy session. Ms. Kelly decides that she needs to check with Mr. Martinez first. Mr. Martinez is very understanding but says that it would not be possible to replace physical education with computers or physical therapy because physical education is required by law and cannot be replaced by any related service. He is very familiar with Chanh's current skills and what she would need to do to improve. Mr. Martinez has been in the district for 12 years and knows that the multidisciplinary team values his opinion. He suggests that instead of computers or physical therapy they add 30 minutes of swimming at the high school pool, which is right next door to their building. In addition, they could implement a trained peer tutor in both her 1:1 APE class and her swimming class. He has started training peer tutors for some of his inclusive classes and has some very skilled tutors in mind to work with Chanh. The added stimulation and motivation may help her extend and look up more to see what is happening. Mr. Martinez writes up his goals and objectives for Chanh's pool class.

Mr. and Mrs. Lu decide that they need to think about the suggestions before anything is implemented. They are familiar with the peer tutor program because Chanh's older brother, Chunlei, was trained and peer tutored 2 years ago, and they understand that this program really helps children with disabilities. They do have some concerns, however: What if the water is too cold and thus affects any potential improvements? What if the changing time causes Chanh to miss her next class after swimming? If she gains these skills in the pool, could they be transferred to land, and could she do them in her wheelchair well enough to use the communication board? How will the instructor ensure that if Chanh has a seizure in the pool she will be safe?

Chanh's parents sit down with her multidisciplinary team and discuss each issue. Regarding the first issue, that the water would be too cold, they learn that the water temperature in the high school pool is typically held at 79 to 80 degrees for swim classes and swim team events. Luckily, Mr. Martinez teaches therapeutic swimming lessons on Thursdays last period at the high school and says that Chanh could join that class. Thursday is also the one day of the week that the school increases the pool's temperature to 84 degrees for this particular swim time. He suggests that on that day Chanh go to swimming last period, the same period that she is supposed to work with Mrs. Malloy. From there she would go straight from the locker room to the bus, so there wouldn't be any concern about her missing a next class.

Another concern is the issue of generalization. Chanh's parents are not sure if the skills she learns in the pool could transfer to land. Mr. Martinez tells them that in his past experience, when using a verbal and a touch cue, students will display the same response even in two different settings. In addition, Mrs. Malloy says that she would come in to the pool and assist with Chanh's lesson. She will work with the peer tutor, Mrs. O'Leary, and Mr. Martinez to encourage purposeful and functional movements in the pool, which will eventually transfer to land and help Chanh with her communication skills. Mrs. Malloy does feel that Chanh will need additional time working on the same goals and objectives at home in order for the plan to work. Mr. and Mrs. Lu and Chanh's older brother, Chunlei, work out their schedule so that when Chanh takes her bath one of them will work on the same goals and objectives in the water two to three additional times each week.

Because Chanh does have active seizures, at times lasting more than a minute, safety is a very important concern. Mr. Martinez decides to order a neck collar flotation device. This device is a life jacket worn around the neck to ensure that the head stays out of the water no matter what the body is doing. This way Chanh can safely work on her extension. The only problem with the neck collar is that it does not help promote head control because it holds the head up itself with no help from the person wearing it. Mr. Martinez, Mrs. O'Leary, and Mrs. Malloy work out a plan that for 5 to 10 minutes of Chanh's lesson they will work 2:1 with the peer tutor on head control and tracking without the neck collar so that Chanh can work on her goals and not be in danger. The good thing about the neck collar is that Chanh will be able to have her head up the entire swim class and see what is going on around her. This will make her want to keep her head up even more when she isn't wearing the neck collar.

The first few weeks of implementing the program are difficult. Chanh is doing a nice job in the pool with her extension and purposeful movement and is even holding her head up for 2 to 3 seconds with minimal physical assistance. The problem is that the swim team enters the locker room right after school while Chanh is being changed, and the noise, movement, and excitement make her so tense that she can hardly get into her clothes. Mrs. O'Leary asks Mr. Martinez what they can do, so he speaks with the female physical educator. The next week Chanh changes in the teachers' locker room and things go much more smoothly.

The program at home is going well with Chunlei and Mrs. Lu taking turns during the week and Mr. Lu assisting with Chanh on weekends. Mr. and Mrs. Lu buy some balls and wands that Chanh likes and reaches for consistently. They send these to school with Chanh so that Mr. Martinez can implement them into the swimming unit. After 2 months, Chanh has achieved purposeful reaching with some grasping, and she can even hold her head up on cue with minimal assistance for 4 to 6 seconds. Mrs. Malloy holds out two to three different objects and Chanh consistently chooses the one she wants. Mrs. Malloy also holds out symbols and pictures so that Chanh can make choices and communicate what she wants throughout her day. Chanh's parents are thrilled with her progress, and after 4 months some of the symbols are successfully used at home.

Resources and References

Block, M. E. (2000). *A teacher's guide to including students with disabilities in general physical education* (2nd ed.). Baltimore: Brooks.

Block, M. E., Lieberman, L. J., & Conner-Kuntz, F. (1998). Authentic assessment in adapted physical education. *Journal of Physical Education, Recreation and Dance, 69*(3), 48–56.

Lieberman, L. J., & Houston-Wilson, C. (2002). *Strategies for inclusion: A handbook for physical educators.* Champaign, IL: Human Kinetics..

Lytle, R. (2000). Learning movement through play. *The Exceptional Parent,* pp. 1–4.

Modell, S., & Cox, A. (1999). Let's get fit: Fitness activities for children with severe/profound disabilities. *Teaching Exceptional Children,* pp. 24–29.

National Spinal Cord Association. (1999). Spinal cord injury statistics. Retrieved November 1, 2000, from www.spinalcord.org.

Preparing for Learning & Teaching

QUESTIONS

CASE 34

SUMMARY OF PARTICIPANTS

Chanh, 8-year-old student with spastic cerebral palsy

Mr. Martinez, APE consultant

Mrs. Malloy, communication specialist

Mrs. O'Leary, Chanh's aid

Mrs. Lu, Chanh's mother

Mr. Lu, Chanh's father

Ms. Kelly, special education director

Chunlei, Chanh's older brother

1. What is the primary issue in this case? Are there related issues? If so, what are they?

2. What are some of the specific elements that contribute to these issues? Medical? Educational? Familial?

3. What role did the characters play in creating/resolving these issues?

4. Did Mr. Martinez, Mrs. Malloy, and Mrs. O'Leary create an appropriate solution? Why or why not? What would you have done differently?

5. The combination of swimming and physical education using a 1:1 or 2:1 approach was very helpful in this situation. What else could the team work on to help Chanh in everyday functioning?

6. What does the law say about physical education for children with severe disabilities?

7. What accommodations are required in physical education, if any?

8. How will the present level of performance for physical education and swimming describe Chanh's performance?

9. What are three appropriate future goals for Chanh?

10. What websites or list serves would be appropriate to find information on developing programming for Chanh?

11. What additional information would the teacher need to know in order to successfully include Chanh with peers her same age?

12. Are there any related topics for discussion?

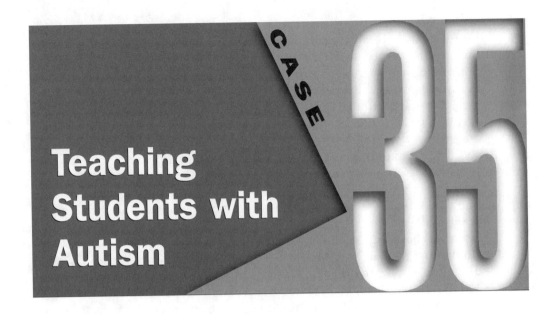

Teaching Students with Autism

For 5 years now, Mrs. Norris has been the physical education teacher at Everglades Middle School in Naples, Florida, and she is considered an effective teacher by most standards. She has established clear rules and routines for the students in all of her classes. In fact, upon entering the gym for class, her students know exactly where to go and what to do to start their daily warm-up activities. To engage her 7th-grade students in activities following their warm-up routine on this particular day, Mrs. Norris has set up several stations on the playing surface just outside the gymnasium and, as appropriate, provided multiple pieces of equipment for each student's use. The stations consist of handball, scoop ball, and punching a tetherball outside on the blacktop. Also prior to class, Mrs. Norris decides to use student peer pairings based on each student's skill and ability level as well as each student's compatibility with his or her peer partner. For example, Jason, a boy with autism, is paired with Ian, a mature, typically developing 7th grader. Mrs. Norris knows that Ian is a very responsible student who has willingly partnered with Jason on previous occasions.

Students either work as peer partners or independently, depending on the activity at that particular station, for about 5 to 8 minutes before they are instructed to rotate. Mrs. Norris briefly explains and demonstrates the skills and structure of the various tasks to the students before each class activity starts, yet Jason seems to have misunderstood the handball and scoop ball tasks. Perhaps that is why on several occasions throughout the lesson, Ian talks with Jason about the activity in which they are to engage. Ian also praises, "Nice catch, Jason" whenever he makes a successful catch while performing the scoop toss task. In fact, Mrs. Norris has noticed that over the past several weeks Jason's peers have increasingly given him praise and feedback such as, "That was good, but try it again." Mrs. Norris is pleased to witness this enhanced degree of interaction and communication between Jason and his peers.

Jason has exhibited autistic behaviors (i.e., marked abnormal development in social interaction and communication) concomitant with moderate mental retardation since he was 2 years old. His receptive and expressive verbal communication is delayed in comparison with his same-age peers (i.e., Jason speaks in two- to three-word bits and usually does not make eye contact with others). Jason's mother, Ms. Singleton, is a single parent. She works two jobs yet still struggles to make enough money to support Jason and pay the bills. Jason's father abandoned them both soon after Jason was born and, despite a longstanding court order, has never provided child support. Moreover, Ms. Singleton has always had difficulty trying to discipline Jason for his inappropriate and increasingly abusive behaviors. Mrs. Norris recalls an earlier time when Jason would often exhibit abusive behaviors (both verbally and physically) with his peers. In fact, on several occasions Jason has challenged Mrs. Norris's authority. To compound this problem, Jason's peers at that time were more likely to criticize and tease him, rather than to interact cooperatively with him, as they now do. Jason often played alone if at all.

However, over the past several months, since the start of the school year, Mrs. Norris and Mrs. Harris, a teacher aide, have carefully followed several strategies[1] recommended for teaching students with behavioral disorders, including autism:

- Mrs. Norris retrieved and reviewed Jason's school records to better understand his disability and search for cues regarding his tendency toward abusiveness.

- Mrs. Norris consulted the APE literature[2] to better understand how to effectively include students with autism and moderate to severe mental disabilities in her classes.

- Early during the school year, Mrs. Norris scheduled a conference to consult with Jason and Ms. Singleton in which she asked questions about Jason's habits, tendencies, and what events or situations tend to trigger his abusive behaviors. Later, Mrs. Norris and Ms. Singleton had a follow-up conference, and now, on a regular basis, they talk by telephone about Jason's progress and occasional setbacks.

- Mrs. Norris talked with Jason and Ms. Singleton about Jason's likes and dislikes in physical education, and together they outlined several behavioral and psychomotor goals for Jason.

- Mrs. Norris makes sure that she puts forward an effort to keep the lines of communication open by actively listening to Jason regarding his needs, interests, and concerns.

- Mrs. Norris has designated peer partners and constantly emphasizes to Jason (and his peers) the importance of working cooperatively, appropriate social interaction, and proper communication between him and his peers.

- Mrs. Norris emphasizes to Jason and his peers the importance of providing one another with genuine and honest praise and the value and use of specific feedback. Jason now feels good about his sport skills and motor abilities following weeks of praise and positive reinforcement.

- Mrs. Norris and Mrs. Harris ensure that Jason receives guidance and support as needed. They also ensure that Jason receives one-on-one tutoring from a peer partner, and in doing so, Mrs. Norris, Mrs. Harris, and most of the students in this 7th-grade class show genuine care and concern for Jason as an individual.

- Mrs. Norris and Mrs. Harris use praise and positive reinforcement strategies (e.g., the Premack principle and token economy[3]) with Jason for appropriately channeling his aggressiveness and on-task behaviors (e.g., punching a tetherball, spiking a volleyball, throwing at a target, verbalizing his feelings). They have also effectively used response cost, overcorrection, and time-out strategies to decrease inappropriate and abusive behaviors (e.g., disrupting equipment, pushing classmates, using abusive language).

- For all her classes Mrs. Norris has implemented Hellison's (1995) Responsibility Model. This has also helped to enhance Jason's (and his peers') self and social responsibility behaviors.

- Mrs. Norris uses conflict resolution strategies[4] as deemed warranted. What seems to work best with Jason is the "talking bench"[5] strategy of allowing Jason and his peer for whom a conflict exists to take time out from the lesson activity and situation that led to the conflict, sit down together for a few minutes to discuss the conflict, and then seek resolution with Mrs. Norris's or Mrs. Harris's guidance.

Much to Mrs. Norris's delight, she now witnesses Jason and his peers playing cooperatively together following months of using these instructional and behavior management strategies. Jason and his peers' increased degree of interaction and level of communication has been gradual across the weeks but significant. For instance, during a recent lesson, one of Jason's classmates jumped with him once and physically held his hand so he would know when to jump. Jason also has had multiple opportunities for interaction with the other students in this class. While working at various stations, Jason and his peer partner would talk with other students at that particular station. However, most of the time, Jason did not initiate such interaction, leaving that to his peers.

As Mrs. Norris had hoped, Jason's use of peer-partnering (tutoring) and station rotation strategies increases the opportunities for interactions between Jason and his peers; however, such interactions are generally unidirectional with Jason as the recipient and rarely as the sender. Mrs. Norris therefore attempts several strategies to promote equal-status interactive behaviors, such as allowing Jason to demonstrate simple skills (e.g., standing long jump) at various stations to his peers. Still, it seems as though

Jason wants to play alone at times. Sometimes, he engages in jumping rope alone, and during the scooter races he tends to pull off to the side by himself, rarely racing with anyone. To hold him more accountable and on-task, Mrs. Norris reemphasizes the importance of cooperation between peer partners in the hope that Jason will participate cooperatively at each station with his classmates.

During class one day, Mrs. Norris takes the class outside on the blacktop. The students participate in basketball (knockout), four square, and kickball. Jason has even more opportunities for interaction with his classmates compared to the previous lessons. Again, he talks with his classmates and is praised "Nice shot" when he makes a basket. On a few occasions throughout the basketball activity, Jason's peer partner calls out his name, usually when it is his turn or when he makes a basket. While Jason plays four square a few classmates help him to place the ball directly in the opponent's square. Jason's overall interactions are relatively high throughout this lesson. This might be because Jason seems to enjoy the basketball activity more than the other activities. Furthermore, this lesson is carried out within a well-structured prearranged environment, with multiple pieces of equipment, and ample opportunities for Jason to have contacts with his peers that are interactive, meaningful, and focused on common goals. Moreover, Mrs. Norris ensures that transition times are reduced from previous lessons.

Overall, again, Jason's peers exhibit appropriate yet generally unidirectional behaviors toward him. Mrs. Norris wonders what more she can do in terms of lesson planning, task structures and modifications, use of peer partners, her own effectiveness as a teacher, plus the implementation of proactive behavior management strategies not only to reduce Jason's tendency toward aggressiveness but also to ensure the development of equal-status relationships between him and his peers. She also wonders if this is even a realistic goal.

Endnotes

1. These strategies for teaching students with autism were adapted from Loovis (2000).

2. A number of APE textbooks provide key information regarding teaching students with autism in physical education contexts (e.g., Block, 2000; Jansma & French, 1994; Lavay, French, & Henderson, 1997; Sherrill, 1998; Winnick, 2000).

3. A *token economy system* allows teachers to delay administering reinforcement for successful performance of the targeted desired behavior; awarded tokens are later exchanged for desired reinforcers (Lavay et al., 1997; McKenzie, 1990). *Response cost* is a punishment strategy whereby the teacher takes away a reinforcer from a student who has misbehaved (Lavay et al., 1997). *Premack principle* is a strategy used for which activities in which students prefer to engage can be used as positive consequences for activities that are less desirable (Lavay et al., 1997).

4. Lavay, French, and Henderson (1997) provide an excellent discussion of conflict resolution (e.g., talking bench) and proactive behavior management strategies.

5. The *talking bench* is an easy-to-use psychodynamic behavior management approach that facilitates conflict resolution in which students who are in conflict with one another are asked to sit down together and talk until they can resolve their misunderstandings or misgivings (Horrocks, 1978; Lavay et al., 1997).

Resources and References

Block, M. E. (2000). *A teacher's guide to including children with disabilities in regular physical education* (2nd ed.). Baltimore: Brookes.

Harrison, J. M., Blakemore, C. L., Buck, M. M., & Pellett, T. L. (1996). *Instructional strategies for secondary school physical education* (4th ed.). Dubuque, IA: Brown & Abuchmark.

Hellison, D. R. (1995). *Teaching responsibility through physical activity.* Champaign, IL: Human Kinetics.

Horrocks, R. N. (1978). Resolving conflict in the classroom. *Journal of Physical Education and Recreation,* 48 (9), 20–21.

Jansma, P., & French, R. (1994). *Special physical education: Physical activity, sports, and recreation.* Englewood Cliffs, NJ: Prentice Hall.

Lavay, B. W., French, R., & Henderson, H. L. (1997). *Positive behavior management strategies for physical educators.* Champaign, IL: Human Kinetics.

Loovis, E. M. (2000). Behavioral disorders. In J. P. Winnick (Ed.), *Adapted physical education and sport* (3rd ed.) (pp. 148–157). Champaign, IL: Human Kinetics.

McKenzie, T. L. (1990). Token economy research: A review for the physical educator. In R. French and B. Lavay (Eds.), *A manual of behavior management methods for physical educators and recreators* (pp. 102–123). Kearney, NE: Educational Systems.

Sherrill, C. (1998). *Adapted physical activity, recreation and sports: Crossdisciplinary and lifespan* (5th ed.). Dubuque, IA: Brown.

Winnick, J. P. (2000). *Adapted physical education and sport* (3rd ed.). Champaign, IL: Human Kinetics.

Acknowledgment

We wish to express our gratitude to Rhea S. Butler for her input on this case. Rhea is an APE specialist at F. C. Hammond Middle School within the Alexandria, Virginia, area.

NOTES

QUESTIONS

Preparing for Learning & Teaching

SUMMARY OF PARTICIPANTS

Mrs. Norris, physical education teacher

Jason, 7th-grade student with autism concomitant with moderate mental retardation

Ian, 7th-grade student who is Jason's peer partner in physical education

Ms. Singleton, Jason's mother

Mrs. Harris, teacher aide

1. What is the primary issue in this case? Are there related issues? If so, what are they?

2. What role did the characters play in creating/resolving these issues?

3. Was it useful for Mrs. Norris to schedule a conference with Jason and his mother? What benefits would such a conference hold? Whom else should Mrs. Norris have invited? Why?

4. Given his condition, what are some goals and objectives that you would have drafted to "successfully" include Jason in your physical education program? Why?

5. How might Mrs. Norris use these strategies (e.g., conferencing with Jason and his parents, using peer partners, implementing Hellison's [1995] Responsibility Model) to impact her physical education pedagogy?

6. What are unidirectional and equal-status relationships? Why is developing equal-status relationships between students with disabilities and their typically developing peers considered important in inclusive physical education contexts?

7. Was Mrs. Norris realistic in her goal of establishing equal-status relationships between Jason and his peers or should she have been satisfied that she had helped Jason significantly decrease his exhibition of abusive behaviors?

8. What guidelines are you aware of for including students with autism in physical education classes? What resources do you have available for such guidance?

Teaching Students with Motor Delays and Mobility Difficulties

Karin is a 10th grader at Woodbridge High School who has mobility difficulties ever since she was in elementary school. She has not been officially diagnosed as having a physical or orthopedic disability such as cerebral palsy or traumatic brain injury, but she does encounter motor problems, stemming from brain (head) trauma as a child. Notably, her right leg is a few inches shorter than the left. Karin wears orthotic shoes (right soles are elevated) so that she can walk without a limp. Her speech is slightly slurred, but intellectually, she is average to above average, personable, and socially well liked by her peers and teachers. Sitting in classrooms engaged in math, English, or social studies is not a problem; however, her motor and mobility difficulties are magnified in PE classes. Because this is an issue that makes her self-conscious about her appearance, Karin wants to work on her motor skills, but without the potential embarrassment of participating with her peers.

Given that Karin doesn't meet any of the criteria for receiving special education services, per any intellectual or academic diagnoses, Mr. Kim, the counselor at Woodbridge High School, feels that a multifactored motor assessment should be conducted to determine her present level of performance. Mr. Kim consults with Mr. Dang, the PE teacher, to get his thoughts and input on Karin's ability. After agreeing that APE might be an option, Mr. Kim contacts Karin's mother, a single parent, to seek her permission to conduct a multifactored motor assessment. Karin's mother asks, "Why is this necessary? What does it mean? Would Karin be considered special education? I don't want that label assigned to my daughter." Karin's mother further argues that this is not the most appropriate thing to do since

Karin is capable of doing everything normally. Mr. Kim concurs with Karin's mother, but he stresses that Karin isn't making gains in motor and mobility skills in her GPE class. Mr. Kim reassures her that Karin will not be removed from GPE. Augmenting APE along with GPE would further develop and even enhance Karin's motor and mobility skills. After much discussion, Karin's mother finally agrees to have Karin assessed by Ms. Kirk, the APE specialist.

Ms. Kirk decides that a multifactored assessment consisting of Prudential FITNESSGRAM[1] and the Bruininks-Oseretsky Test of Motor Proficiency (BOTMP)[2], will be completed. The assessment sessions last 1 hour per day across 3 days. Ms. Kirk wants to make sure that nothing out of the ordinary is done to disrupt Karin's typical school day. As such, most of the assessment sessions take place first thing in the morning. The results of the Prudential FITNESSGRAM indicate that Karin scored average on flexibility, below average on upper-body strength (push-ups) and endurance (curl-ups), and below average on cardiovascular endurance; skinfolds were not taken.

For the BOTMP assessment, Karin's gross motor composite sum of 51 converted to a composite score of 44 equating to the 27th percentile with a stanine of 4. A stanine of 4 suggests that for gross motor, Karin is low average when compared with peers her own age. For balance, subtest 2, Karin scores 12 of a possible 32 points. This finding suggests that Karin is average to slightly below average on balancing skills. Some of the more difficult skills include closing her eyes while standing on a balance beam with her preferred leg and walking forward heel-to-toe on the beam. These two items clearly are weaknesses for Karin. Items related to bilateral coordination involve moving the foot and fingers simultaneously for 90 seconds. Karin is not able to perform the tapping feet alternatively while making circles with fingers, tapping foot and finger on same side synchronized, and tapping foot and finger on opposite side synchronized. Drawing lines and crosses simultaneously was not administered. The strength portion consists of arm and shoulder strength, abdominal strength, and leg strength. Karin scores 14 of a possible 42 points. This means that Karin performs slightly below peers her own age. Specifically, knee and full push-ups are low. Abdominal strength as measured by curl-ups is also low. Standing long jump is slightly below average. Karin scored 16 of a possible 21 points. She does extremely well in upper-limb coordination. She also demonstrates average eye-hand coordination by catching a thrown ball, bouncing and catching a ball with both hands, and catching and tossing a ball with preferred hand and both hands. The results of the strength portion of the BOTMP indicate an overall strength for Karin.

Based on the assessment results, Ms. Kirk recommends (a) that Karin should continue to have GPE and receive APE direct service once a week for 45 minutes each session, (b) that she should participate in activities that address abdominal strength, and (c) that she should participate in activities that stress gross motor skills. All activities received from APE would be in agreement with the goals and outcomes as stated by Mr. Dang. Another assessment Ms. Kirk decides to do is an interview with Karin. In this interview, Ms. Kirk asks open-ended questions about how Karin feels about PE and her motor difficulties. Karin says that she likes Mr. Dang, but she feels self-conscious about not being able to run, walk, throw, and catch like the rest of her classmates. Karin asks Ms. Kirk, "Am I special education?" Ms. Kirk quickly replies, "Special education is not a thing, or object. Special education is a service that is mandated to all students with an individualized education program. This label is very misleading and oftentimes causes misunderstanding and misconceptions." Karin explains, "Although my classmates don't tease me and are actually rather supportive, I just don't feel right." Ms. Kirk asks, "What would you like to accomplish during this extra session of physical education?" "I want to do everything that my classmates are doing without feeling stupid or embarrassed," replies Karin. Paraphrasing this information, Ms. Kirk writes up goals and objectives for Karin's IEP. Within a few weeks, the official IEP meeting is held.

Karin's mother is told her rights as a parent and quickly acknowledges her understanding of these rights. Because the IEP has only physical education goals and objectives, she feels comfortable and readily accepts the document. Services are to begin next week. Scheduling is another issue that Ms. Kirk and Mr. Dang have to address.

It is agreed that Karin will receive APE every Monday from 8:15 to 9:00 A.M., so that she doesn't miss out on any of her classes. Her GPE class is normally scheduled right after lunch, so there are no conflicts. Ms. Kirk consults with Mr. Dang about his current PE curriculum. After reviewing this information, she modifies the activities in order for Karin to work on her mobility difficulties. During the first session, Ms. Kirk has Karin walk up and down the court. Karin focuses on the lines of the court at first, then fixates her eyes on an object on the wall. Ms. Kirk tells Karin to try to walk in a straight line. Upon completing the walking activity, Ms. Kirk has Karin jog up and down the court. Once she gets the hang of jogging, Ms. Kirk has Karin jog to the soccer ball, stop, and kick it as hard as she can. This goes on for almost the entire session. Karin, breathing heavily and perspiring, feels that she has accomplished a lot. Ms. Kirk asks Karin, "Are you tired?" Karin replies, "No." Ms. Kirk suggests, "Karin, take a water break since the gym is warm, humid, and stuffy. Walk normally over to the water fountain." As she does, Ms. Kirk notices that her limp is getting more and more pronounced. Could it be that too much motor activity was causing Karin some discomfort? Ms. Kirk asks Karin, "How do you feel?" Karin replies, "I feel fine, but my right leg feels a little stiff." Ms. Kirk believes that this is enough for one session and realizes that there is much work to be done. Interestingly, Karin is motivated to do more so that she can participate without the fear of not being able to accomplish simple motor tasks like her classmates.

After taking Karin back to the locker room to change, Ms. Kirk writes down some notes about Karin's performance. She feels that Karin is slowly getting her self-esteem back, because she can participate, by herself, in motor activities without the fear of embarrassment. Later that day, Ms. Kirk decides to observe Karin in her GPE class. Mr. Dang has the students playing a game of speedball, so the skills that she is practicing allow for more repetitions during APE class. Karin is smiling and laughing with her class-mates. She isn't aware that Ms. Kirk is observing her. During a partner drill of trapping, picking up the ball with both feet up to the hands, Karin tries her best. Interestingly, many other students are having difficulty with this skill. In fact, most of Karin's classmates are having problems. Ms. Kirk smiles and thinks to herself, "Maybe the entire class needs APE."

Endnotes

1. Cooper Institute for Aerobics Research. (1999a). *Prudential FITNESS-GRAM software.* Dallas, TX: Author.

2. The BOTMP can be secured from American Guidance Services, 4201 Woodland Road., Circle Pines, MN 55014. Normed-referenced test of motor ability for children/youth ages 4.5 to 14.5. Website: www.agsnet.com.

   Caution is advised when selecting the BOTMP for testing purposes. Although the BOTMP is normed referenced and still widely used in APE, normative data are well over 20 years old.

QUESTIONS

Preparing for Learning & Teaching

1. What is the primary issue in this case?

2. What are some of the factors that contributed positively and negatively to this case?

3. How was Karin's motor delay really a problem? From whose perspective?

4. What contributed to her motor and mobility delays? Was the use of orthotics an issue?

5. Do you think having an IEP specifically for only APE is necessary? Is it possible to provide APE services without an IEP? If so, would this be cost-effective?

6. What do you think Mr. Dang could have contributed to improving Karin's motor and mobility difficulties?

7. Do you think Mr. Dang provided enough adaptations and modifications for Karin to participate successfully in GPE?

8. What would you do if you were Karin's PE teacher?

9. What were your thoughts when Karin's mother asked, "Will she be special education?" Why do you think she had that question in mind?

10. Was it appropriate for Mr. Kim, the counselor, to suggest APE services for Karin?

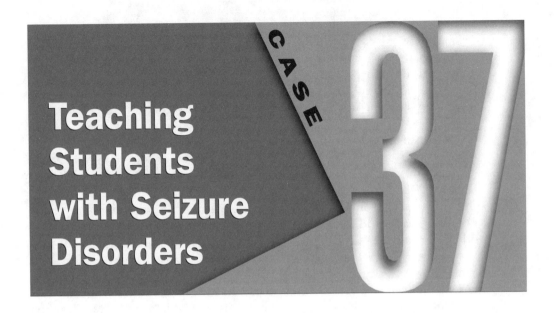

Teaching Students with Seizure Disorders

C A S E

37

rs. Mario is an induction teacher with less than 5 years of teaching experience. Although she teaches GPE at Northside Middle
School in the Northside school district, she has taken and passed
the Adapted Physical Education National Standards (APENS)
Certification Examination.[1] Despite her relatively limited amount
of teaching experience with students with disabilities, Mrs. Mario believes
that certification and accountability are essential in her professional development. Being versatile, flexible, and open minded will make her a better
PE teacher to all students, including those with disabilities. Mrs. Mario is
well liked and respected by the school administrators and fellow teachers,
and she has a knack for getting students to perform their optimal best.
Classroom teachers and students get excited each time Mrs. Mario comes for
physical education activities.

This particular day starts out like any other day with Mrs. Mario arriving 15 minutes before class, setting up for the volleyball lesson. Yet, Mrs.
Mario has a nagging concern for this class, because Ricardo's seizures appear
to have worsened each week. Ricardo is a 7th grader, articulate, friendly,
and generally well liked by his classmates and teachers. He has been known
for his seizure episodes for years. A few years ago, Ricardo was put on medication to control these seizures, but, over time he was taken off the medication. As a 6th grader, his seizures were minimal. Over the course of 1
year, his seizures reemerged randomly from time to time with an apparent
increase in severity. For example, one day it might be an absence type of
seizure, and another day it might be a more tonic-clonic type of seizure.
Absence seizures are described as day-dreaming, a flaccid look, eyes rolling

upward, and impaired consciousness, whereas tonic-clonic seizures are more recognizable. Although there are a myriad of phases associated with tonic-clonic seizures, a tonic phase accurately describes Ricardo's latest attack. This condition is described as continuous contraction of muscles. Specifically, Ricardo's body starts shaking, he crumples to the floor, and he loses body control and fluids, which may cause physical, irreversible damage to Ricardo.

Northside Middle School is a fairly new school with excellent resources. For example, Mrs. Mario has at her disposal a spacious state-of-the-art indoor gymnasium, ample storage space, lots of equipment, and other available resources. The gymnasium is well lit, with lots of space. Mrs. Mario prepares the volleyball lesson in a round-robin tournament format, which incorporates four teams and two games. Ricardo's team is called the Giants, and the others are called the Panthers, Sting Rays, and Hawks. The tournament play between the Giants and Hawks goes without incident for the entire first game. However, during the second game, with the Hawks serving, the volleyball flies directly over the net toward Ricardo. Ricardo does not move as the ball approaches him; instead, he stands motionless as the ball hits the ground. He makes no attempt to retrieve the ball. He just stands there swaying back and forth, eyes glassy and saliva running from his mouth. His teammates yell out but Ricardo doesn't respond. A teammate yells, "Come on Ricardo, we just lost that point. The ball came right at you." His stoic look confuses the students. They immediately shout, "Mrs. Mario, Mrs. Mario, come quick. Ricardo is sick." Mrs. Mario drops her clipboard and runs over to Ricardo. Guiding Ricardo to the side of the gym to sit, Mrs. Mario tries to communicate with him. With a gaze and starry-eyed look, Ricardo doesn't respond. Immediately, Mrs. Mario sends a student to the health room to find Ms. Brown, the school nurse aide.

Mrs. Mario tries to maintain order in the class. Students are congregating around Ricardo, staring and asking Mrs. Mario, "What's wrong with Ricardo?" No one can really answer this question. After the class is over, Mrs. Mario visits Ricardo in the health room. His mother is coming to pick him up and take him to the doctor. Ms. Brown indicates that Ricardo's mother also expresses concern about Ricardo's condition, because his attacks are getting worse. For the rest of the day, Mrs. Mario worries about Ricardo's health and well-being.

Surprisingly, the next day Ricardo appears in class. Mrs. Mario is really glad to see Ricardo back in school. She walks over to him and asks, "How are you feeling today?" "I feel fine. I'm really sorry about what happened in class yesterday," he replies. Ricardo is very embarrassed about the entire situation. He is aware that students in his PE class have been staring at him from the beginning of class, not wanting to interact with him, and even talking behind his back. What's more, some of them are actually afraid of coming near him; others appear to be oblivious to what happened. Nevertheless, Ricardo is determined not to let his physical condition control him. He wants to show his peers that he can do anything he wants to, and that he is skilled in doing so.

The unique thing about Ricardo is that he enjoys school, his friends, and teachers. Moreover, he has aspirations of participating in interscholastic athletics when he gets to high school. Football is his favorite sport. Ricardo believes that he can be an all-district quarterback and perhaps earn a scholarship to attend college. He practices throwing the football with his dad almost every day after school. He often thinks he's Joe Montana passing to Jerry Rice for exciting touchdowns. Ricardo likes to dream big, but, unfortunately, he doesn't seem to realize that his condition may limit his participation in contact sports.

The next unit is team handball. Ricardo feels that this will give him the opportunity to regain some of the trust and respect he lost when he had convulsions during the volleyball tournament. The students are assigned pinnies to identify teams. Employing the tactical approach[2] to teaching team sports and games, Mrs. Mario has the students create 3 vs. 3 games. She provides the objective, parameters, and equipment. The students must create their own game within these parameters (questioning the students, probing each other for solutions). The students go to their assigned areas to play the game.

Maneuvering around the gym, Mrs. Mario provides feedback and cues to each group. Eventually, the teams become more and more competitive, with balls flying everywhere. Mrs. Mario soon realizes that someone might be hit by these balls. She is just about to call order and probe the class with questions when Ricardo has another tonic-clonic attack. It appears that none of the flying balls has hit him, but the excitement of his running around, and actually being quite good at this activity, has triggered another seizure. This time, Mrs. Mario asks everyone to clear the area. A gymnastics mat is on the floor adjacent to the playing area, so Mrs. Mario and another student assist Ricardo to the mat to let the seizure run its course. After a minute, the seizure stops and Ricardo eventually falls asleep. The expressions on the students' faces reveal their concern for Ricardo. Ms. Brown had previously indicated that Ricardo should remain where he is during a seizure and have someone call her instead of bringing him to the health room, so Mrs. Mario has a student summon her. Some time passes before Ricardo awakens to an empty gym with Mrs. Mario and Ms. Brown kneeling beside him. He feels better, but he repeatedly says how embarrassed he is about his condition.

Mrs. Mario returns to her office to contemplate what to do next. She wonders, "Maybe Ricardo should be placed back on medications to control his condition. Maybe he should just not participate in physical education. Maybe he should do more academic tasks in physical education." All these "maybes" worry her. What could she do? Where could she get some advice, and how should she continuously deal with Ricardo, who is such a great kid to have in class? Finally, Mrs. Mario thinks to herself, "One isolated seizure is really not an issue, but multiple seizures within such a short time frame is cause for concern. I wonder what the doctor or Ricardo's mother has to say about this?"

Endnotes

1. For information and application materials regarding the APENS Certification Examination, call 1-888-APENS-EXAM, contact apens@twu.edu, or visit the APENS website at www.twu.edu/o/apens.

2. The tactical games approach "emphasizes game play and places skill learning within its game context, allowing students to see the relevance of skills to game situations" (Griffin, Mitchell, & Oslin, 1997, p. ix).

Resources and References

American Medical Association: www.ama-assn.org/cgi-bin/feedtool.pl.

Epilepsy Foundation of America: www.epilepsyfoundation.org.

Griffin, L. L., Mitchell, S. A., & Oslin, J. L. (1997). *Teaching sport concepts and skills: A tactical games approach.* Champaign, IL: Human Kinetics.

QUESTIONS

Preparing for Learning & Teaching

CASE 37

SUMMARY OF PARTICIPANTS

Mrs. Mario, GPE teacher

Ricardo, 7th-grade student with seizure episodes

Ms. Brown, school nurse aide

1. What is the primary issue in this case?

2. What are some of the factors that contributed to this case?

3. What could Mrs. Mario do with respect to handling students who are seizure prone?

4. How could a student with seizures deal with such a condition and reduce or eliminate his or her embarrassment?

5. Do you think it was necessary for Mrs. Mario to alter her teaching tactics? Was it effective?

6. Did Mrs. Mario handle the situation properly?

7. What significance did Mrs. Mario's passing the APENS examination bring to this case?

8. Would you have done anything differently?

9. What next step would you take regarding preparing yourself for students who have seizures?

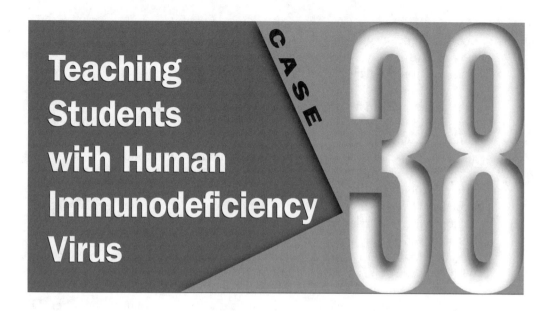

Teaching Students with Human Immunodeficiency Virus

CASE 38

Piedmont Hills is a middle school located near Atlanta, Georgia. Mr. Simms recently entered his second year of teaching physical education at the school. He thrives to help children do the best that they can at all times. The school has a large population of African American students and faculty. In fact, the student population comprises 73 percent African Americans, 7 percent Hispanics, 17 percent White Americans, and 3 percent other backgrounds. The community is made up of lower- to middle-class families.

Mr. Simms's fourth-period 7th-grade PE class is made up of 38 children, including several who have disabilities. Mr. Simms has limited experience working with children with disabilities and feels that students with disabilities need to be "watched closely" during class. Nevertheless, he works enthusiastically to encourage each student with a disability to participate fully. One such student is Shanika, an African American girl who was born with sickle-cell anemia[1] and who later contracted the human immunodeficiency virus (HIV) from contaminated blood during a blood transfusion. She is now a carrier at Stage 1 HIV[2] infection (i.e., a symptom-free condition lasting several years). On numerous occasions throughout her childhood, she has been hospitalized for to severe aplastic crises (i.e., intense pain, jaundice, labored breathing, aching bones, chest pains, swollen joints, and fatigue) as a result of the sickle-cell anemia.

Mr. Simms decides that he should attend the next scheduled meeting with the IEP team to discuss the purpose and objectives of including Shanika in physical activities. At that meeting, he uses data from the Brockport Physical Fitness Test[3] to talk about concerns regarding Shanika's low physical fitness level. It is also pointed out that she is underweight, does not move well, or have adequate coordination. Moreover, she must be very careful not to injure herself during physical activity and should avoid excessive jumping tasks and contact sports. Mr. Simms states his concern that any injury to Shanika that results in bleeding presents a risk of infection to her classmates. He questions whether ethical and legal responsibilities should be weighted against Shanika's right to privacy in discussing her condition with her classmates. Shanika's mother, Ms. Robinson, states that she would prefer that Mr. Simms help Shanika talk about her condition with the other students. Ms. Robinson sees this as an opportunity for the other students in the class to learn more about Shanika and for her to explain why she misses so many school days. Mr. Simms explains that, although he is worried about Shanika's chances of injury, he wants to keep her involved in physical activities with her classmates as much as possible. He adds that having Ms. Robinson's permission and having Shanika talk with her classmates are important steps. This will enable him to keep her involved in physical activities and everyone will be aware of the need for precautions for the safety of both Shanika and her classmates. The other IEP team members agree.

Mr. Simms feels that exhibiting a positive attitude and demeanor toward including Shanika in class activities with her classmates is important. Consequently, at every opportunity he will encourage her to perform the same activities, with some modifications and a few exceptions (e.g., avoiding excessive jumping and contact in sports), as all the other children. For example, Shanika will be encouraged to perform the badminton skills and drills with her classmates. Mr. Simms will pay close attention to the activities she performs. If he thinks that an activity could lead to an injury or a problem, he will either modify the activity (e.g., use cones to demarcate a self-space only for Shanika to move in), instruct her to avoid physical contact with classmates, or explain to her that she may need to be more careful to avoid injuries, and perhaps stop. Mr. Simms firmly believes that Shanika should be allowed to participate as fully as possible with caution and safety at the forefront of everything she does in class. He will remind her of the importance of monitoring herself carefully as she participates in the class's activities.

Mr. Simms also knows that appropriate hygienic practices are required for the safety of all. For instance, if an injury or a bleeding episode (e.g., nosebleed) does occur during class activities, the school nurse is to be immediately called using Mr. Simms's cellular phone. At the start of the school year, he had informed all of the students that if Shanika were injured or bleeding, only he or the school nurse should have direct contact with her, and that in such situations all who do come in contact with her must wear rubber gloves. Mr. Simms also will make sure that blood-soaked items are placed in leakproof bags for disposal or washing.

As the school year continues, Shanika is absent from school more often than most students because she "feels bad." But when she is there, Shanika is very much involved in most physical activities with most classmates, who interact with her without hesitation. Only a couple of classmates distance themselves from Shanika out of concern for HIV infection. From time to time, Shanika takes a break from some of the more vigorous activities, but she understands her limits. Nonetheless, Mr. Simms is always watchful, but no major problems occur and he is pleased to have Shanika included in his PE class.

Endnotes

1. *Sickle-cell anemia* causes red blood cells to have a sickle shape in individuals, mostly African Americans, who have defective hemoglobin. This sickling effect can cause cell destruction and impair circulation in capillaries and small blood vessels (Surburg, 2000).

2. *Stage 1 HIV infection* refers to an acquired "symptom-free condition lasting several years that is diagnosed by a positive antibody test that indicates HIV in the blood serum" (Sherrill, 1998, p. 500). Individuals with this condition have defective immune systems and cannot resist certain types of infections or rare malignancies (Sherrill, 1998; Surburg, 2000).

3. The Brockport Physical Fitness Test (Winnick & Short, 1999a, 1999b) is a health-related, criterion-referenced physical fitness test validated for use with children/youth with and without disabilities who are ages 10 to 17 years. The test may be purchased from Human Kinetics, P.O. Box 5076, Champaign, IL 61820; telephone: 800-747-4457; website: www.humankinetics.com

Resources and References

Centers for Disease Control and Prevention. (1999). *1999 HIV/AIDS surveillance report.* Available: www.cdc.gov/hiv/ldhap.htm.

Eichner, E. R. (1993). Sickle cell trait, heroic exercise, and fatal collapse. *The Physician and Sportsmedicine, 26,* 75–85.

Sherrill, C. (1998). *Adapted physical activity, recreation and sports: Cross-disciplinary and lifespan* (5th ed.). Dubuque, IA: WCB McGraw-Hill.

Spence, D. W., Galantino, M., Mossbert, K. H., & Zimmerman, S. O. (1990). Progressive resistance exercise: Effects on muscle function and anthropometry of a select AIDS population. *Archives of Physical Medicine and Rehabilitation, 71,* 644–648.

Surburg, P. R. (2000). Other health-impaired students. In J. P. Winnick (Ed.), *Adapted physical education and sport* (3rd ed.) (pp. 247–248). Champaign, IL: Human Kinetics.

Winnick, J., & Short, F. (1999a). *The Brockport physical fitness test manual.* Champaign, IL: Human Kinetics.

Winnick, J., & Short, F. (Eds.). (1999b). *The Brockport physical fitness training guide.* Champaign, IL: Human Kinetics.

NOTES

QUESTIONS

Preparing for Learning & Teaching

SUMMARY OF PARTICIPANTS

Mr. Simms, physical education teacher

Shanika, 7th-grade student born with sickle-cell anemia who later contracted HIV

Ms. Robinson, Shanika's mother

1. What is the primary issue in this case? Are there related issues? If so, what are they?

2. What were Mr. Simms's greater concerns relative to Shanika and her classmates? What are some solutions to these concerns?

3. What ethical or legal responsibilities did Mr. Simms have in discussing Shanika's condition with her classmates?

4. In what ways was it important that Mr. Simms exhibit a positive attitude and demeanor for the successful inclusion of Shanika in physical education with her classmates?

5. Why would Mr. Simms keep a cellular phone handy during PE class? In addition to the school nurse's cellular and office telephone numbers, what other emergency telephone numbers should be on file for immediate contact in the event that an injury, severe aplastic crisis, or other emergency situation were to occur?

6. Why was it important that Mr. Simms participate in a meeting with the IEP team to report Shanika's fitness data and discuss his concerns as well as the purpose and objectives of including her in physical education? Who should be invited to attend such a meeting?

7. What guidelines are you aware of for including students with sickle-cell anemia or HIV infections in PE classes? What resources do you have available for such guidance?

Teaching Students with Exercise-Induced Asthma

39

ichele Benson is an induction teacher starting her second year of teaching GPE at East Side High School in Durham, North Carolina. Michele is also an advocate for the inclusion of students with disabilities and other health impairments in her classes. However, she has never actually taught such students other than those few students with disabilities during her practicum experiences in college. So, when informed by Mr. Simmons, the school principal, that Abu, a 9th-grade student with severe exercise-induced asthma (EIA), is to be included in her third-period class, she is excited and yet somewhat apprehensive. These feelings both stem from the fact that Abu will be the first student with a disabling condition to be included in her PE program. Michele worries whether she is competent enough to effectively teach a student with EIA, or any other disabling condition for that matter. Will she know what to do if Abu has an asthma attack? What activities can he safely participate in during physical education? What activities are contraindicated for Abu? Michele has many questions.

To help answer these and other questions, Michele immediately pulls out one of her APE resource textbooks. She had purchased this particular book a year earlier while taking a graduate course at the local university. Much to her relief, this book proves once again to be an excellent resource; it provides information and guidelines for teaching students with asthma in physical education. Michele knows that if she follows these guidelines, she can provide Abu with safe, successful, and satisfying learning experiences in her PE classes. She also understands that some of her students with more severe disabling conditions might require the use of support personnel and other accommodations. But she is willing to take on such challenges and to do whatever is necessary to be an effective teacher.

In preparation for Abu's arrival to her class, Michele makes sure that she reviews the guidelines she has read about in her APE and sport resource book. Further, she contacts Ms. Sansbury, the school nurse, and Mr. and Mrs. Amahs, Abu's parents, to schedule a conference. The conference is scheduled for the next day at noon, a time most agreeable to all parties. However, Mrs. Amahs is out of town on a business trip and will not be available to attend. Therefore, Michele, Ms. Sansbury, Mr. Amahs, and Abu will meet at school during the lunch hour block.

Prior to the scheduled conference, Michele reads through Abu's school and medical records. She learns that Abu and his parents had moved from Ghana, Africa, to the United States several years ago while Mr. Amahs attended graduate school at Duke University. Moreover, both Mr. and Mrs. Amahs now work in the Research Triangle Park area outside of Durham, North Carolina. Further, Abu has had EIA since he was 7 years old, and he takes medication using an inhaler to help control his condition. Michele is impressed to learn that Abu has received several academic awards and honors. Abu also is fluent in speaking several languages. Unfortunately, however, other than a statement that he had "received regular physical education," there are no annual goals, objectives, or information about Abu's actual involvement in physical education.

After introductions at the start of the conference, Michele again explains to Mr. Amahs and Abu the purpose of the meeting. Next, Ms. Sansbury explains that Abu's medication should be taken (inhaled) 30 minutes to 1 hour before Abu participates in vigorous physical activities or sports. Mr. Amahs agrees and points out that in his earlier years, Abu frequently suffered from asthma attacks. However, with a look of disappointment, Mr. Amahs says, "But even now we still don't have Abu's asthma attacks completely under control. Abu can participate only for brief periods in physical activities and sports. His favorite sports are soccer, basketball, and baseball." Abu smiles and nods his head in agreement. Mr. Amahs quickly points out, "Abu is very apprehensive about participating in PE classes." Michele asks, "Abu, what would you like to do in PE if you could decide?" Abu replies, "I would like to play soccer." "Okay," responds Michele. "You will have a chance to play soccer during our team sports unit when we learn about soccer participation." She continues, "What else would you like?" "Hmm . . . I like basketball. I can beat my dad!" Abu excitedly answers. Michele then explains that she will involve Abu in various roles in soccer, basketball, and baseball, in addition to other team sports within the sport education model[1] that she employs in her PE program. Both Mr. Amahs and Abu are quite pleased.

As the meeting continues, Michele explains the purpose and use of the sport education model to Mr. Amahs and Abu. In doing so, she asks Abu what his feelings about participating in physical education are. She assures him that they all—Michele, Ms. Sansbury, his parents, and others—will work together to ensure that he will be successful in her PE program. She asks Mr. Amahs and Abu to start thinking about goals for Abu's physical education experience. At that point Michele opens her adapted resource book to go over the guidelines with Ms. Sansbury, Abu, and Mr. Amahs. Together they discuss goals and objectives mindful of the those guidelines[2] and the sport education model:

- All students including Abu will engage in daily warm-up activities and class closure including a cool-down period.

- PE classes at East Side High School follow a block schedule. Michele typically frames her class periods into several separate 12- to 15-minute activity sessions and at times engages students in station work with timed rotations. However, as recommended for students with EIA, Abu (and his peers) will engage in short-burst (anaerobic) or short-duration activities such as softball, baseball, and tennis.

- Abu and his classmates will have opportunities to participate in soccer play and "shoot hoops" in basketball. Although Michele will not avoid engaging her students (including Abu) in aerobic-type activities such as soccer participation, she will make sure that Abu has regular opportunities to take rest breaks interpolated throughout each activity. Further, Abu will be allowed to take a 2- to 3-minute rest break whenever he feels the need to do so. Moreover, Abu will be taught how best to pace himself during physical activities.

- In Michele's classes, she emphasizes physical fitness involving cardiovascular and muscular strength conditioning exercises at the start of the school year as well as sport-related conditioning at the beginning and throughout each new sport unit introduced. In doing so, she will structure her class sessions to gradually increase the level of exercise intensity, frequency, and duration for all her students, including Abu, to improve and maintain their physical fitness levels.

- Michele will encourage Abu to practice breathing control exercises while at school and Mr. and Mrs. Amahs will encourage him to do so at home. Since no swimming pool is available at East Side High School, Abu will swim at the local community recreation center in the evenings on a regular basis.

- Abu will be allowed to visit Ms. Sansbury's office and take his medication at least 30 minutes prior to going to his PE classes.

- Michele, Abu, and Ms. Sansbury will establish and practice emergency procedures for coping with episodes in which Abu might experience an asthma attack. In that vein, Mr. and Mrs. Amahs's work phone and cell phone numbers will be exchanged. Michele will select several students from her third-period class whom she considers responsible and designate them as "runners." Designated "runners" will be responsible for immediately contacting Michele and/or Ms. Sansbury in the event of an emergency situation.

- Through the use of the sport education model, Michele will be able to ensure that all her students, including Abu, will better understand the value of cooperation, enjoyment, and role responsibility, as well as gain a healthy appreciation for sport participation and competition.

- Michele understands that a healthful environment is important for all students, particularly those students with asthma, allergies, or other breathing-related concerns. For example, she regularly cleans the PE equipment and keeps the equipment storage room well organized and clean. She will also make sure that Abu has tissues, a trash receptacle, and a spittoon available so that he can dispose of coughed-up mucus. Further, she will remind the school custodian to clean the gym floor, locker rooms, and floor mats regularly.

- Abu will be required to stop activity immediately at the onset of an asthma attack and be instructed to take two breaths of his medication while seated in a quiet and comfortable position. Michele will monitor his condition and call for Ms. Sansbury. In addition, Abu will not be required nor allowed to participate in vigorous physical activities on days when he has flu or cold symptoms.

After reviewing the guidelines, there is a heightened level of understanding and agreement among Michele, Ms. Sansbury, Abu, and Mr. Amahs regarding Abu's future involvement in physical education. Everyone is pleased with and encouraged by the information that they have shared. In fact, Michele leaves the conference with a greater understanding of what she needs to do to successfully include Abu in her PE class. She returns to her office, again refers to her adapted resource book, turns on her computer, and types up the goals and specific objectives for Abu within the framework of the guidelines and sport education model that they had discussed during the conference.

Endnotes

1. Siedentop's (1994) sport education model is "a curriculum and instruction model developed for school physical education programs" (p. 3) and is used to promote positive sport experiences for students at various age levels. Siedentop's (1994) *Sport Education: Quality PE Through Positive Sport Experience* provides an excellent discussion of this model.

2. Guidelines for teaching students with asthma were adapted from Surburg (2000).

Resources and References

Block, M. E. (2000). *A teacher's guide to including children with disabilities in regular physical education* (2nd ed.). Baltimore: Brookes.

Harrison, J. M., Blakemore, C. L., Buck, M. M., & Pellett, T. L. (1996). *Instructional strategies for secondary school physical education* (4th ed.). Dubuque, IA: Brown & Abuchmark.

Sherrill, C. (1998). *Adapted physical activity, recreation and sports: Cross-disciplinary and lifespan* (5th ed.). Dubuque, IA: WCB McGraw-Hill.

Siedentop, D. (Ed.). (1994). *Sport education: Quality PE through positive sport experience.* Champaign, IL: Human Kinetics.

Surburg, P. R. (2000). Other health-impaired students. In J. P. Winnick (Ed.), *Adapted physical education and sport* (3rd ed.) (pp. 240–241). Champaign, IL: Human Kinetics.

NAME   DATE

Preparing for Learning & Teaching

SUMMARY OF PARTICIPANTS

Michele Benson, GPE teacher

Mr. Simmons, school principal

Abu, 9th-grade student with severe EIA

Ms. Sansbury, school nurse

Mr. and Mrs. Amahs, Abu's parents

1. What is the primary issue in this case? Are there related issues? If so, what are they?

2. What role did the characters play in creating/resolving these issues?

3. In what ways might an APE resource textbook provide guidance and, in turn, enhance Michele's sense of competency relative to teaching students with disabilities and other health impairments?

4. How might Michele's use of resources, conferencing with relevant persons (e.g., the student with the disabling condition, school nurse, parents), and a heightened sense of competency impact her physical education pedagogy?

5. Why was it important for Michele to schedule a conference with the school nurse, Abu, and Mr. Amahs? What benefits would such a conference hold? What was the purpose of inviting the school nurse to the conference? Who else should have been invited? Why?

6. During the conference was it necessary for Michele to take time out to discuss with Abu and Mr. Amahs the purpose and use of the sport education model? Was it appropriate to discuss goals for Abu's physical education experience at this meeting? Why or why not?

7. What guidelines are you aware of for including students with asthma in PE classes? What resources do you have available for such guidance?

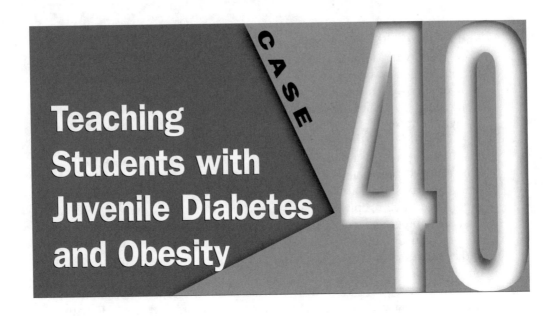

Teaching Students with Juvenile Diabetes and Obesity

Having recently moved from the city, Roland is excited about entering 9th grade at Benjamin Parker High School this year. He feels that having a change of environment, making new friends, and having new teachers will be especially beneficial, because his experiences at Hyatt Middle School were not at all positive. Roland wonders about what his English teacher will be like, how much work he or she will have him complete, and to what extent he can participate in writing for the school paper.

At Hyatt Middle School, Roland was teased a lot, constantly bombarded with "fat person" jokes, and even threatened with bodily harm. Part of Roland's issues dealt with his weight—he was clearly obese. In addition, Roland has juvenile diabetes. Diabetes is a potentially life-threatening condition that causes a high sugar (glucose) content in the blood and urine. Very few individuals at Hyatt Middle School knew about this disease, but everyone was aware of Roland's obvious weight problem. Being the target of "fat" jokes eventually took its toll on Roland to the point where he literally did not want to attend school, wished that he was desperately ill so he could rid himself of his excess weight, and even considered suicide. This led to various mood swings and an increase in eating to alleviate depression and anxiety. While school authorities tried to be persuasive and helpful, the physical education teacher at Hyatt did little, if anything positive, to assist Roland with his weight problem. As a result, Roland hated PE class.

Roland's parents view the move from the city and Roland's transfer to Benjamin Parker High School positively. They hope that a change of venue will increase Roland's perception of himself, aid in his schoolwork, and prompt him to pursue school activities (e.g., writing for the school paper) and to address his weight problem. Their excitement is substantiated when they meet with Mrs. Matthews, the principal of Benjamin Parker High School. She is warm and welcoming, taking Roland and his parents on a tour of campus, introducing them to staff, and making them feel right at home. Mrs. Matthews highlights some of the things that the school is doing in light of receiving several grants. Excitedly, she indicates that Ms. Patton, the physical education teacher and department chair, has received a grant to increase physical activity across the lifespan. Her program will incorporate nontraditional activities (i.e., bowling, hiking and camping, fishing, cross-country skiing, and orienteering) into the existing PE programs to promote more lifelong physical activities. Roland and his parents are amazed that such programs exist in physical education. Roland thinks to himself, "Yeah, I can do those things." As Roland and his parents leave Benjamin Parker High School, they feel relieved and reassured that things will work out just fine.

The first day of school does not arrive soon enough. As Roland walks toward his first class (math), the other students stare at him. He thinks to himself, "Being in a high school environment sure doesn't make much difference." Academically, Roland feels comfortable with his performance—physical education is his biggest problem. Roland's second-period class is PE. Ms. Patton meets with her 9th-grade PE class and explains that this year, Benjamin Parker will try something different for physical education. She explains that new activities will be offered as units for physical education; however, everyone will be involved in a physical fitness unit before any nontraditional activities will be offered. Roland is shocked. He immediately recalls all his troubling experiences at Hyatt Middle School. As his anxiety rises he feels an insulin reaction (hypoglycemic attack) coming on. He starts to perspire, his heart rate and breath rate increase, and he feels faint. Ms. Patton is unaware of his condition, so she thinks little of it. Roland, having had such experiences before, takes out a Snicker's bar and starts eating it. One of the students in class yells, "Hey, fat boy, no one is supposed to eat in the gym." All of his classmates laugh hysterically, but Roland continues to eat the candy bar and starts to feel better.

At the end of the period, Ms. Patton sits down with Roland and asks, "What was wrong, Roland? Is there anything I can do?" Roland explains, "I'm diabetic and take insulin shots daily. Sometimes when I get stressed, I have to eat something sweet." He continues, "I feel embarrassed during PE class because everyone teases and laughs at me. I really want to lose weight, but I can't seem to get very far. All the students teased me at Hyatt Middle School, but I thought I would feel more accepted in high school." He further explains that he is very excited about all the nontraditional activities that Benjamin Parker has to offer in physical education. He has bowled only once in his life and is anxious to see if he can get better at it. His family frequently goes on hiking and camping trips, so this is right up his alley. Yet, he was told that he would have to participate in a physical fitness unit before participating in any nontraditional activities. Tears start rolling down Roland's face. In an attempt to calm and console him, Ms. Patton tells

Roland that perhaps some kind of an arrangement for all students during 2nd period can be worked out.

Later, Ms. Patton recalls that some students who are health risks or even disabled under the Individuals with Disabilities Education Act Amendments (IDEA) of 1997 fall under the category of "Other Heath Impairments." Having taken a recent course at the local university, she remembers that such students need accommodations in order to meet their educational needs. Ms. Patton wonders which of her students might have health problems or disability issues that hinder their education. Apparently, Roland fits into the "Other Health Impairments" category and may require APE services if his physical education needs cannot be addressed in her GPE.

Ms. Patton anticipates that Roland will feel "out of place" in the physical fitness unit, so she decides to assist him with a specialized physical fitness program. Most important, she will need to make sure that Roland has received all his necessary medications and is able to participate. She decides that prior to class she will visit with the school health aide to determine what effect diabetes will have on his physical education performance. She also reads up on various "dos and don'ts" about diabetes and excessive obesity. To ensure that the program will be beneficial, not stifling, she decides to design it so that there will be no strenuous activities for Roland. For example, Roland could walk around the track, timing himself every lap. If he feels okay, he could then begin to jog. This would be left solely up to him. "This might be an excellent idea for the other students, too," she thinks to herself.

The next day is the start of the physical fitness unit. When the class finally arrives, Ms. Patton informs everyone that they will do a 12-minute run, jog, or walk. Various students who don't want to run, exercise, or stretch let out moans and groans. They want to know when they can play, bowl, fish, and so on. In response, Ms. Patton emphasizes that the most important thing is to keep moving. She has in place various exercise modalities such as pull-up bars, stretch and stepping benches, and dip bars. Students are free to utilize all modalities as long as they can document what and how many they did. Ms. Patton also asks Keith, a classmate who did volunteer work with young children over the summer, to walk with Roland during the class. She keeps a watchful eye on Roland to make sure things are going well. On the one hand, Ms. Patton worries that he might have another attack, and on the other, she hopes that he will start feeling better about himself. However, she acknowledges that she needs to learn more about his weight problem and juvenile diabetes.

As the period ends, Ms. Patton asks Roland, "How do you feel?" He replies, "Class wasn't too bad. Keith is a cool guy and we have similar interests. We plan to go hunting for birds in a few weeks." As Roland walks to the locker room, Ms. Patton decides that she should consult with his parents to stress the need for a combination of diet and exercise at home and at school. During this consultation, she plans to point out how helpful it would be for them to do physical activity with him at home and to help her monitor his weight problems. By communicating with Roland's parents, Ms. Patton feels that they can effectively address his obesity and diabetes, which will better enable him to participate in class activities.

NOTES

QUESTIONS

Preparing for Learning & Teaching

1. What is the primary issue in this case?

2. What are some of the factors that contributed positively and negatively to this case?

3. How did Roland feel about school in general? What were his feelings about physical education? Why was he looking forward to physical education in high school?

4. What do you think Ms. Patton contributed to improving Roland's participation in the physical fitness unit? Do you think she provided enough support and input? How influential was the school's administration?

5. What are your thoughts about everyone having to participate in a physical fitness unit prior to participating in nontraditional activities?

6. Can Ms. Patton address Roland's health-related and self-esteem problems alone? What would you do in such a situation?

INDEX

ABCD model, 14–16

Abdominal strength, assessing, 232

Absence seizures, 237–238

Abusive behavior, 224

Academic learning time in PE (ALT-PE), 126, 127

Activities, lack of after school, 113–114

Adapted dance, 163

Adapted Physical Education National Standards (APENS) Certification Examination, 67, 237

Adapted physical education, see APE

Adapted physical education teacher, itinerant, 183–186

ADD, 54, 145, 163

ADHD, 157–158, 163

Adults, recreation centers and, 113–115

Advocacy, 7–12

Aerobics program, 22, 120

African American students/families, 16, 145, 243

Afrocentric educational system, 145

After-school activities, lack of, 113–114

After-school programs, 139–140

Aggressiveness, 8–10, 28, 41, 158
  cerebral palsy and, 105–109

Allport, G. W., 178

Americans with Disabilities Act, 192

Amputation:
  congenital double leg, 93
  congenital single leg, 126

Anger, in students, 8 (see also Aggressiveness, Behavior management)

Anxiety, 255

APE (adapted physical education):
  creating and conducting a program of, 33–38

itinerant teacher and, 183–186

masters degree in, 7

preschoolers and, 183–184

specialist, 9

visual impairment and, 197–201

Aplastic crises, 243

Aquatics program, 63, 87–90 (see also Swimming)

Asperger disorder, 22, 23, 151

Assessment, 14–15, 28, 106
  authentic, 45–52, 53, 56
  BOTMP, 232, 234
  Brockport Physical Fitness Test, 199
  FITNESSGRAM, 199
  MOBILITEE, 106–107
  multifactored motor, 231
  peer, 53–60
  rubric, 45–49
  TGMD-2, 184

Assistive technologies, 83

Asthma, 145, 151, 249–252

Attention deficit disorder (ADD), 54, 145, 163

Attention deficit hyperactivity disorder, 157–158, 163

Attention deficits, 151 (see also ADD, ADHD)

Attitudes:
  changing, 1–6
  positive, 113–114
  striving to improve, 146

Attitudinal theory, 178, 182

Audience, behavioral objectives and, 15

Authentic assessment, 45–52, 53, 56

Autism, 7–12, 22, 27–30, 34, 40–42, 45, 47, 67, 140, 163, 223–227
  crowded spaces and, 42